LIVING TO SOME PURPOSE

Also by Adnan Pachachi:

Muzahim al-Baja'ji: Sirah Siyasiyyah
(Muzahim Pachachi: A Political Biography). In Arabic only.
London: Markaz al-Watha'iq wa-'l-Dirasat al-Ta'rikhiyyah, 1989

Iraq's Voice at the United Nations, 1959–69: A Personal Record.
London: Quartet Books, 1991. Arabic edition: *Sawt al-'Iraq fi'l-Umam al-Muttahidah, 1959–1969*. Beirut: Al-Mu'assasah al-'Arabiyyah li-'l-Dirasat wa-'l-Nashr, 2002

Fi 'Ayn al-I'sar
(In the Eye of the Storm). In Arabic only.
Beirut: Dar al-Saqi, 2012

LIVING TO SOME PURPOSE

MEMOIRS OF A SECULARIST IRAQI AND ARAB STATESMAN

ADNAN PACHACHI

FOREWORD BY PETER SLUGLETT

Arabian Publishing

Living to Some Purpose:
Memoirs of a Secularist Iraqi and Arab Statesman
By Adnan Pachachi

© Dr Adnan Pachachi 2013

Produced and published in 2013 by Arabian Publishing Ltd
4 Bloomsbury Place, London WC2A 2QA
Email: arabian.publishing@arabia.uk.com

Edited by William Facey

The moral right of the author has been asserted according to the Copyright,
Designs and Patents Act 1988

All rights are reserved. No part of this publication may be reproduced, stored or introduced into a retrieval system, or transmitted, in any form, or by any means (electronic, mechanical, photocopying, recording or otherwise) without prior permission in writing of the publisher and copyright holder.

A catalogue card for this book is available from the British Library

ISBN: 978-0-9571060-3-1

Typesetting and digital artwork by Jamie Crocker, Artista-Design, UK
Printed and bound by TJ International, Cornwall, UK

This book is dedicated to my compatriots
in Iraq and the United Arab Emirates

A share in two revolutions is living to some purpose

Thomas Paine (1737–1809), English radical and secularist,
in a letter to George Washington, 16 October 1789

CONTENTS

	Acknowledgements	viii
	List of Photographs	ix
	Foreword by Peter Sluglett	xi
	Introduction	1
1	Childhood, 1923–34	3
2	Secondary School and University, 1934–43	9
3	Iraqi Embassy in Washington, 1945–49	18
4	Director of the United Nations Department, Iraqi Ministry of Foreign Affairs, 1950–53	24
5	Iraqi Embassy in Washington, 1953–57	28
6	Director General of the Department of International Affairs, Iraqi Ministry of Foreign Affairs, 1957–59	33
7	Ambassador and Permanent Representative to the United Nations, 1959–65	38
8	Foreign Minister of Iraq, 1965–67	58
9	The Arab–Israeli War of 1967	84
10	Resignation from the Iraqi Foreign Service, 1969	102
11	Service in the United Arab Emirates, 1969–93	106
12	Iraqi Expatriate Opposition, 1991–2003	114
13	Return to Iraq, 2003–10	125
	Epilogue	153

Appendices

1	Arab–American Relations (memorandum, June 1953)	157
2	The Gulf War of 1990–91 (*Guardian*, 1991)	167
3	Human Rights, the United Nations, and Weapons of Mass Destruction (speech, 1993)	175
4	Iraq's Route to a Democratic Future (*Financial Times*, 2003)	179
5	An Essay on Palestine (written in 1994 and brought up to date)	182
6	Islam and Modernity (speech, 2005)	202
7	A Lecture on Iraq given at St Antony's College, Oxford (2005)	205
8	The Situation in Iraq at the Height of Sectarian Strife (*Financial Times*, 2006)	211
9	Index of Speeches at the United Nations	214
	Index	221

Acknowledgements

I AM PROFOUNDLY GRATEFUL to my sister-in-law, Ellen Jawdat, for reading the manuscript and offering valuable advice, which greatly improved the text. Many thanks go equally to Dr Frauke Heard-Bey, the well-known author and scholar, for her constructive suggestions, and to my daughter, Maysoon, who was most helpful in reading and revising the manuscript. Finally, I owe a debt of gratitude to Analyn Yamson, who typed and retyped the manuscript several times over and patiently incorporated all the changes that I kept making over a period of several months.

Adnan Pachachi

PHOTOGRAPHS

Between pp. 116 and 117:

1. The author with his father, Muzahim Pachachi, in 1934.

2. The author as a boy in Geneva, 1935.

3. The author at ten years of age.

4. The author as a young diplomat in Paris with Norwegian lawyer and politician Trygve Lie, first Secretary-General of the United Nations, November 1951.

5. The author greets Nikita Khrushchev, Premier of the Soviet Union, New York, 1960.

6. US President John F. Kennedy greets the author, with Adlai Stevenson, US Permanent Representative to the United Nations, New York, 1961.

7. The author presiding over the United Nations Economic and Social Council, Geneva, 1965.

8. The author with Pope Paul VI, Vatican City, October 1966.

9. Egyptian President Jamal Abdul Nasser and the author, Cairo, 1966.

10. Dr Adnan and Mrs Pachachi with Indira Ghandi, Prime Minister of India, New Delhi, March 1967.

Photographs

11. The author as Foreign Minister of Iraq in discussion with Andrei Gromyko, Foreign Minister of the Soviet Union, Moscow, April 1967.

12. The author as Foreign Minister of Iraq, in discussion with the foreign ministers of Jordan and Morocco in the UN Security Council, on the eve of the adoption of Resolution 242 for the settlement of the Arab–Israeli conflict after the 1967 June war, November 1967.

13. The author makes a point to HH Sheikh Zayed bin Sultan Al Nahyan, Founder and President of the United Arab Emirates, 1971.

14. The author with his wife and three daughters, London, 1983.

15. The author shares a joke with HM King Abdullah II of the Hashemite Kingdom of Jordan, Amman, 2003.

16. The Governing Council of Iraq in 2004: the author with Jalal Talabani, Massoud Barzani and Ghazi al-Yawar.

17. HH Sheikh Sabah al-Ahmad al-Jabr Al-Sabah, Emir of Kuwait, greets the author in 2006.

Foreword

ADNAN PACHACHI, now nearly ninety years old, can look back on a long and eventful life, mostly as an Iraqi diplomat and statesman who served his country at the United Nations with vigour and determination, and defended the Arab cause passionately in the same forum. But for an extraordinary outburst of pettiness and small-mindedness he might well have become the first president of post-Saddam Iraq, a position that he would have occupied with far greater distinction than any of those who have filled it since.

Dr Pachachi – as he explains, his family name is a corruption of *parchachi*, meaning dealers in a particular kind of embroidered cloth – was born in Baghdad in 1923, and attended Victoria College Alexandria, the American University of Beirut, and Georgetown University. In 1945 he entered the Iraqi Foreign Service, joining the Iraqi Embassy in Washington and representing Iraq at the UN in New York, where he spent much of the next twenty-five years. He is clearly an unrepentant member of the pre-1958 old order, *al-'ahd al-ba'id*, who, like him, "cherish the memory of the monarchy, under whose secular and tolerant government the people of Iraq found peace and security" – a sentiment with which one can empathize without necessarily sharing it.

Dr Pachachi's many years at the UN have convinced him of the profound importance of that institution, without blinding him to its limitations. At the young age of thirty-seven he became chair of the UN Committee on Decolonization. Throughout his career at the UN he was highly regarded by his colleagues, as evidenced by the many Foreign Office despatches testifying to his integrity; in the context of the discussions on Aden in the late 1950s and 1960s he is described as a tough but worthy adversary.

These memoirs contain many interesting reflections on Iraqi foreign policy, Israel, Palestine, and American policy in the Middle East. The author berates the US for its failure to use its influence to restrain Israel, and sees little in common between the broad inclusiveness of US domestic policy and Israel's narrow intolerance. Although there are few revelations, there are interesting accounts of the author's meetings with President

Johnson and senior members of his administration at the end of May 1967, apparently in an attempt on the administration's part to convince the Arab world that Israel would not launch a pre-emptive strike (which of course it did). Dr Pachachi describes the Arab defeat in June 1967 as a "traumatic experience from which I have never really recovered".

In January 1969, shortly before a series of public hangings of Jews and other 'enemies of the people' in Baghdad, Dr Pachachi resigned from the Foreign Service. Almost immediately, he was invited to Abu Dhabi where he built up the emirate's administration and later the UAE's diplomatic service, and represented the UAE at various international forums for many years. His wry account of meetings with Shaikh Zayed is especially enjoyable: "I greatly enjoyed these sessions but I have to admit that sitting on the ground is something I have never found easy to do".

Probably of interest to most readers is the part of these memoirs concerning the author's activities in the Iraqi opposition in the 1990s and in Iraq itself after 2003. Dr Pachachi wanted to create or be part of a secular centrist opposition. Quite rightly, as subsequent events were to show, he was always profoundly suspicious of the US favourite, Ahmad Chalabi, who he saw as unrealistic, vainglorious and over-ambitious. The author was also deeply distrustful of the neo-conservatives at the US Department of Defense. His account of his meeting with Saddam Hussein a few hours after the latter's capture is a study in contrasts, with Adel Abdul Mahdi and Muwaffaq al-Ruba'i reviling the prisoner while Pachachi calmly asked him why on earth he had not retreated from Kuwait in 1990 when he could obviously have done so. His distress at his own marginalization and that of his secular and non-sectarian colleagues in 2004 is palpable, and his fears of the excessive influence of certain elements in the Iranian government have been amply justified.

Iraq is fortunate to have had a public servant of such integrity and honesty: it was tragic that he was prevented from using his talents to assist in guiding Iraq out of chaos and onto the path of recovery. While wishing him many happy years of retirement, those of us who care deeply about Iraq and its people know that we shall probably not see his like again.

Peter Sluglett
Middle East Institute
National University of Singapore

Introduction

My family and friends have for a long time urged me to write an autobiography detailing and commenting on the main events and developments in a life which has spanned nine decades and moved constantly between cultures. In my role as a politician and diplomat, I have often been fortunate to find myself as an active participant in some of the major political transformations of my day – both in the Middle East and elsewhere in the developing world. It is my hope that my experiences and the insights I may have gained along the way will be of interest to those seeking to understand something of the present political state of our world.

My life falls into four distinct phases. The first, beginning with my birth in 1923, ended in 1943 when I finished my undergraduate university studies. The second began in 1944 and ended in 1969, a period during which I served as an Iraqi diplomat, Ambassador to the United Nations and Foreign Minister of Iraq, and was active in the historic efforts of the UN to end colonialism and help many countries to attain their freedom and independence. During that same period, I became deeply involved in the Palestine question and was active in the strenuous United Nations efforts to end the Israeli occupation of Arab territories after the Six-Day War of June 1967.

The third phase began in 1971 when I was appointed Minister in the Government of Abu Dhabi and Personal Representative of the President of the United Arab Emirates, and ended in 1993 when I retired at the age of seventy. I was fortunate to have been able to play a modest role in the creation of the UAE.

Introduction

The fourth phase began in 1991 and ended in 2010. This period is divided into two parts, the first when I was active in expatriate Iraqi opposition politics, and the second after my return to Iraq in 2003. During the latter period I was a member of the Governing Council, its President in January 2004, a member of the Interim National Council in 2004–05, and a member of the Iraqi Parliament from 2006 to 2010, and actively participated in the efforts to make Iraq a democratic, pluralist, tolerant and civilized modern society. I strove with others to give Iraqis a system of government under which they could freely enjoy the fundamental human rights denied them for so long. I dreamt of a country where the rule of law reigned supreme and justice was administered by an impartial and independent judiciary under laws prohibiting torture, the death penalty, arbitrary arrest and abduction. When I returned to Iraq in 2003 after an absence of thirty-five years, I was fortunate to have with me a group of dedicated idealists who shared my hopes and dreams. We failed in part because of our own ineptitude as politicians, but chiefly because the Iraqi people were not yet ready to shed their sectarian and ethnic prejudices. My seven-year odyssey in Iraq, with its failures and frustrations, is the subject of the final chapter of this book.

This memoir follows the chronological sequence of the four distinct phases of my life set out above. I have also included, as appendices, an internal Foreign Ministry memorandum on Arab–American relations which I wrote in 1953, an essay I wrote on the conquest of Palestine between 1948 and 1967, and several articles and speeches on various subjects, as well as an index of the principal speeches I made at the United Nations on the Arab–Israeli conflict and colonial questions.

1

Childhood, 1923–34

I WAS BORN IN BAGHDAD on 14 May 1923 by Caesarean section, probably the first such birth in Iraq. The operation became necessary when my mother, a few days before I was due, had an accident that fractured her pelvis. There were few doctors in Iraq at that time and the facilities in the one and only hospital were rudimentary at best. The doctor who performed the operation was Dr Noel Braham, a British physician, who a year earlier had operated on King Feisal I's appendix. He was regarded as a skilled surgeon when he was sober, which was not very often. Many years later when I was a healthy-looking teenager of seventeen, I met Dr Braham again. He reminded me of his role in bringing me into the world and expressed the hope that I would be like Julius Caesar, who had been born in the same way. I laughed and said that he was expecting too much, but that I would try not to disappoint him.

I was born into power, wealth and privilege. My family, Al-Pachachi, was among the most prominent old families of Baghdad. It traced its origins to the 'Abdah branch of the Shammar tribe, which had migrated to Iraq from its home in Najd (now central Saudi Arabia) and settled during the 17th century in an area west of Mosul between the Tigris and Euphrates rivers. One of our ancestors married into a prominent merchant family in Mosul, the Kalabdouns, who were also known as the Parchachis because their business was in fine and elegant gold-embroidered pieces of cloth, which in Turkish are called *parcha*. Thus they became known in

Mosul as the Parchachi family. They left Mosul at the end of the 18th century and settled in Baghdad, where they had a successful and thriving business and their wealth enabled them, over the years, to become large owners of property and agricultural land. Their titular head, Nu'man Al-Pachachi, a merchant/landowner, rose to prominence as acknowledged leader of the business community and is remembered for his philanthropy and generosity. He helped the people of Anbar and Baghdad at a time of famine, with the result that that year was known as 'the Year of Al-Pachachi'. In 1813, Nu'man became involved in a struggle for power between various leaders of the Mamluks who had ruled Baghdad since the middle of the 18th century. He sided with the governor, who was toppled and killed by a new Mamluk leader, Daoud Pasha, who wanted to execute Nu'man and his friend and colleague, Daoud Abdullah Sassoon, a prominent member of the Jewish community and treasurer of the province of Baghdad. Upon their release from prison, they were saved by bribing the new governor of Baghdad and his cronies and fleeing the country. Sassoon, subsequently the founder of the well-known Sassoon family in Britain, urged Nu'man to go with him to India and China, to start a new life and a new business career. Nu'man declined, feeling he wanted to spend the rest of his days in a Muslim country. He died and was buried in Damascus. A story circulated in Baghdad that when Nu'man fled, he left a bag of gold buried under the cellar of his house by the Tigris. Nothing was found when, many years later, the house was demolished and a hotel built in its place.

I was conscious very early in life that I belonged to the ruling elite of the country and enjoyed advantages denied to most other Iraqis. Consequently I felt I was duty-bound to serve the country and its people. The tradition of selfless service established by the founding fathers of modern Iraq was their legacy to my generation.

As an only child I was spoiled and overprotected. My health was fragile compared to that of other boys my age. I was a lonely and unhappy child, believing that I was responsible for my mother's pain and suffering. Those around me compounded this feeling of guilt by constantly reminding me that my difficult birth was the cause of my mother's misfortunes and that, in order to atone for it, I should achieve success in my life and fulfil all the high hopes my father had for me. I carried this burden of guilt well into adulthood. I loved my mother and tried to repress my anger at what had happened to her. This anger exploded occasionally and flared up whenever I saw someone, even if I had no idea who they were, being unfairly treated and subjected to physical violence and abuse. My father and mother were different in many ways, for while my mother was a simple, uneducated and devout woman, my father, Muzahim Al-Pachachi (1890–1982), was among the best-educated politicians in Iraq, a true Arab nationalist who would become Prime Minister in 1948–49. There were also differences in temperament. All this affected me profoundly and as a result I became a strong advocate of equality between men and women.

Baghdad at the time of my birth was no more than a large village lacking in all essentials: no electricity, no clean water, only one or two roads, a single primitive hospital and few schools. Other cities in the region, such as Cairo, Alexandria, Beirut, Jerusalem and Damascus, were far more developed. As a child I remember that on rainy days when the streets became a sea of mud, people would hire porters to carry them on their backs from one side of the street to the other. This shows how primitive Iraq was after four centuries of Ottoman misrule.

As I grew up, Iraq was undergoing rapid change. There was hope that after centuries of stagnation it would become part of the modern world. New schools, especially for girls, were opened and students were sent abroad to complete their higher education. There was tremendous interest in science, literature, the arts, music and drama. People were eager to learn and change their way of life.

I have many graphic memories of my childhood years, notably of two surgical operations: a tonsillectomy, and my circumcision in 1928 when I was five years old. The operations were performed not in the hospital but at home on my father's large desk, which was covered with clean sheets. I have an alarmingly clear memory of the gleaming surgical instruments being neatly laid out close by me before I sank into chloroform-induced unconsciousness.

When I was seven, we went to Lebanon to spend the summer holidays and I vividly recall my astonishment at seeing the sea for the first time in Beirut. I was struck by its immense size compared to our River Tigris, in which, at the age of ten, I learned how to swim. I was in a class of about ten boys and our swimming teacher was a Baghdadi Jew, Haroun, who was proud of belonging to the ancient Jewish community believed to have settled in Iraq in the 6th century BC. They were descendants of the Hebrews who were brought in captivity to Iraq by Nebuchadnezzar, king of Babylon, after his conquest of Jerusalem in 586 BC. Over the centuries, many Jewish prophets and rabbis were born and lived in Iraq, and it was there that the Babylonian Talmud evolved, which is an essential part of Jewish lore. Haroun was an amiable and modest man, who loved music. While he was teaching us how to swim we joined him in singing the latest songs of the famous Egyptian musician, Muhammad Abdul Wahhab, so we learned to swim as we sang. Haroun's method of teaching was a traditional one which perhaps dates back to Babylonian times: four pieces of the buoyant base of the date palm frond were tied around our bodies to enable us to float, and they were taken off one by one as our skill progressed. As a final proof of my ability I had to swim right across the Tigris – a very wide river.

Other memories centre on the movies. Cinema had just arrived in Iraq and from the age of six I became a regular visitor to the few movie theatres then existing in Baghdad, most of the time accompanied by a man employed by my father to look after me, Yusuf Micha, a Christian from the village of Telkeif near Mosul. With Yusuf I saw most of the early classics, such as one said to be the first talkie, *The Jazz Singer* starring Al Jolson, as well as Marlene Dietrich in *Mata Hari* and *The Blue Angel*, *Queen Christina* with Greta Garbo, Gary Cooper in *Beau Geste*, and, above all, the films of Laurel and Hardy and the early westerns, which I enjoy to this day. I remember how the audience would cheer and applaud when the hero vanquished the 'baddie'.

An incident engraved on my memory took place in 1931, when I was eight years old, during the Iftar feast at the end of Ramadan, the month of fasting. Yusuf and I went to visit the shrine of the Shi'a Imam Musa Al-Kadhim, the revered seventh imam of the Shi'a sect. Visiting the shrine was a Baghdadi tradition even among Sunnis like us. After the visit, we went to a popular restaurant famous for its kebab. As we started eating, a man approached shouting that Yusuf was a Christian, an unclean infidel, and therefore should not eat in a Muslim restaurant. A crowd gathered within seconds and started beating him. I screamed and yelled and cried and tried to protect him, but there was nothing I could do. Luckily the police arrived just in time to save him. This incident had a profound effect on me and since that day I have detested any form of bigotry and discrimination.

That same year there was a general strike directed against the government and in particular at the Minister of the Interior, who happened to be my father. Demonstrators tried to enter our house but were repulsed by the police. This was my first experience of the rougher side of Iraqi politics.

In 1928 I entered the American School for Boys in Baghdad, which had been established by a Protestant minister named Dr Calvin K. Staudt. Although it was ostensibly a religious school, in fact there was little effort to convert anybody. It was a multi-faith school where Muslim, Jewish and Christian pupils studied together. At school I showed some aptitude for history and geography and a notable weakness in maths and science. My father employed private teachers to improve my performance in these subjects. He was extremely concerned about and interested in my education and he encouraged me to use his extensive library to read many Arabic as well as English history books. I also learned early in life to read newspapers and magazines. I had a precocious interest in politics and history and must have seemed rather serious compared to other boys of my age who were naturally more interested in play and sports. History was my passion, and my unusually retentive memory enabled me to memorize names and events in a way that impressed my fellow students and elicited a remark from a friend later in life that my mind was a storehouse of trivia!

Those early years made me aware of the political situation in Iraq and I met many prominent political figures who visited our home. Iraq was in the process of rapid transformation from a remote and neglected province of the Ottoman Empire to a vibrant modern state. This momentous change began with the arrival of the British in 1914. By the end of the First World War the whole country was under military occupation and was administered by a group of highly motivated British officers belonging to the Indian Civil Service. They established a structure of a modern government, but faced resistance from the Iraqi people, who demanded complete independence. During the First World War, the Arabs had fought on the side of the British and now there was anger at Britain's reneging on its promise to help the Arabs gain their freedom and sovereignty. When the League of Nations mandate for Iraq was awarded to Britain in 1920, revolt broke out in many parts of the country. This resulted in a drastic reversal of British policy. Instead of keeping Iraq attached to British India, it was decided to establish a semi-independent kingdom with close links to Britain. Winston Churchill, the Colonial Secretary at that time, obtained the approval of the British Cabinet for this new policy championed by well-known Arabists such as T. E. Lawrence and Gertrude Bell.

There were several candidates for the throne of the new kingdom. The most prominent and acceptable among them was Feisal, son of King Hussein of the Hijaz, Commander of the Arab Regular Army in the revolt against Turkish Ottoman rule during the First World War, and Ruler of Syria from 1918 to1920. After his accession to the Iraqi throne in 1921, the struggle to end the mandate and attain full independence continued with renewed vigour. Iraqis had to wait eleven years before their country became a fully-fledged sovereign state and a member of the League of Nations. Britain, however, retained some military bases in accordance with the Treaty of Alliance and Friendship concluded in 1930.

The British maintained their influence in Iraq through close relations with the monarchs, with the exception of King Ghazi (ruled 1933–39), and with some politicians, the foremost among whom was Nuri Al-Said who believed Iraq needed British help and guidance to stand on its feet as an independent and sovereign state. The British, on their part, created the structure of a modern state and instituted a tradition of honesty and integrity in government, which gave Iraq, until the Gulf Wars of 1991 and 2003, the most competent and least corrupt civil service in the region. Many Iraqis who welcomed the revolution of 1958 today cherish the memory of the monarchy, under whose secular and tolerant government the people of Iraq found peace and security.

2

SECONDARY SCHOOL AND UNIVERSITY, 1934–43

MY GRADUATION FROM PRIMARY school in 1934 coincided with my father's appointment as Permanent Delegate of Iraq to the League of Nations in Geneva and also Minister to Italy and Germany. He wanted me to stay in the Arab world but not in Baghdad, where I would be spoiled by my mother and aunts. So on the advice of some friends he decided to send me to Victoria College, the well-known English public school in Alexandria, Egypt, founded in 1902. King Edward VII laid the cornerstone while he was in Egypt on his way to India to be crowned Emperor. The school was modelled after English public schools like Eton, Harrow and Winchester. The British Empire was then at its zenith and the aim of the school's founders was to give the native populations in the East the benefit of an English education, which they considered the best in the world. The aim was to form close links with the peoples of the region which would benefit Britain and protect its vital interests.

Victoria College was a new experience for me. I found it difficult at first to conform to the strict rules of the school. The English I had learned at the American school in Baghdad was clearly inadequate and I had to learn the language all over again. I was also a failure at sports such as football and cricket. This affected me deeply because sport has always been very important in English public schools. I admired and envied those who excelled at it and it took me quite a while to overcome the feeling of inadequacy induced by my poor showing. However there was one day, engraved on my memory, when I unexpectedly and miraculously took four wickets against a team of British soldiers stationed at a nearby base.

I enjoyed the high level of education and the skill of our excellent teachers at Victoria College. I fell in love with the English language and I was taught to speak English as it should be spoken. I even made great strides in mathematics, thanks to our teacher, Mr Rider, who was also my housemaster. But what I enjoyed most was history and literature (except poetry). I acquired a good knowledge of English and European history, and took advantage of the opportunity to study in depth and to appreciate the works of such great figures of English literature as Shakespeare, Milton, Thackeray, Dickens, Walter Scott and others.

While at Victoria College I made several trips to Europe during the summer holidays of 1935, 1937, 1938 and 1939 to see my father, who held diplomatic posts in Geneva, Rome and Paris. My first trip, at the age of twelve, in 1935 was a memorable one. I travelled by ship from Alexandria to Naples and it was the first time that I experienced the pleasure and luxury of a sea voyage. In Rome a close friend of my father, Paul Hindou, an Iraqi priest belonging to the Syriac Catholic Church, took me at my father's request to the historic sites and famous churches of Rome. He was extremely well versed in history, art and architecture. He opened my eyes to the wonders of the Renaissance and taught me a great deal about Roman history. We visited St Peter's Basilica and the Vatican and Borghese museums as well as the Sistine Chapel and the Basilica of St Paul Outside the Walls. Of the works of Michelangelo, I recall the *Pietà*, the Sistine Chapel and the statue of Moses, and I have a special memory of the works of Bernini and Raphael. Hindou took me to the catacombs where he expounded on the early rise of Christianity. Later that summer, I went by car with my father from Rome to Geneva. On the way we visited Siena, Florence, Bologna and Milan and saw more art treasures, including Michelangelo's *David* and Leonardo da Vinci's *Last Supper*.

Shortly after our arrival in Geneva, my father was instructed to go to Berlin to open the Iraqi Legation and present his letters of credence to the German head of state, Adolf Hitler. I accompanied him on a memorable trip by car from Geneva to Berlin and back. It took about two weeks because we stayed in various German cities such as Munich, Augsburg,

Leipzig, Stuttgart and Baden-Baden. Our driver Joseph was a Polish Jew who had German nationality. He was apprehensive when we entered German territory but my father assured him that he would be safe because we had diplomatic immunity. He was, like the Iraqi priest in Rome, very well informed about history and art. Shortly after our arrival in Berlin, I went with Joseph to the museum housing the famous Ishtar Gate of Babylon. We also went to Potsdam and visited Sanssouci, the palace of Frederick II (the Great), King of Prussia. We had to cut short our visit to Germany because my father was unable to present his credentials to Hitler, who was spending the summer at Berchtesgaden in the Bavarian Alps. My father decided to return to Switzerland via the Black Forest, which gave us an opportunity to visit the University of Heidelberg. My father then relinquished his post in Berlin, which was reassigned to an uncle of King Ghazi of Iraq, Prince Zaid.

During the first week of September 1935, I went with Joseph to Paris, London, Amsterdam and Brussels. Because of my interest in history, I was very keen to visit the places in Paris connected with Napoleon and the French Revolution. Joseph also took me to the Louvre and other museums, where we saw some of the treasures of ancient Mesopotamia, as well as Leonardo da Vinci's *Mona Lisa* and masterpieces of the Impressionist school of painting. In London, I was thrilled to see the places I had read about in my history books, such as the Tower of London, Westminster Abbey and St Paul's Cathedral. We visited the National Gallery, the British Museum, the Natural History and Science Museums and, inevitably, Madame Tussaud's. Our cultural pilgrimage included art museums in Amsterdam and Brussels.

Father Hindou and Joseph, so different in background, had a common love of art that they instilled in me. Because of my youth I was unable to absorb all that I saw and heard, but from that early time of my life I was drawn to European culture and civilization. This attachment to Europe and everything European grew stronger with the passing years. European values and standards are universal and are now a beacon of light to all nations striving to improve the lives of their citizens. The European Union has surpassed most other regions of the world in upholding the rule of law and protecting fundamental human rights. Few places in the world have comparably advanced health, educational and social welfare systems. The creation of a united Europe committed to peace, tolerance and the freedom and wellbeing of the individual, irrespective of his or her religious beliefs or ethnic origins, will go down as one of the great achievements of the 20th century.

During those European travels I recall that in 1938, when I was a little over fifteen and was spending holidays in the French Alps, a man asked me whether I was interested in joining the International Brigade fighting for the Republican Government against the forces of General Franco in the Spanish Civil War. I said, Yes, I would, because I supported the Republican regime. My father was understandably opposed to the whole idea because of my age and the fact that the Republican cause was already lost; and General Franco was on the verge of seizing power and proclaiming victory. Thus I missed my only chance to experience fighting in actual combat conditions.

In 1939, my mother went to Berlin to consult a famous orthopedic surgeon, Professor-Doctor Ernst Ferdinand Sauerbruch. Her brother, my uncle and I stayed with her in Berlin for about three weeks, during July and August 1939. I found life in Berlin quite normal and was completely unaware of the heavy hand of the totalitarian dictatorship ruling Germany at that time; the sordid side of the regime was well concealed from us. On 10 August my mother and I went to Paris to join my father at his new post and I was there when the Second World War broke out in September. My father decided to send me back to Alexandria for my final year at Victoria College. I travelled by the Orient Express from Paris to Istanbul in a private compartment. It was quite an eventful and pleasant journey through Switzerland, Italy, Yugoslavia and Bulgaria. From Istanbul I took a two-day trip by train to Aleppo in Syria. In contrast to the luxury of my private compartment on the Orient Express, I shared my third-class accommodation with Turkish peasants and their animals – sheep and chickens, who slept all over the floor during what seemed to me an endless journey.

During the six years I spent at Victoria College I followed the important developments taking place in Palestine, where an armed revolt against British rule raged for three years from 1936 to 1939. From those early days I was awakened to the Palestine question and the terrible injustice inflicted on its Arab population. From then on, Palestine became a central issue in my life and career. I also followed with interest and consternation the developments in Europe and in Germany in particular, where within the short space of six years Hitler had recovered Saarland, incorporated Austria and the Sudetenland, and rearmed and remilitarized the Rhineland in violation of the Treaties of Versailles and Locarno.

Also at that time, there was a good deal of nationalist agitation in Egypt against the continued British military presence in the country. Thus, on the eve of the Second World War, anti-British feeling in the region was running high. Although I supported the nationalist anti-colonial movements in Palestine, Egypt and Iraq, I was not anti-British, as such. I had learned enough about the British to admire their democracy and way of life. My subsequent clashes with British representatives at the UN on colonial issues did not affect my enduring fondness for Britain.

At Victoria College, the attitude of our teachers and those in the administration was secular. They did not try to inculcate Christian values in those of us who were Muslim, for example. Although they upheld basic British principles of democracy and fair play, the pre-eminence of British literature and so forth, they did not try to justify British policies in Palestine or throughout the Empire. At the same time as I was learning about British and European literature, culture and history – and indeed, we did not study Arab, Indian or Chinese culture or history – I was reading a great deal in Arabic, especially political and cultural publications such as *Al-Risale*, Arab history, and the writings of Taha Hussein and of Aqad and Tawfiq Al-Hakim. I somehow did not expect to learn about these things at Victoria College. There, I learned other things – about European literature and political systems for example – and I learned to question things. In fact, we were encouraged to do so. I could see that the way we were taught European history was often slanted to show the 'superiority' of the British – at the battles of Agincourt and Crécy, Waterloo and Trafalgar, for instance. But I became an admirer of the French revolution, of *Liberté*, *Egalité* and *Fraternité*, and of Napoleon who fought alone against the entrenched and outdated monarchies of Europe.

In August 1940, I obtained the Oxford and Cambridge School Certificate. The headmaster of Victoria College, Mr Reed, had applied on my behalf for a place at Oxford, at either Magdalen or Balliol College. But I was unable to travel to England because that year France fell and Italy declared war. The Mediterranean became a dangerous war zone and the Battle of Britain was reaching its climax, putting air travel out of the question. I had to find an alternative to Oxford. I consulted my father, at that time in Vichy as Iraqi Minister to France. He suggested the American University in Beirut, where I was I enrolled as a sophomore in October 1940. Before leaving Alexandria, I had my first experience of war when a bomb exploded in the sea in front of the hotel to which the school had transferred after its main building had been taken over by the British authorities for use as a military hospital. There were no casualties, but I was excited to be made one of the air raid wardens in the school. There was not much for us to do, however, and it was only after I left Alexandria that real military operations took place.

The American University of Beirut (or AUB as it is called) opened up a new world for me. Despite its name it was to all intents and purposes an Arab institution. A majority of the students were Arabs, mostly from Lebanon, Syria, Palestine and Iraq, and it preserved its Arab character despite English being the language of instruction. It was and still is a centre of intense nationalist activity and this had a profound and lasting effect on my political development.

I studied mainly history and political science. AUB was very different from Victoria College, where the emphasis was on English history and literature, whereas at AUB I was exposed to European and Arab political and literary writings. At the same time, my attachment to Western classical music deepened and was soon to become one of the great passions of my life. AUB was fortunate to have the services of distinguished musicians who had fled Europe to escape the war. There used to be weekly and monthly concerts and, once a year, a performance of Handel's *Messiah* in the university chapel.

During my first year at AUB war broke out between Iraq and Britain. What started as a difference in interpretation of certain provisions of the Anglo-Iraqi Treaty of 1930 soon led to armed conflict. In Iraq, Prime Minister Rashid Ali Gailani was brought to power by a group of nationalist officers who sympathized with the Axis powers because of Britain and France's colonial role in the region, especially in Palestine and Syria. When Italy declared war in 1940, the British asked Iraq to break off diplomatic relations with the country. Gailani refused to do so. At the same time, the

British asserted the right to station troops on Iraqi territory. But the Iraqi government maintained that under the Treaty of 1930, British troops were only allowed the right of passage through Iraqi territory. Winston Churchill, however, rejected this argument. He was leading Britain alone in its "finest hour" against an apparently victorious Germany and was determined not to allow a pro-German, or even a strictly neutral, regime in Iraq. In Beirut, I and other Iraqi students and sympathizers demonstrated, denouncing British aggression and supporting the nationalist stand of the Iraqi government headed by Rashid Ali Gailani. I went back to Baghdad and volunteered for the Youth Brigade, whose duty was to maintain law and order in Baghdad. The unequal contest ended in Iraq's inevitable defeat. Soon thereafter, in June 1941, the British and the Free French under General de Gaulle occupied Syria and Lebanon. On my return to Beirut to resume my studies at AUB, I experienced war conditions for the first time. These fortunately were quite tolerable despite the blackout and shortages in some goods and services. I remember, for example, that coins completely disappeared from circulation and we had to use matchsticks to pay for transport or small purchases. I graduated from AUB on 7 June 1943, and returned to Iraq.

After three years in Beirut, my attachment to the ideals of Arab Nationalism intensified, as did my love for books and music. In Baghdad I applied for a post in the Iraqi Foreign Service, only to be barred from taking the Foreign Ministry exam. The reason, as I learnt later, was a report from the CID (Criminal Investigation Department) that I had supported Rashid Ali Gailani, had taken part in the demonstration in Beirut, and had volunteered for the Youth Brigade. It was not to be the last time I found myself on the wrong side of the authorities. It was a year before I could join the Iraqi Foreign Service.

During that period I read extensively in philosophy and history, as well as in English, European and Arabic literature. I was greatly influenced by such philosophers and writers as Ibn Khaldun, René Descartes, John Locke, John Stuart Mill and Alexis de Tocqueville. The concept of fundamental human rights and the primacy of the individual, which had been born in England and developed and spread over the centuries, became my guiding principle not only in politics but life in general. I became a firm believer in the values and ideals of the Enlightenment, which laid the foundations of modern secular democracies and opposed sectarianism and the encroachment of religion upon government; and as a firm believer in science, logic and reason, I rejected the superstitions and falsehoods inherited from the ages of darkness and ignorance.

While at Victoria College, I had taken piano lessons with an elderly Russian countess who had settled in Egypt after the Russian revolution of 1917. Sadly I lacked the patience and capacity for hard work that a proper musical education demands, but am happy to report that in 1938 I gave a public performance in Alexandria of one of Mendelssohn's *Songs Without Words*, the "Gondoliera" or "Venetian Boat Song" from Book 2, an admittedly easy piece.

In music, my personal tastes can perhaps best be described as traditionalist and conservative. Bach, Beethoven and Mozart top the list though I enjoy many other composers of the 18th- and 19th-century baroque, classical and Romantic movements. I have yet to be converted to 20th-century composers who, with the exception of Richard Strauss, have so far failed to impress me. That is my deficiency, naturally. I am sure I am missing a great deal and hope to fill this serious gap in my musical knowledge and appreciation. Music is an essential and indispensable part of my existence and I cannot conceive of life without it. I have been privileged personally to meet some outstanding musical figures, among them Herbert von Karajan, Leopold Stokowski, Zubin Mehta, Vladimir Horowitz, Leonard Bernstein and Daniel Barenboim. I recall with most pleasure my encounter with Yehudi Menuhin with whom, at a dinner given in 1991 by the famous French-Polish painter Balthus in his grand chalet near Gstaad, I had the pleasure of talking about music, of course, and Palestine. I was delighted to receive a letter from him next day in which he wrote: "It was fascinating and most encouraging to meet you and establish contact with a remarkable and ancient civilization. I was amazed at your knowledge of music and now find it corroborated learning of your annual visits to Salzburg." Lord Menuhin did not mention my other annual musical journey, to the Wagner Festival in Bayreuth.

At the Salzburg Festival I ran into many prominent people. My meeting with the British Prime Minister, Mrs Margaret Thatcher, and her husband Denis in particular stands out in my mind, at a luncheon given in her honour by Princess Marianne Fürstin zu Sayn-Wittgenstein-Sayn. Among the guests were our very close friends Prince and Princess Sadruddine Aga Khan. Inevitably, our discussions focused on the situation in the Middle East, which seemed to concern Mrs Thatcher. In the course of our exchange of views, I ventured to ask her why British ambassadors retire at the early age of sixty, just when they are at the peak of their abilities. She agreed with me and said she was trying to do something about it. At another luncheon given to celebrate the 70th birthday of Leonard Bernstein, I found myself sitting next to the guest of honour; he discussed Mozart's opera *The Marriage of Figaro* and explained to me some of the finer musical points in that sublime work of art. I recall also my talks with former British Prime Minister Sir Edward Heath, an accomplished musician in his own right. The two operas he loved most were Mozart's *Cosi Fan Tutte* and Beethoven's *Fidelio*. He was also fulsome about Tchaikovsky's orchestration. Our discussion naturally drifted from music to Iraq and the Middle East. He spoke at length about his meeting with Saddam Hussein and his success in persuading the Iraqi dictator to release a number of British subjects on the eve of the Gulf War in 1990–91. He seemed to believe that Saddam Hussein was popular in Iraq and enjoyed the support of its people. I tried without success to correct these misconceptions, which were widely shared at the time in some influential Arab and Western circles.

In Baghdad during the last two years of the Second World War, I had opportunities to meet various British and American literary figures, as well as soldiers and diplomats, in the house of Badia Afnan, a lady of culture and refinement who worked with me later in the United Nations. She held a salon where Iraqi and foreign intellectuals met for wide-ranging discussions on political and cultural matters. I was a listener and tried to learn and absorb as much as I could. A cherished memory from those years is of my deepening friendship with Jawad Salim, the foremost Iraqi artist of the 20th century. We were both in our early twenties and used to spend evenings talking about art and life and articulating our dreams, hopes and aspirations. I was in New York in 1960 when I heard about his sudden and premature death. I was devastated and shared with every Iraqi the grief and sadness at this irreparable loss. Jawad will live through his art long after the rest of us are forgotten.

3

Iraqi Embassy in Washington, 1945–49

I WAS APPOINTED TO THE IRAQI Foreign Service on 11 December 1944, and assigned to the "Western Section" of the Political Department at the Ministry of Foreign Affairs. I started work with great enthusiasm and pride. My training began by drafting diplomatic notes mostly relating to our old and special relationship with Britain and our new relations with the United States of America. Unexpectedly, late in January 1945, the Minister of Foreign Affairs decided to transfer me to the Iraqi Legation (later Embassy) in Washington. I was delighted, but felt uneasy about leaving my mother. Before my departure, the US Envoy in Iraq, Loy Henderson, invited me to a tête-à-tête lunch during which he congratulated me on my appointment and asked me not to pay any attention to the attempts to prevent my appointment to the Iraqi Foreign Service. He assured me that I would find the United States a society with deeply rooted anti-colonial traditions, and a reverence for freedom and equality and the rule of law.

Travel from the Middle East to the United States during the war was restricted and only aircraft of the United States Air Force were allowed to fly. I had previously experienced air travel when I flew in 1939 and 1940 between Egypt and Iraq in flying boats and slow, unpressurized propeller aeroplanes. It took two days to fly from Cairo to Washington because of long stops at American military bases in Casablanca, the Azores and

Bermuda. The flight from Cairo to Casablanca took twelve hours in a DC3 Dakota two-engined aeroplane, which stopped en route at Benghazi, Tripoli, Tunis, Algiers and Oran. I was the only civilian on board, all the other passengers being American soldiers. From Casablanca to the Azores and Washington, I travelled on a DC4 which, unlike the DC3, had seats. I remember a group of Saudi diplomats in the passenger waiting room in the Azores, on their way to San Francisco for the opening of the United Nations scheduled for 23 April 1945. At Bermuda, the last stop before Washington, where I stayed another day and part of the night, I remember searching high and low for a barber on the US base where I was staying who might give me a shave – but to no avail. The barbers, it seemed, were allowed to minister only to military personnel.

I arrived in Washington, unshaven, on the evening of 6 April 1945 and the first person I bumped into was Selwa, the daughter of the Iraqi Envoy, Ali Jawdat Al-Ayyubi (1886–1969), the eminent Iraqi statesman and Arab nationalist who, among many other posts, served his country three times as Prime Minister between 1934 and 1957. I had been in love with Selwa ever since we were teenagers. While I was at AUB and she was at the American College for Women, I used to see her occasionally, but not often enough. Our feelings and sentiments had had their ups and downs, but when I saw her that evening in Washington all my suppressed feelings of love and longing were unleashed. For more than a year our love for each other grew ever stronger. We were married on 16 November 1946; we have been together for sixty-five years so far and our love for one another has never faltered. We were both very young and naturally had our differences and disagreements. She shared many of my ideas but could be occasionally critical. I appreciated her intelligence and abilities. Her higher education had been cut short by our marriage when she left the Harvard School of Design (The College of Architecture) after only one year. The premature suspension of her graduate education left her feeling deprived. This feeling was compounded by the childhood problem of being a single girl between two boys who, she felt, were more favoured than her.

Maysoon, the first of our three daughters, was born in Washington. Her early years were spent travelling with us back and forth between the US and the Middle East, shifting between languages and cultures. This was true of all our children, but especially so of Maysoon. My wife and I, particularly my wife, were committed from the beginning to providing our daughters with a solid education with which to face the world. And perhaps this education and their early experiences of seeing life from more than one cultural perspective gave them a questioning, critical attitude. I have to admit that has not always been easy to manage. Sometimes we have not fully comprehended what our children were doing, but they have largely charged ahead anyway. Although, we were in broad agreement on many things, we have had many arguments about politics and social issues over the years, and I have always been proud of my children's independence of thought even if I utterly disagreed with them. Maysoon attended the Brearley School in New York and eventually came to live in London, receiving a degree in Philosophy from University College London before going on to do an MA at the London Film School and becoming a documentary filmmaker. Perhaps because Maysoon is the oldest and spent more of her life in Iraq than her sisters did, she has concentrated, in her film work on the region and especially on the lives of women there. In 2004, she travelled to Iraq with me and made a film about her return. It was the first time she had been back in thirty-five years. At that time she also co-founded, with a colleague, a free-of-charge school in Baghdad to train and teach basic filmmaking to young Iraqis. Our daughters all have a strong sense of justice, they are compassionate, tolerant and generous, and for us they are a precious gift.

A few days after my arrival in Washington, President Franklin D. Roosevelt died, and I witnessed at first hand the love and respect the American people had for him. Greatness was certainly thrust on this man, who saved the United States from economic disaster and led his country to victory in war. He has taken his place among the greats such as Washington, Jefferson and Lincoln.

When I first arrived in Washington in April 1945 as a young diplomat, my knowledge of the United States had come from studies of American history at university and my reading of some of the classics of American literature. I was also influenced by the image of America as projected in Hollywood films, which I soon found out did not accurately reflect the realities of American life. The United States was then at the pinnacle of its power and prestige. As a young man not yet twenty-two years of age, I was dazzled and seduced by that extraordinary country, which seemed to me so far ahead of any other in the world. The United States was indeed the land of opportunity for all, irrespective of ethnic origin or religious belief. This is the America that I admired. I was naturally disappointed by the racial segregation being rigorously enforced in Washington at that time. I also remember an incident in the sweltering hot summer of 1945, when I and two of my colleagues at the Iraqi embassy headed off to a country club on the Chesapeake Bay where we were told the swimming facilities were superb. After driving for an hour and a half, we pulled up at the gates, full of enthusiasm and ready for that swim, only to be met by the guard. "Can't you read?" he said, pointing to the big sign: *Only Gentiles of North European Ancestry Allowed*. We were stunned and, shaking our heads, we climbed back into the car and headed back to hot, humid Washington. Though it was painful for me to see racial discrimination of this kind practised daily and in so many offensive ways, it nonetheless failed to change my overall impression of the country in which I was destined to live for eighteen years of my youth and adult life. I appreciated the freedom and vigour of its open and egalitarian society, the warmth and friendliness of its people and the enduring strength of its institutions.

While in Washington I attended, as an observer, the National Conventions of both political parties in 1948 and followed as well as I could the twists and turns of American domestic politics. I also participated in two international meetings, the First Conference of the Food and Agriculture Organization in Quebec City in Canada in October 1945, and the Inaugural Meeting of the International Bank for Reconstruction and Development and the International Monetary Fund in Savannah, Georgia, in March 1946. There I witnessed John Maynard Keynes, the great economist, eloquently rebutting the attacks against him launched by the American Assistant Secretary of the Treasury, Harry Dexter White, who was later exposed as a member of the Communist Party working closely with the Soviet Union. Another event I recall during my stay in Savannah was the St Patrick's Day parade on 17 March 1946. It was the first time I had experienced such a typically American tradition: a particular ethnic group expressing its national identity. Later, in the '60s, when I was living in New York, there were many such manifestations.

Those early conference experiences had a profound effect on me. I discovered that I had a natural and instinctive preference for multilateral diplomacy; being a shy young man I was a rather awkward practitioner of bilateral diplomacy and felt much more at ease in large gatherings of people.

During my four years (1945–49) in the Iraqi Embassy in Washington, a major upheaval occurred in the Arab world when the Zionist movement succeeded in creating a Jewish state in Palestine. Soon after my arrival in Washington, I became aware of the power of the Zionist movement and the Arabs' ineffectual response to its pervasive influence in the United States. The main demand of the movement at that time was to allow a hundred thousand Jewish refugees from Europe to migrate immediately to Palestine. This demand was strongly supported by the new President, Harry Truman, as well as the US Congress. The State Department, however, warned that unqualified support for Zionist demands would harm vital American interests in Arab and Islamic countries. This clear difference in attitude and approach to the Palestine question between Congress and the State Department persisted for many years, a feature of the American political scene. Eventually and gradually, the pro-Israeli bias of Congress became the policy of the United States under both Republican and Democrat Presidents.

The new British Foreign Secretary, Ernest Bevin, was initially, like his Labour Party, an avowed supporter of Zionist ideology and aims. But gradually he realized that there were two sides to this question and refused to accede to the American and Zionist demands as long as the United States was unwilling to share the burden of maintaining peace and order in Palestine.

An Anglo-American Committee of Enquiry was established in 1946 and held its first meeting in Washington. I attended as an observer and saw hundreds of prominent figures in political, economic, media and academic circles supporting the Zionists' demands without reservation. Arab spokesmen were few and they did their best to confront the avalanche of pro-Zionist speeches and written statements. An Arab office had just been established in Washington by a prominent Palestinian, Musa Al-Alami, a native of Jerusalem and a man of high principles and ideals. The office was largely funded by the Iraqi government under my uncle, Hamdi Pachachi, a lifelong supporter of the Palestinian cause. It included among its members many highly qualified people from Palestine, Iraq and

Lebanon. In spite of their valiant efforts, they could do little to stem the tide of Zionist propaganda.

The Anglo-American Committee, after extensive travels in Europe and the Middle East, recommended that a hundred thousand Jewish refugees be allowed immediately to enter Palestine, and that the country should remain united under international trusteeship until both sides agreed on the constitution of a United State of Palestine. These two recommendations were not implemented because of opposition from all sides. Finally, Britain brought the whole problem to the United Nations General Assembly. Being in Washington, I followed the debates at the United Nations in New York and made frequent visits there to see the Iraqi and Arab delegates. I was intensely interested and I shared with my Arab compatriots their frustration and terrible sense of failure as the Zionist movement emerged victorious and was able to establish the State of Israel on more than three-quarters of the land of Palestine.

4

Director of the United Nations Department, Iraqi Ministry of Foreign Affairs, 1950–53

While at the Iraqi Embassy in Washington I attended Georgetown University, from which I graduated with a PhD degree in June 1949. The subject of my thesis was the development of Arab nationalism in Iraq during the period 1908–21. Five days after I received my degree, I flew with Selwa and Maysoon from Washington to Cairo to take up my new post as Iraqi consul in Alexandria. I was met by my father at the airport. It was the first time we had seen each other for ten years and it was a difficult encounter. The last time we had met I was a sixteen-year-old high school student. Now, in 1949, I was already a married man with a two-year-old daughter and a job as consul in the Iraqi Foreign Service. In the ten years we had been apart, I had become very westernized in my behaviour and attitudes and, although my father was politically progressive, socially he was a conservative. He didn't like many of my closest friends and was suspicious of them. He tried to interfere in my personal life and influence my decisions and we had many fierce arguments, but I stood my ground and eventually he gave up. It was never an easy relationship but essentially we loved one another, and I was grateful, in the end, for his deep care for me and in his interest in my welfare and future.

After a short stay in Alexandria as Iraqi Consul, I was transferred to the Foreign Ministry in Baghdad. My new appointment as head of the United Nations Section at the Ministry marked the beginning of my long association with the UN.

Over the years I have become ever more convinced that the United Nations, despite its occasional failures, is essential for world peace. The world needs the UN and no effort should be spared to make it more relevant and effective. I am fortunate to have been actively involved in its work, conscious of the privilege of being part of a vast undertaking to ensure a better world built on the rule of law, justice and respect for human rights, a world free from the scourge of war, poverty, ignorance and exploitation. In spite of disappointments and failures, the ideals enshrined in the Charter of the United Nations, which eloquently express the eternal yearnings of mankind, are as meaningful and pertinent today as they were when the United Nations came into being amid the wreckage and carnage of the Second World War.

Our second daughter was born in Baghdad. We named her Reema, which was also the name of my paternal grandmother. Always a creative, inventive child, she grew up to be an intelligent, charming and vivacious woman, and is now a well-known jewelry designer with a flair for original, beautifully crafted work. She completed her high school education in New York and the United Nations School and, like Maysoon, eventually settled in London, where she studied at the Central School of Art and then at postgraduate level at the Royal College of Art. She has had her own shops in London's Belgravia and currently Notting Hill Gate and, in 2001, she became Creative Director of the De Beers–Vuitton jewelry joint venture for two years, one of the most high-profile jobs in the jewelry industry.

Reema suffered a devastating loss when her eldest son Said died prematurely at the age of twenty-three. Her sorrow and grief will forever remain but she is getting on with her life supported by the love and devotion of her children, parents and sisters. We were present at Said's funeral in September 2004, during which my daughter Leila sang two of his favourite songs, "Summertime" from Gershwin's opera *Porgy and Bess*, and an aria from Mozart's Opera *Zaide*. It was a most moving occasion, which I still cannot recall without tears in my eyes. Reema's daughter Aisha graduated with honours from Sussex University and is now doing her graduate studies at the School of Oriental and African Studies in the University of London; she is studying international law and planning a career in promoting human rights awareness and the understanding of environmental problems caused by global warming. Reema's younger son, Kareem, has made a name for himself as a poet, dramatist, musician and political activist.

I was appointed a member of the Iraqi Delegation to the Sixth Regular Session of the United Nations General Assembly, which began on 6 November 1951 in the Palais de Chaillot in Paris. The main items on the agenda were the question of Palestinian refugees, the independence of Tunisia and Morocco, and the Korean problem. I was assigned to represent Iraq on the Fifth Committee, which was concerned with financial and budgetary questions. Though a newcomer to the world of high diplomacy, I handled my tasks as well as I could. I vividly recall my fascination and awe as I watched all those diplomats strutting about on the world stage. I spent three months in Paris living in the luxurious surroundings of the Hotel de Crillon on the Place de la Concorde, in the heart of that incomparable city. There was plenty of work, mixed with pleasure. My wife spent a month with me and we visited most of the art museums and exhibitions. In music, a concert devoted to the works of Claude Debussy given by the famous German pianist, Walter Gieseking, lingers in my memory. Of course we also indulged in the culinary delights that only Paris can provide, and I took my wife and friends to many famous restaurants. It was for me a time of discovery and indulgence.

The Seventh Regular Session of the UN General Assembly was held from October to December 1952 in its new building on the East River in New York. I travelled with the other members of the Iraqi Delegation on the ocean liner, *Queen Elizabeth*, from Southampton to New York. It was my first experience of the great luxury available to first-class passengers on those wonderful ships. I crossed the Atlantic by sea four times until, sadly, liners were supplanted by jet air travel, culminating in *Concorde*, on which I was a passenger four times before it was grounded. I mention all these things to show how privileged I was early in my life. In New York, work at the UN was mixed with a great deal of social and cultural activity. New York remains unique. I loved the city and everything it had to offer. Little did I expect in 1952 that I would spend ten years of my life in that great metropolis. The main issues before the General Assembly at that time were, again, Korea, the Palestinian refugees, Moroccan and Tunisian independence, and other colonial questions as well as the apartheid policies of the government of South Africa.

In June 1953, the newly appointed Iraqi Ambassador in Washington wanted me to accompany him to his new post. My wife disliked the idea of going back to Washington but I agreed and took my young family to America. I had just been promoted to the rank of First Secretary, having successfully passed an exam that included a so-called thesis, written in English, as required by regulations. Entitled "The Presidency of the United States", it gave me a greater insight into the workings of the American system of government.

5

Iraqi Embassy in Washington, 1953–57

During the four years of my second tour of duty in Washington, our third daughter Leila was born. Early in life she showed an interest in and love for music. I still recall with enormous pleasure her sitting on my lap as a seven-year-old, listening to Bach with me. She started her piano lessons at the age of eight with an excellent teacher. She made great progress in her musical studies and became an accomplished pianist. In 1979 she graduated from the Music Academy in Wurzburg, Germany, and went to live in Munich with her husband, her former piano teacher. In time they had two sons. Soon after her arrival in Munich, she discovered that she had a good mezzo-soprano voice. She embarked on intensive voice studies and gave recitals in Munich, Utrecht, London, Abu Dhabi, Stuttgart and Prague, and in 1994 in Hamburg she sang the title role in a full operatic production of *Carmen*.

Her husband, Peter Schulz-Thierbach, died in 1993 of a sudden, massive heart attack. There had been nothing to indicate that he had any health problems. My wife and I and our two other daughters attended his funeral, at which a chamber music ensemble played the second movement of Schubert's String Quintet in C major. It was a very sad and moving occasion. With two young sons to raise on her own, Leila found it difficult to continue her career and for a long time stopped singing altogether, which saddened me. Her elder son Adnan loves watches and has an impressive collection of some unusual ones. He treasures his collections and is now working and settled and seems to be contented. Her younger son Faris discovered his love for singing and developed a fine deep bass voice. He has been training, having already sung the role of Don Basilio in Rossini's *Barber of Seville* and that of Sparafucile, the assassin, in Verdi's *Rigoletto*, and performed in Gian Carlo Menotti's opera *Amahl and the Night Visitors*. His performance in Munich on 14 May 2011 as one of the soloists in Mozart's *Requiem* was very well received and he subsequently sang the role of Sarastro in Mozart's opera, *The Magic Flute*. Our love for and dedication to music has created a special bond between me and my daughter Leila. It is one of the things I cherish most and has given me immense pleasure. After Leila's birth, and in spite of social and family pressures to try for a son, we decided we were more than content with our three daughters.

At the United Nations I became involved in colonial questions when I was assigned to represent Iraq on the Fourth Committee, on which all members of the United Nations were represented. I welcomed this assignment because it was the committee that discussed the role of the UN in accelerating the progress of countries under colonial rule towards freedom and independence. The guiding principle of my work on colonial questions was my belief in the right of every people to self-determination. That is why, unlike most other Iraqi politicians, I openly supported this right for the Kurdish people in Iraq.

My speeches in the Fourth Committee and in the plenary meetings of the General Assembly on colonial questions are on record. They dealt with every aspect of the difficult journey towards freedom and independence of such territories as the Portuguese colonies, Aden, Togo, the Cameroons, Southern Rhodesia (Zimbabwe), South-West Africa (Namibia), Northern Rhodesia (Zambia), Nyasaland (Malawi), Tanganyika and Zanzibar (Tanzania), Rwanda, Burundi and the Congo. I recall in 1962, while we were discussing the future of the Belgian trust territory of Rwanda-Urundi, the Prime Minister of Belgium, Paul-Henri Spaak, saying that he regarded me as his most dangerous adversary. I considered that quite a compliment.

My duties at the Embassy were concerned with Iraqi–American relations. These greatly improved in 1955 after Iraq joined the Baghdad Pact, an anti-communist alliance with Turkey, Pakistan, Iran and Britain.

The influential US Secretary of State, John Foster Dulles, was especially pleased by Iraq's rejection of neutralism. But the main affair overshadowing all others was the Suez Crisis of 1956–57. The events of that fateful year followed an important decision in 1955 by the Egyptian leader, Jamal Abdul Nasser, after months of futile negotiations with the United States on military co-operation and assistance. In April 1955 Nasser attended the Bandung Conference of independent Afro-Asian states, where he took a strongly neutralist stand and attacked the alliances with which John Foster Dulles sought to surround and contain both the Soviet Union and China. While at Bandung, Nasser learned from the Chinese Premier, Chou En-lai, that the Soviet Union would be willing to supply Egypt with large quantities of arms. Nasser informed the US Ambassador in Cairo that unless the United States fulfilled its promises, Egypt would be compelled to get the military hardware it needed from the Russians. Nasser's warnings went unheeded, and in September 1955 an agreement with Czechoslovakia was signed whereby Egypt would receive 80 million dollars' worth of military equipment.

That agreement greatly enhanced Nasser's prestige and strengthened his claim to be the undisputed leader of the Arab world. The Israelis were quick to exploit the widening rift between the United States and Egypt by launching frequent attacks on Egyptian positions in the Gaza Strip. As usual they overplayed their hand and the escalating violence in the Middle East coupled with fear of further Soviet political gains persuaded the United States to adopt a more conciliatory attitude towards Egypt. As a first step, the US administration rejected Israel's request for arms, then expressed its readiness to finance with the World Bank and the United Kingdom the construction of the Aswan High Dam. An agreement was concluded with the World Bank in February 1956 for a loan of 200 million dollars contingent on a financial grant to be given by the United States and the United Kingdom. Dulles had hoped that the Aswan Dam deal would encourage Nasser to start indirect negotiations with Israel. When Nasser declared his unwillingness to deal with Israel from a position of weakness, Dulles, who had always disliked the Egyptian ruler for his neutralism and for bringing the Soviet Union into the Arab world, decided not to resist the pressures against a deal with Nasser that were building up in Congress. For five months he kept the Egyptians waiting for the grant agreement. During that period, Egypt recognized the People's Republic of China which, in Dulles's eyes, was evil incarnate and the archenemy of the United States.

This was the *coup de grâce* for the Aswan Dam deal and, despite Nasser's belated withdrawal of his reservations regarding some of the conditions of the agreement, Dulles informed the Egyptian Ambassador in Washington that the United States was no longer interested in financing the building of the dam because of Egypt's alleged inability to bear the financial burdens involved in such a huge project. Nasser was justifiably incensed at what he perceived to be American perfidy, compounded by a gratuitous insult. He retaliated by nationalizing the Suez Canal Company, an act greeted with tremendous acclaim throughout the Arab world. Thus, Nasser became the acknowledged leader of the Arab masses and the authentic voice of their aspirations for freedom and dignity. Britain and France, the major users and shareholders in the Canal Company, reacted with extreme hostility and threatened military action. President Eisenhower objected to the use of force and was extremely annoyed by the threats emanating from London and Paris; he was determined to defuse the crisis by peaceful means and, if need be, economic pressure.

This conciliatory American position greatly contributed to improving US–Egyptian relations and Nasser pinned his hopes on the United States being able to dissuade its French and British allies from undertaking any military action against Egypt. For this reason he responded favourably to American proposals and co-operated fully with the United States in the weeks preceding the Anglo-French-Israeli attack. As is well known, Eisenhower was kept completely in the dark about the collusion of Britain and France with Israel, and when the Israeli attack began on 29 October 1956 the Americans were as much taken by surprise as everyone else. Nasser asked the United States for help, having despaired of any effective military assistance from the Soviet Union which urged him, in fact, to come to terms with the British and French. The United States, under a President of impeccable honour and integrity, rose to the occasion and led the campaign to confront the aggressors in the United Nations. Eisenhower compelled the British to halt their military operations after threatening to impose severe economic sanctions, which Britain's fragile economy would be unable to withstand. It is therefore only fair to acknowledge that Eisenhower saved Egypt in 1956. A great opportunity thus presented itself for significant improvement in US–Egyptian relations, with far-reaching consequences for the future. Nasser was the first to seize this historic opportunity and offered the hand of genuine friendship to the United States, but unfortunately John Foster Dulles had never forgiven him for steering the Arabs away from alliances inspired and dominated by the West, and for moving them towards neutralism and friendship with the Soviet Union. As a result, he did everything in his power to wreck the rapprochement with Egypt, turning down the request for emergency relief and refusing to release 27 million dollars of blocked dollar balances belonging to Egypt.

The defeat of the tripartite aggression made Nasser the hero of the Arab masses and undisputed leader of the Arab world. The United States should have realized by then that the only way to improve its position and that of the West in the Arab world was to reach some kind of accommodation with Nasser who, despite the rebuff from Dulles, was still anxious to improve relations with the United States. Dulles on the other hand embarked on a policy the aim of which was to isolate Nasser. Saudi Arabia and Jordan became the target of Dulles's relentless pressure to break away from Nasser's camp and join Iraq in a grand monarchical coalition against the two republics of Egypt and Syria. The overthrow of the Syrian regime, which had recently seemed to be veering dangerously towards communism, became Dulles's main concern during 1957. Various CIA-inspired plots were hatched in which Iraq and the pro-Western Lebanese President Camille Chamoun took part. The Eisenhower Doctrine, with its proclaimed purpose of preventing the spread of communism in the Middle East, became the new American instrument for mobilizing anti-Nasser forces in the Arab world.

6

DIRECTOR GENERAL OF THE DEPARTMENT OF INTERNATIONAL AFFAIRS, IRAQI MINISTRY OF FOREIGN AFFAIRS, 1957–59

IN JUNE 1957 I WAS TRANSFERRED to the Foreign Ministry in Baghdad to take up the post of Director General of the Department of International Organizations. My father-in-law, Ali Jawdat, was Prime Minister at that time, and suggested that I should be seconded to his office as head of the Department of Political Affairs. In that new position I studied the reports and dispatches sent to the Prime Minister's office, and I urged on him that the government should try to improve relations with Egypt and end the divisions in the Arab world. He fully agreed, and as a first step asked the King, Feisal II, to dissolve Parliament and hold new elections in order to defuse discontent and public anger at the failure of the previous government of Nuri Said to respond effectively to Britain's alliance with Israel against Egypt. The King was under the influence of his uncle, Crown Prince Abdul Illah, who had been Regent of Iraq for fourteen years and wielded real power even after the end of his Regency. Ali Jawdat's request to dissolve parliament was turned down, forcing him to resign. My secondment was terminated and I returned to my job at the Foreign Ministry.

Soon after that we moved to our new house on Ali Jawdat's property in Karadat Mariam in West Baghdad, now the so-called Green Zone. The house was designed by my brother-in-law's wife, Ellen, a graduate of the Harvard School of Design and a well-known architect who had many buildings in Baghdad to her credit. A few weeks later, thieves broke into the house and held us at gun- and knifepoint. They heaped us with insults and stole some valuables. What was odd was that they engaged us in political discussion, accusing us of exploiting the poor – an accusation I vehemently denied. Baghdad society was shocked; some suspected the thieves of working for government intelligence and that the burglary had been a warning to me to stop criticizing the government and advocating close relations with Egypt. I have no evidence to support such suspicions.

In February 1958, the union of Egypt and Syria was announced. The new United Arab Republic (UAR) was welcomed with enormous enthusiasm by the overwhelming majority of the Iraqi people. I myself was overjoyed and hoped that this historic breakthrough would be followed by others, as indeed came about almost immediately when a federal union between Jordan and Iraq was proclaimed. I supported this new move towards Arab unity but it was greeted with indifference by the Iraqi public, who considered it merely a desperate attempt by the Iraqi Government to improve its image. Nuri Said, by now Prime Minister again, proposed to the British government that Kuwait should join this new Arab union in a tripartite Federation, but the British as well the Ruler of Kuwait rejected this proposal. Nuri Said felt betrayed by his erstwhile friend, Britain, in his hour of great need. He warned the British Foreign Secretary, Selwyn Lloyd, that Western policies would in the end ruin and destroy the West's staunch friends in the region. I was asked to prepare a memorandum about Kuwait joining the Federation, but I am sad to say it was overlooked.

While we were busy at the Foreign Ministry preparing for the creation of a unified diplomatic service for the Arab Federation (between Iraq and Jordan), I was visited by a senior official of the Development Board. He was a friendly British gentleman who suggested that I should take a temporary leave of absence from the Foreign Ministry to establish and direct a new department of the Board dealing with social issues and the effects of the new economic projects on the everyday life of Iraqis, especially in the rural areas. I welcomed the idea but declined the offer because I felt I was not qualified by education, training or inclination to undertake such a pioneering task. I also wanted to continue in my diplomatic career and began to look forward to a post of chief of mission. I wondered whether the offer had been made to remove me from the Foreign Ministry because of my anti-colonial activities at the United Nations and my alleged Nasserist leanings.

In June 1958, I went to Amman as a member of an Iraqi delegation to discuss with the Jordanian government the details of merging the Foreign Services of the two countries. The Jordanians insisted on an equal division of the diplomatic posts. We protested on the grounds that Iraq, unlike Jordan, had a well-established and experienced Foreign Service, and that Iraq had wider international interests. I went to see Nuri Said privately and complained about the Jordanian position. I found him sad and pensive, and he said we should go along with Jordanian demands because it was essential that the union be maintained and strengthened. This was the last time I saw him; a few months later he was dead, a bitter and frustrated man.

The situation in Iraq was rapidly reaching boiling point. We heard rumours about army officers, inspired by Pan-Arabism and Egypt's example in 1952, plotting to overthrow the government. When Nuri Said and Prince Abdul Illah were informed of this, they dismissed the rumours as unfounded and reaffirmed their trust in the loyalty of the Armed Forces. They soon found out, at the cost of their lives, how mistaken they were. I was grief-stricken by the massacre of the Royal Family. Abdul Illah paid with his life for having hanged the four Colonels who had led the coup against him in 1941. I was also devastated by the brutal murder and mutilation of Nuri Said, whom I had known since childhood. He and his wife were frequent visitors at our home in Baghdad, and I was close to his nephews and those of his wife – the sons of Jafar and Tahsin Al-Askari. I remember, when we were children, Nuri used to take us out on a boat on summer nights, when the moon was full, to a small island in the middle of the Tigris called Al-Jazra. It used to completely disappear in the winter and only reappear in summer when the level of the river went down. We used to swim and play and eat delicious *masgouf* fish – a particular Iraqi river carp – while Nuri told us jokes and funny stories. He always urged me to be less bookish and to indulge more in sports. As I grew up to be a fervent Arab nationalist, I opposed his policies, but that did not affect our personal relations. I never doubted his love for his country and his devotion to the ideals of Arab nationalism, which he espoused early in his youth and from which he never wavered. He was a brave soldier who fought for Iraqi and Arab independence. Undoubtedly, like any politician, he was guilty of errors of judgement, such as his obsession with the exaggerated communist threat to Iraq. He also depended on Britain's friendship even when such a friendship was politically suicidal. After the 1956 attack on Egypt he had an opportunity to retrieve much of his popularity but he let it slip: he could have withdrawn from the Baghdad Pact Alliance in 1956 after Britain joined France and Israel in waging war against another Arab country.

The military coup by the Free Officers on 14 July 1958 soon developed into a full-scale revolution that changed Iraq completely and for ever. I was in Baghdad that fateful morning. The night before, I had been informed that my name had been removed from the list of Foreign Service officials of the Iraq–Jordan Federation. I protested to the then Foreign Minister, Tawfiq Al-Suwaidi, who blamed Abdul Illah and Nuri Said. The day following the coup, 15 July, all government officials were ordered to report to their ministries and departments. I went to the Foreign Ministry and met the new Foreign Minister, Abdul Jabbar Jomard, who was friendly and courteous. He asked me to join a committee set up to investigate Foreign Service officials and remove those whose loyalty to the new republican regime was doubtful. I tried to protect as many of my colleagues as I could and am happy to say that only a few were dismissed. The Minister of Information asked me to censor all outgoing media dispatches. I tried to be as liberal as possible and co-operated in a very friendly fashion with the hundreds of correspondents flocking to Baghdad to cover the momentous drama unfolding in Iraq.

Soon after the fall of the monarchy, Iraq's new Republican Government withdrew from the Baghdad Pact and declared their intention to co-operate closely with the United Arab Republic. This led Camille Chamoun, President of Lebanon, to request US troops to help him repel any attack by his enemies in the civil war then raging in his country. A similar request by King Hussein of Jordan to the British government caused the whole matter to be transferred to the United Nations Security Council. As it was unable to agree, a special session of the General Assembly was convened. The new Minister decided to lead the delegation, of which I was a member.

We left Baghdad on 12 August 1958, barely four weeks after the revolution; it had been a period full of tension and uncertainty. We flew to Copenhagen and the contrast between the peaceful, cool and beautiful Danish capital and the extreme heat, violence and fear in Baghdad was stark. I felt as if I had moved to another world. In New York the Iraqi delegation was cordially received. Jomard gave his speech in French as translated from an English text which Ismat Kittani and I had written. The Minister asked me to stay in New York to join the Iraqi delegation to the Thirteenth Session of the UN General Assembly scheduled to begin in September 1958. My family in the meantime had gone to Europe a few days after my departure from Baghdad and I decided to bring them to the United States. We stayed during the three months of the session in a modest hotel in the Upper East Side of Manhattan.

During the session I was very active in the Fourth Committee, dealing with such thorny problems as the Portuguese colonies, the future of the Cameroons under French and British trusteeship, and South-West Africa, which we tried to save from the clutches of the racist apartheid government of South Africa. At the end of the session in December 1958, I received orders from the government to proceed immediately to Moscow, where I was to be Counsellor of the Embassy which had just been opened with a new Ambassador, a leftist politician, at its head. It was an unpleasant surprise for me. I was already deeply concerned by the strong communist influence in Baghdad. I also felt that I was by now entitled to head a diplomatic mission and not to continue as a number two, even in an embassy as important as that in the Soviet Union.

So I resigned and applied for a job in the United Nations Secretariat. While my application was being considered, a cabinet reshuffle occurred in Baghdad in which Hashim Jawad was appointed Foreign Minister. One of his first acts was to refuse my resignation and appoint me as representative to the resumed General Assembly session dealing with the issue of the Cameroons. I went to New York and was very active in the debates on that question, taking a strong stand in favour of the opposition parties against a French-appointed government. A few days after the end of the session, I was informed of my appointment as Counsellor and Acting Permanent Representative to the United Nations in New York, a dream finally come true.

7

AMBASSADOR AND PERMANENT REPRESENTATIVE TO THE UNITED NATIONS, 1959–65

As soon as I took up my new post I was met with unrelenting hostility by the Iraqi Consul General, Izzedine Al-Rawi. He was unable to accept someone who had belonged to the defunct regime being given such an important position. The communist newspapers in Iraq echoed his hostility towards me. I did not cave in; I fought back and won, thanks to the support of Hashim Jawad who appreciated my work and the excellent reputation I had established with the anti-colonialist bloc at the United Nations. Rawi was transferred back to Baghdad and I have not heard of him since. And in order to avoid any friction in future, a Consular Officer under my authority was entrusted with consular matters. That enabled me to devote all my time to representing Iraq in a manner that would better serve the interests of my country and enhance its international reputation. I had the good fortune to be helped by two outstanding Iraqi foreign service officials, Ismat Kittani and Faiha Kamal.

Early in 1960, I decided to seek the chairmanship of the Fourth Committee. My candidacy was strongly opposed by the colonial powers. Among the documents of the British Foreign Office which were opened to the public at the British National Archives (previously the Public Record Office) at Kew, in west London, I saw several dispatches between the British mission at the United Nations and the Foreign Office in London.

The first, dated 2 February 1960, was signed by A. R. Moore and addressed to Mr Tahourdin, in which the UK mission stated:

> It would not be easy to accept Pachachi's candidacy. He is one of our foremost adversaries on colonial questions. He is clever and capable and knowledgeable in matters of procedure and while it would be important to have a competent chairman of the fourth committee (and Mr Pachachi is that) it would be preferable if somebody else will assume the chairmanship of the committee.

Another dispatch, dated 12 March 1960 from the Foreign Office to the British mission in New York, sent by Tahourdin to A. R. Moore, stated:

> I share your dislike of the idea of Pachachi's chairmanship of the fourth committee. While he may be competent, he would be unable if not unwilling to be neutral. I agree that it is in the interest of UK, that the chairman of the committee should not only be competent but also neutral if possible.

This dispatch was signed by Douglas Hurd, who much later would become Foreign Secretary. And another, dated 18 March 1960, said: "We are against as a matter of principle that the chairmanship of the fourth committee should be given to a rabid anti-colonialist like Mr Pachachi." Those efforts failed and I was elected unanimously to the chairmanship of the Fourth Committee on 21 September 1960 after a graceful speech of nomination delivered by Sir Andrew Cohen, the British representative.

A few weeks earlier, I had been given the rank of Ambassador and presented my credentials to the Secretary-General of the United Nations, Dag Hammarskjold, as Permanent Representative of Iraq to the UN. This was undoubtedly a turning point in my life and career. I was thirty-seven, and perhaps one of the youngest ambassadors at the United Nations. Most of my colleagues were senior diplomats at the pinnacle of their careers or politicians who had held important positions in their countries. During the eight and a half years in which I served as Iraq's representative to the UN I was privileged to work with many outstanding personalities of world stature, and always tried to live up to the high standards prevailing in the UN at that time. I was fortunate in having a beautiful wife of exquisite taste and great dignity and class. She contributed in no small measure to whatever success I achieved. I am also happy to say that I maintained the best of relations with all those who worked with me in the Iraqi mission. Among them I must mention my deputy, Ismat Kittani, who subsequently had a distinguished career both in the United Nations Secretariat and in the service of his country, reaching the position of Assistant Secretary-General of the United Nations and later becoming Permanent Representative of Iraq, besides being elected President of the General Assembly in 1981. I should also mention Adnan Raouf, a brilliant man who later held senior positions in the UN Secretariat, and Faiha Kamal, a gifted and capable woman who went on to become a senior UN official. Without their help and co-operation it would have been impossible for me to discharge my duties as Permanent Representative. To them and my other colleagues in the mission, I owe a debt of gratitude that no words can adequately express.

When I was appointed Permanent Representative, the United Nations had only eighty members, less than half of its present membership. It was an organization dominated by the United States and its allies. We had to fight very hard to get any favourable decision on issues like Palestine or colonialism. During my tenure, deliberations at the UN were dominated by the Cold War, a factor that greatly diminished the efficacy of the world organization. As a founding member of the movement of non-aligned countries, Iraq co-operated closely with such countries as Yugoslavia and India. I also maintained excellent personal relations with the representatives of the Arab states and of the two military blocs, and endeavoured to enhance Iraq's importance at the UN. In so doing, I did not hesitate to adopt a clear and forthright position on most issues. Such a stand, I believe, earned the respect of many delegations. There were those who criticized me for over-exposure and believed that a lower profile would have been more appropriate in the light of Iraq's size and relative insignificance on the world stage. I disagreed with this view because the only way for a small country like ours to carry any weight in international affairs is to have a role in the United Nations, the only forum where small countries can make their voices heard.

During my first two years as Permanent Representative, I was concerned mainly with colonial questions. At the Fifteenth Session in

1960, as I indicated, I was elected chairman of the Fourth Committee and took part in the drafting of the declaration on the granting of independence to colonial countries and peoples. I am proud to have been involved in the international efforts to expedite the historic march towards freedom. My stand against colonialism and racism was appreciated by many African leaders and American activists in the field of human rights. One of them was Ralph Bunche, a close friend of mine who was for many years in charge of the Trusteeship Department in the UN Secretariat. He invited me to go with him to a meeting of the National Association for the Advancement of Colored People (NAACP), where I met Roger Wilkins, the well-known figure in the civil rights movement in America. I also met Malcolm X, one of the most prominent leaders in the struggle against racism in the United States. We had a long talk at a gathering to which various other UN ambassadors had been invited. At a meeting in South Chicago in 1968 I vividly recall meeting Elijah Mohammed who, in contrast to Malcolm X, was a black racist and a firm believer in total segregation. As a result of my consistently anti-colonialist stand at the United Nations I have often been accused of being anti-Western. This is an unjust accusation. In their handling of colonial questions, the Western powers have often violated their own principles and values. The ideals of justice, freedom and equality, so loudly trumpeted by them, were frequently ignored when it came to the colonies. What I did was to point out, a little forcefully perhaps, the inconsistency of their proclaimed beliefs and objectives with their actual policies and practices.

It was at the momentous Fifteenth General Assembly Session in 1960 that I met such world leaders as Jamal Abdul Nasser, Jawaharlal Nehru, Nikita Khrushchev, Josip Broz Tito, Fidel Castro, Ahmed Sukarno, Harold Macmillan and Dwight Eisenhower. In late September 1960, Khrushchev gave a luncheon in honour of the President of the General Assembly, Frederick Boland of Ireland, and the seven chairmen of the main committees; I attended as chairman of the Fourth Committee. Immediately after lunch, during which Mr Khrushchev drank prodigious amounts of vodka, we all went to the meeting of the General Assembly at which he famously banged his shoe. I have often wondered whether the heavy drinking at that luncheon had something to do with the incident. A few days later, we gave a big reception at the Iraqi mission in honour of the Algerian delegation, which was unexpectedly attended by Khrushchev himself. This was a memorable occasion: the Soviet leader, with a throng of uninvited journalists in his train, gave an impromptu press conference. The leader of a superpower using the Iraqi mission to speak to the world press made quite a spectacle.

The burning issue during the Fifteenth Session in 1960–61 was the Congo problem. On 30 June 1960, the Congo, which had been a Belgian colony since the turn of the century, acceded to independence. No adequate preparations had been made for the orderly transfer of power, and the seething anger and resentment of the native population against their Belgian masters soon erupted in violence all over the country as Congolese soldiers mutinied and attacked their Belgian officers. On 10 July, Belgian airborne troops intervened and the Congolese government, under Patrice Lumumba, appealed to the United Nations for help. The Belgians countered by encouraging Moise Tshombe to declare the secession of the mineral-rich province of Katanga from the rest of the Congo. There ensued an almost complete collapse of law and order with a massive breakdown of essential services and economic activity. Belgian troops occupied parts of the capital, Leopoldville, and Dag Hammarskjold, the Secretary-General of the UN, convened a meeting of the Security Council on 15 July 1960 to consider the situation. The Council authorized the Secretary-General to provide the Congolese government with military assistance.

The Congo operation was thus launched, and it immediately encountered great difficulties. The UN force entrusted with the task of maintaining law and order in the whole of the Congo was initially refused entry into the province of Katanga. A further resolution of the Security Council had to be adopted before it was allowed to enter Katanga and replace the Belgian forces that had been withdrawn. However, the Katanga secession did not cease and the main issue that arose was whether the UN troops were entitled to end it by force or would have to treat it as a purely internal matter outside the UN mandate. Hammarskjold adhered to the latter opinion because he wanted to avoid bloodshed. Both sides in the Congo – the supporters of Lumumba and his opponents – tried to use the UN force to their advantage. Hammarskjold steadfastly refused to be drawn into internal Congolese conflicts. Then, in September, Mobutu's junior officers in the Congolese army, with the assistance of the CIA, staged a coup and took over power in the capital of the Congo. The situation became polarized between the supporters of the Western powers and the Soviet Union. The United Nations was caught in the middle, and the Secretary-General pleased neither side, but the majority of the smaller states supported him. I was one of his most enthusiastic supporters, although the government of Iraq at the time, under pressure from the Soviet Union, wanted me to express disapproval of the Secretary-General's actions. This I refused to do, with the approval of the Foreign Minister, Hashim Jawad. The Secretary-General was being attacked for his stand by the Soviets and, less stridently, by the West. He greatly appreciated a statement I made in September 1960 in support of him and his actions. Lumumba was arrested by Mobutu with the approval and encouragement of the Western powers. In December 1960, Hammarskjold, fearing that the United Nations force would be dragged into a military confrontation with the Congolese army of Mobutu, took no action to save Lumumba and he was killed in January 1961. The Soviet Union accused Hammarskjold of complicity and declared that it no longer recognized him as Secretary-General of the UN.

About the same time – it was 24 January 1961 – Hammarskjold called me to his office and said he wanted someone at his side to direct and co-ordinate the whole Congo operation from New York; he wanted to entrust me with this responsibility and to appoint me Under-Secretary for Special Political Affairs – the first Arab to be offered such a senior post at the UN. After some hesitation I accepted, and the Secretary-General formally asked the Iraqi government to release me for service in the United Nations. At first the Prime Minister and Iraqi leader, Abdul Karim Qassim, was inclined to approve my secondment to the UN but then, under strong Soviet pressure, he changed his mind and turned down the Secretary-General's request.

On 13 September 1961, despite its refusal to use force, the United Nations contingent was drawn into a military confrontation with the secessionist government of Katanga. The Western governments severely criticized the UN's handling of the problem and threatened to withdraw economic and logistical support. Hammarskjold arrived in Congo the day the fighting erupted in Katanga and tried to retrieve the situation, but as the fighting continued he decided to go to Katanga himself to meet Tshombe, leader of the secessionist group. They were to meet at Ndola in Northern Rhodesia, still a British colony and under the authority of the racist government of Roy Welensky. Hammarskjold never reached Ndola. He was killed when his plane crashed as it was approaching the airport on 18 September 1961.

I cannot describe the shock and grief I felt. Dag Hammarskjold inspired both love and admiration, and I felt, and feel to this day, after all these years, a sense of deep personal loss. I shall never forget the memorial meeting held in the General Assembly hall when the Philadelphia Orchestra under Eugene Ormandy played two of the greatest musical masterpieces – Hammarskjold's favourites (and mine): the final chorus of Bach's St Matthew Passion and the fourth, choral movement of Beethoven's Ninth Symphony. It was a very moving occasion and I suspect there were not many dry eyes among those present.

In retrospect, and with the benefit of hindsight, I believe Dag Hammarskjold attributed too much importance to the Congo problem. It was an exaggeration to consider it a major threat to international peace and security. The danger of a confrontation between East and West did not materialize because neither side attached that much importance to the country. Hammarskjold was wrong to plunge headlong into the complexities of tribal politics in a newly independent African country, though of course the size and great wealth of the Congo made it one of the most important countries on the continent. Hammarskjold always wanted to break new ground for the United Nations and so confer on the Secretary-General increased authority and initiative. He was encouraged by the Suez experience, but here the circumstances were vastly different. Whereas in Suez there was a real possibility of great-power confrontation, and two great powers actually deployed their armed forces against a member state of the UN, no such risks were presented by the Congo. It was essentially an internal problem in which, admittedly, outside powers were interested, but not a situation where the UN should have intervened. Yet, having done so, Hammarskjold was right to pursue it to the end.

In April 1961, I became involved for the first time in the UN debates on Palestine. I spoke on the question of property rights of Palestinian refugees and made a detailed reply to the statement of the representative of Israel, and a further statement in the plenary meeting of the General Assembly on 21 April 1961 on the proposal to appoint a custodian for Palestine refugee properties. My interventions elicited the following observations in the *Jewish Observer* in its issue of 28 April:

> But an outstanding figure during these debates was Dr Pachachi, the Iraqi delegate. He is rated as probably the ablest and most impressive of the Arab delegates among the many who have been and still are at the United Nations.

At the same time I intervened in the debate on the "Bay of Pigs" fiasco in Cuba. In April 1961, Cuban dissidents, with the help of the United States, invaded Cuba, and were annihilated in the Bay of Pigs. The Cuban government of Fidel Castro lodged a complaint that was considered in the First Committee of the United Nations General Assembly on 19 April. The speech that I made on the subject was warmly received by most of the Latin American countries and, naturally, by the Soviet bloc. I was rewarded with a magnificent large box of the best Cuban cigars sent to me with the compliments of Fidel Castro.

Soon thereafter, on 19 June 1961, a crisis erupted when the British government recognized the independence of Kuwait. On 25 June the Iraqi leader, Abdul Karim Qassim, declared that Kuwait was an integral part of Iraq and refused to recognize its independence. The ruler of Kuwait then requested British military assistance and British troops landed in Kuwait on 1 July. At the same time, the United Kingdom lodged a complaint with the Security Council on behalf of Kuwait against Iraq, and we promptly lodged a counter-complaint against the United Kingdom. The Security Council discussed these two complaints between 2 and 7 July 1961.

It must be emphasized that the situation in which I was involved in 1961 was very different from the one in 1990, when Iraq invaded and annexed Kuwait. Iraq's claims were based on the fact that Kuwait had been juridically part of the Ottoman province of Basra, which subsequently became part of the Iraqi state.

This position was maintained and vigorously reaffirmed from the inception of the modern Iraqi state in 1921 until 1963. Successive Iraqi governments have asserted those claims and unsuccessfully sought to solve the problem in consultation with the British government. In 1938 there was a strong popular movement in Kuwait calling for union with Iraq, and King Ghazi encouraged and supported that movement. In 1961, when Kuwait's independence was proclaimed, the Iraqi government's refusal to recognize that independence was supported by the Iraqi people. Even the opposition groups whose leaders were in exile in Cairo asserted in the strongest possible terms the legitimacy of Iraq's claims to Kuwait and supported Qassim's stand, despite the fact that they were plotting to overthrow him.

It is against this background that we should consider Iraq's position in the United Nations in 1961. My interventions on the Kuwait issue in 1961 are part of history and are fully documented in the records of the United Nations. In 1963, the situation changed radically with Iraq's recognition of Kuwait's independence, followed by the establishment of normal diplomatic relations with it as a fellow member of the Arab League and the United Nations, and it was apparent by that time that the people of Kuwait wanted independence and no longer supported union with Iraq. Subsequently these relations had their ups and downs because of the still unresolved border problem: during the Iran–Iraq war, their relations were close, as both countries co-operated to confront Iranian ambitions in the Gulf. After the war, relations rapidly deteriorated again because of the border problem, exacerbated by what Iraq considered to be Kuwait's insensitivity to the severe difficulties arising from the long war with Iran and the sharp fall in oil prices. These problems should not have been allowed to fester, but should have been resolved quickly. If that had been done, relations between the two countries could have been normalized and raised to the level expected of two neighbouring Arab countries with common interests and aspirations.

Before the year 1961 ended, I took part in the first summit meeting of the Movement of Non-Aligned Countries in Belgrade, where I worked closely with my friend and colleague, Ambassador Mahmoud Riad of Egypt, to include in the final communiqué a strong endorsement of the Arab position on Palestine.

The non-aligned movement was born in the late 1950s, at the height of the Cold War. The founding fathers of the movement were President Tito of Yugoslavia, Prime Minister Nehru of India and Presidents Nasser and Sukarno of Egypt and Indonesia. They invited leaders from Latin

America, the Middle East, Asia and Africa to join them at the inaugural summit meeting of the movement in Belgrade in 1961, in which I participated as a member of the Iraqi delegation, as I would do again in Cairo in 1964 and Algiers in 1973, but this time representing the UAE. There was a genuine fear that the two military alliances, NATO and the Warsaw Pact, might plunge the world into a nuclear holocaust and the non-aligned movement expressed the collective desire of many nations, particularly the newly independent countries of Asia and Africa, to meet the challenges and problems created by the Cold War. The state of permanent crisis which characterized the Cold War was felt in every country and by every people with a degree of intensity and immediacy that made international affairs a matter of everyday concern for the average man and woman the world over. Small countries like Iraq were reluctant to be drawn into military alliances, but at the same time they could not stand aloof and allow their destiny to be decided by others. The broad objectives of the movement were the following:

1. To strengthen the UN and enable it to preserve peace and thus obviate the necessity for military alliances.

2. To support by all means, the struggle for independence and the suppression of all forms of racial discrimination.

3. To give the UN and its specialized agencies greater power and responsibility in promoting economic development with the ultimate aim of eradicating poverty all over the world.

In late October 1962, one of the most memorable episodes at the United Nations during those earlier years was the Cuban missile crisis. I followed very closely the debates in the Security Council on this question, and participated in continuous meetings of the group of non-aligned countries in an effort to defuse the crisis. There was a time when we believed that a nuclear confrontation between the two superpowers was inevitable. It was therefore with great joy and relief that we greeted the decision of the Soviet Union to withdraw their missiles from Cuba. That humiliating retreat was the beginning of the end of Khrushchev's rule in the Soviet Union. I have always retained a soft spot for Khrushchev because of his support for the Arab position in the Arab–Israeli conflict and the Algerian war of independence. Although I totally reject communism, both as a political doctrine and as an instrument for economic development and social equality, I appreciated the military, political and economic assistance the Soviet Union had rendered to the Arab world. It would be an act of crass ingratitude on our part if we failed to recognize this.

That same year I was able to have Iraq nominated to membership of the Special Committee on Decolonization, which became known as the Committee of 24. I again encountered some difficulty as the British government tried to prevent Iraq from becoming a member. Though their efforts failed it might be useful and interesting to quote official British documents on this subject.

First, an excerpt from telegram no. 9, dated 5 January 1963, sent by Sir Patrick Dean, British Ambassador and Permanent Representative of the United Kingdom, to the Foreign Office:

> And in some ways the presence of Iraq on the committee makes it more desirable that we should continue to serve in order to combat Pachachi's mischief making as far as possible. I have again made my view about the undesirability of Iraq quite clear to the President of the General Assembly and so has my Australian colleague and it is just possible that the former may think again. But I believe, invitations have been issued and acceptances received and the threat from us not to serve will be unlikely to lead to the replacement of Iraq by a more amenable Asian. Iraq is certainly preferable to Indonesia but will cause us serious and continued trouble.

Second, excerpts from dispatch number 10724/10/63/B107/3, dated 4 April 1963, sent by the United Kingdom mission to the United Nations to the Foreign Office and signed by A. H. Campbell, Head of Chancery:

> We should nonetheless be giving thought to what our attitude should be if Pachachi is successful in getting these territories (Persian Gulf Sheikhdoms) added to the agenda of the committee of twenty-four. He's an able and persistent fellow who often succeeds in getting his way. ... Pachachi of Iraq is a persistent character and he may well try to bulldoze his point of view through the working group.

Iraq's membership of the Committee of 24 began on 1 January 1963, and barely five weeks later a military coup in Baghdad overthrew the regime of Abdul Karim Qassim, who was executed the following day. As a matter of principle I oppose the death penalty, which I consider a relic from a barbaric past. The Western powers as well as Egypt, Kuwait and other Arab states welcomed the change of regime and the accession to power of the Ba'ath party in Iraq. The Soviet representative in New York contacted me and offered me asylum in Moscow. I thanked him for his offer but told him that I intended to remain in my post serving Iraq and the Arab countries. I was very saddened by Qassim's tragic end. He was decent and honest, but certainly lacked the experience and ability to govern. Nine months after the Ba'athist coup of February 1963, Abdul Salam Aref, who was president at the time, toppled the Ba'ath Party from power and took over the real authority of governing the country. It should be noted that the only time in Iraq's recent history free of executions and murders for political reasons was during the rule of the Arif brothers – that is to say from 18 November 1963 to 17 July 1968.

In March 1963 a Ba'athist coup in Syria toppled its democratically elected government. A new and unprecedented opportunity presented itself for a giant step forward on the road to Arab unity. Talks began between Egypt, Iraq and Syria to set up a federal state in the heart of the Middle East. Unfortunately the negotiations failed because of the mutual distrust between Nasser and the Ba'athists. Nasser had never trusted the Ba'ath Party in Syria after they joined the secessionist conspiracy in 1961 which ended the United Arab Republic, a union between Egypt and Syria. The conflict was not really about trust or the lack of it, but about power. Neither Nasser nor the Ba'athists could accept sharing power with anyone else.

Meanwhile, I introduced the question of Aden in the Committee of 24 (the Decolonization Committee). The question of Aden was, in fact, the question of Southern Arabia, which included in addition to the city of Aden itself, the vast territory of Hadhramaut, and stretched from the Red Sea to the Arabian Sea – in other words, much of the southern Arabian Peninsula. There was a conflict between the nationalist parties, which demanded immediate independence and union with Yemen, and the various tribal chiefs and 'sultans' who formed, with the encouragement and protection of the British government, the South Arabian Federation. Iraq and most Arab countries supported the nationalist parties and considered the South Arabian Federation a colonial creation of Britain. I proposed setting up a sub-committee to visit the Crown Colony and Protectorates and to ascertain the wishes of the inhabitants. The sub-committee of five members (including myself) was prevented by the British authorities from entering Aden, so we went to Yemen, Iraq, Egypt and Saudi Arabia to hear Adenis' petitions. In Yemen, we drove from Hodeida to Sana'a, and I was appalled and upset by the extremity of the poverty and underdevelopment I could see from the windows of the car. In Sana'a we were assigned to a guesthouse which, as it turned out, had another thirty inhabitants at the time – and just a single bathroom. As we approached the building, the ambassador from Madagascar exclaimed: "Mais, c'est formidable comme odeur!" Our saviour was Ibrahim Al-Wali, the Iraqi Chargé d'Affaires. I suggested that he invite us all to stay at his house, which he graciously did. And there we all took hot baths, one after the other, before sitting down to eat a nice dinner, while the music of Bach and Beethoven played in the background. The British Ambassador at the United Nations, Sir Patrick Dean, was in constant touch with his government about the activities of our sub-committee. The following are excerpts from his reports to the Foreign Office. First, from telegram no. 748, dated 23 May 1963:

> I am not entirely confident that Pachachi who is a clever and unscrupulous opportunist would not attempt to divert the sub-committee nearer to Aden and the frontier of the Federation of South Arabia.

Second, from his report dated 6 August 1963 to the Foreign Secretary, the Earl of Home, FO dispatch number 2815/20/15463:

> The whole debate on Aden was masterminded by the Ambassador of Iraq who led with a keynote speech denouncing every aspect of our policy in the territory and openly advocating its incorporation in Yemen. He introduced two petitioners who painted a lurid picture of British rule and finally he tabled a draft resolution calling for a sub-committee to visit Aden and the neighbouring countries. The sub-committee visited Yemen, Baghdad and Cairo

with the Ambassador of Iraq as its mentor and guide. As was to be expected, the sub-committee completely endorsed the picture of Aden presented by the Ambassador of Iraq.

During the Eighteenth Session of the General Assembly in 1963, the question of Aden was discussed in its plenary meeting and I spoke at length, reviewing the work of the sub-committee and calling for the adoption of the resolution recommended by the Special Committee of 24. The General Assembly adopted those recommendations in Resolution 1949 (XVIII).

In the summer of 1964, the special sub-committee on Aden again visited the region and met hundreds of petitioners, who warned us that the situation in Aden was getting out of hand and that, unless the United Nations took action, the whole area would be engulfed in chaos and bloodshed. In October 1964, I attended the second Conference of Non-Aligned Countries in Cairo, where I was able to obtain the support of the movement for Aden's independence. Fortunately, the new Labour government that came to power in Britain in October 1964 was more responsive and willing to co-operate with the United Nations. In this changed situation I made a comprehensive statement couched in more conciliatory terms.

The new British attitude was made clear when I later met with Anthony Greenwood, the British Colonial Secretary, and Lord Beswick, as well as Lord Caradon (Hugh Foot), the United Kingdom representative at the United Nations, and had detailed discussions with them on Aden.

We tried to soften somewhat the resolution in order to make it more acceptable to the British, and the following is the text that was adopted by the General Assembly on 8 November 1965 (Resolution 2023 (XX)):

2023 (XX). Question of Aden
The General Assembly,
Having considered the chapters of the reports of the Special Committee on the situation with regard to the Implementation of the Declaration on the Granting of Independence to Colonial Countries and Peoples in respect of the Territory of Aden [A/5800/Add.4 and A/6000/Add.4], which includes, in addition to Aden, the Eastern and Western Aden Protectorates

as well as the Islands of Perim, Kuria Muria, Kamaran and other off-shore islands.

Recalling its resolutions 1514 (XV) of 14 December 1960 and 1949 (XVIII) of 11 December 1963, and the resolutions adopted by the Special Committee on 9 April 1964 [A/5800/Add. 4, para. 166], 11 May 1964 [ibid., para. 202], and 17 May 1965 [A/6000/Add. 4, para. 300]:

Having heard the statements of the petitioners,
Having taken note of the declarations of the representative of the administering power,
Deeply concerned at the critical and explosive situation which is threatening peace and security in the area, arising from the policies pursued by the administering Power in the Territory,

1. Approves the chapters of the reports of the Special Committee on the Situation with regard to the Implementation of the Declaration on the Granting of Independence to Colonial Countries and Peoples in respect of the Territory of Aden and endorses the conclusions and recommendations of the Sub-Committee on Aden;
2. Endorses the resolutions adopted by the Special Committee on 9 April 1964, 11 May 1964, and 17 May 1965;
3. Deplores the refusal of the administering Power to implement the resolutions of the General Assembly and the Special Committee;
4. Further deplores the attempts of the administering Power to set up an unrepresentative regime in the Territory, with a view to granting it independence contrary to General Assembly Resolutions 1514 (XV) and 1949 (XVIII), and appeals to all States not to recognize any independence which is not based on the wishes of the people of the Territory freely expressed through election held under universal adult suffrage;
5. Reaffirms the inalienable right of the people of the Territory to self-determination and to freedom from colonial rule and recognizes the legitimacy of their efforts

to achieve the rights laid down in the Charter of the United Nations, the Universal Declaration of Human Rights and the Declaration on the Granting of Independence to Colonial Countries and Peoples;
6. Considers that the maintenance of the military bases in the Territory constitutes a major obstacle to the liberation of the people of the Territory from colonial domination and is prejudicial to the peace and security of the region, and that the immediate and complete removal of these bases is therefore essential;
7. Notes with deep concern that military operations against the people of the Territory are still being carried out by the administering Power;
8. Urges the United Kingdom of Great Britain and Northern Ireland immediately to:
a) Abolish the state of emergency;
b) Repeal all laws restricting public freedom;
c) Cease all repressive actions against the people of the Territory, in particular military operations;
d) Release all political detainees and allow the return of those people who have been exiled or forbidden to reside in the Territory because of political activities;
9. Reaffirms paragraphs 6 to 11 Resolution 1949 (XVIII) and urges administering Power to implement them immediately;
10. Appeals to all Member States to render all possible assistance to the people of the Territory in their efforts to attain freedom and independence;
11. Draws the attention of the Security Council to the dangerous situation prevailing in the area as a result of British military action against the people of the Territory;
12. Requests the United Nations High Commissioner for Refugees, the specialized agencies and the international relief organizations to offer all possible assistance to the people who are suffering as a result of the military operations in the Territory;

13. Requests the Secretary-General to take such action as he may deem expedient to ensure the implementation of the present resolution and report thereon to the Special Committee;
14. Requests the Special Committee to examine again the situation in the Territory and to report thereon to the General Assembly at its 21st Session;
15. Decides to maintain this item on its agenda.

My discussions with the British Government continued for another two years until the country became an independent state separate from Yemen. I will revert to this subject when dealing with my activities as Foreign Minister of Iraq during 1966–67.

In July 1965, I presided over the meetings of the Economic and Social Council in Geneva and tried to reaffirm its authority and restore its central role in the economic and social activities of the United Nations. During the Twentieth Session of the General Assembly, I spoke on the Palestinian issue on 28 October 1965. It must have been quite effective, since the *Jewish Chronicle* of 5 November 1965 commented: "In many respects, the debate has been worse than previous ones because Adnan Pachachi, the Iraqi Delegate, has been leading for the Arabs. He is a clever debater and gives the appearance of being moderate." Finally, in 1965, I spoke on the Cyprus question. The new Iraqi Prime Minister, Abdul Rahman Al-Bazzaz, whose cabinet I was later to join, wanted to improve relations with Iraq's non-Arab neighbours such as Turkey and Iran. That is why we supported the Turks on Cyprus. Lord Caradon, the British Permanent Representative, in dispatch no. 22722–1–66 dated 7 January 1966, commented as follows:

> The Turks were lucky in having the Permanent Representatives of Iraq and Afghanistan as their spokesmen. Ambassador Pachachi, the Iraqi Permanent Representative and now to become the Minister of Foreign Affairs, is one of the shrewdest and most effective debaters the United Nations has seen as well as being a master of UN procedure.

On 11 December 1965, I was appointed Iraqi Minister of State for Foreign Affairs. Before I left New York at the end of December, I received many letters of congratulations. I have selected two of them. Following are excerpts from the letter of Lord Caradon, the British Permanent Representative:

> Dear Adnan,
>
> I doubt if there is any delegate in the past decade who has made a more consistent or more valuable contribution here at the United Nations than you have. Your speeches were always clear and eloquent – I remember many occasions when you spoke with an inspiring force and persuasiveness – and, what is even rarer at the United Nations, your speeches were always based on a very thorough preparation and understanding of your subject. What is more, you brought to many different subjects at the United Nations, a freshness and originality which always made it a pleasure to listen to you.
>
> But there is something much more than that. There is a good number of delegates here who represent their countries ably. The real test of outstanding performance at the United Nations, it seems to me, is the test of whether a delegate not only serves his own country well but also serves the interests and increases the authority of the United Nations. This you certainly did and you did so in many varied fields – not forgetting the valuable contribution you made recently in the Economic and Social Council.
>
> Those of us who have had the privilege to work with you will not forget the force of your oratory or the width of your interest or the elegance of the style with which you performed all your duties here. Nor shall we forget the privilege of your friendship.
>
> We know that you go to an even more exciting task. We wish you good fortune in that adventure. As you set out on this greater enterprise you carry with you the gratitude and admiration of us all.
>
> Yours ever,
Hugh [Caradon]

The second letter was from Philippe de Seynes, UN Undersecretary for Economic and Social Affairs, and formerly an Inspecteur des Finances in

France, who was especially grateful for my efforts while I presided over the Economic and Social Council:

> 16 December 1965
> My dear Adnan,
> I would like to offer my warmest congratulations on your new appointment. All those who have watched you over the last years cannot but rejoice over this elevation which is a timely recognition of everything you represent for us.
>
> At the same time I would be less than frank if I did not confess to a certain ambivalence in my feelings, having in mind certain parochial interests with which you were recently associated – to such a remarkable effect. In this respect I can only hope – and indeed I am quite confident – that you will keep a place in your heart, and perhaps also on your agenda for ECOSOC.
>
> As a veteran of this important organ, which is so much the centre of my own life, I would like to express my most sincere gratitude for your quite unique contribution. For you came to ECOSOC at a time of danger, when it was seriously threatened to fade away as an effective instrument entrusted with great responsibilities. I am not saying that we are as yet out of the woods. But I can testify, I believe with some authority, that your presence was decisive in this near crisis. Not only did you bring to it a clear and rational vision of things but you were able to impress it on a somewhat unruly audience, thanks to the forcefulness of your presentation, and also to the charm and skill in human relations which might be called the "diplomatic knack" (and how to get it?) which is so necessary to effective action.
>
> I wish you great success and happiness.
>
> Yours sincerely,
> Philippe de Seynes

But most of all I valued a plaque presented to me by the Palestinian Liberation Organization, on which was inscribed the following:

PRESENTED TO
His Excellency Dr Adnan M. Pachachi
in recognition and appreciation
of his dedication to and distinguished service for
Palestine
in the
United Nations
by the Palestine Liberation Organization
in New York, December 1965

I have often been asked how was I able to continue in my post as Permanent Representative under several different regimes. The answer is simple. I felt I was not serving any particular government but my country, Iraq. Fortunately, on the major questions before the United Nations, the positions of the successive regimes in Iraq were identical. I was given full freedom and discretion and very rarely did I receive specific instructions. I made all the decisions and never had to change any position I had already taken.

8

FOREIGN MINISTER OF IRAQ, 1965–67

THE CABLE INFORMING ME of my appointment as Minister came as a complete surprise. The Prime Minister, Abdul Rahman Al-Bazzaz, had come to New York to lead the Iraqi delegation to the Twentieth Session of the General Assembly the previous September, but had said nothing about his wish to offer me a post in his Cabinet. He had dropped several hints about the country needing my services and so forth, but had said nothing specific.

I had known Abdul Rahman Al-Bazzaz for many years. We had, in fact, both been members of the Iraqi delegation to the Seventh Session of the General Assembly in 1952. I knew him to be a conservative Arab nationalist and a deeply devout Muslim. He was a highly educated scholar, an eloquent speaker and an extremely self-confident man.

At first I was not too happy about leaving the United Nations, and on my arrival in Baghdad on 4 January 1966 I immediately spoke to various people who were close to the President of the Republic, Abdul Salam Aref, to try to learn the real reasons for my appointment to the Cabinet. I was considered to be a non-political, competent professional who had done excellent work for Iraq at the United Nations, but why should I now become a minister? I had no connection whatever with the various parties and groupings that were active on the political scene. I was, in fact, an outsider, and felt as such from the moment I assumed my responsibilities, which had not been spelled out in detail since the Prime Minister himself was, at the same time, Foreign Minister. From the information I obtained from various sources, the picture became clear and the reasons for my appointment were as follows.

It was not Dr Al-Bazzaz who had chosen me. My name had been suggested to him by President Aref. Although I had met the President only once, during the Conference of Non-aligned Countries in Cairo in October 1964, he was told by the Egyptians, who greatly appreciated my work at the United Nations, that they thought it would be a good idea to have someone in the government who was an Arab nationalist, and at the same time had plenty of experience in international affairs. The Egyptians were not too happy with the policy of Al-Bazzaz, who was trying to improve relations with Saudi Arabia, Turkey and Iran, and was an enthusiastic advocate of Islamic solidarity, which was, in those days, believed to be directed against Nasser. Al-Bazzaz also intended to dismantle the socialist structure created in July 1964 and to restore the private sector to its previous prominence. Said Sleibi was the Military Commander of the Baghdad District and a close friend of President Aref; he had been instrumental in bringing him to power in November 1963, and in thwarting an attempted coup against him in September 1965 by the pro-Egyptian elements within the armed forces. It was Sleibi who had informed me that I had originally been scheduled to be appointed Foreign Minister. But Al-Bazzaz had refused and instead, as a compromise, I had been given the position of Minister of State. The military establishment disliked Al-Bazzaz, for he sought to curtail its influence and return the country to civilian rule. Because Aref was seeking to mend fences with the Egyptians, he was only too happy to accept their recommendation of my appointment in the government, and so all these cross-currents contributed to my elevation to ministerial rank. However convoluted and far-fetched this may seem, I could find no other plausible explanation.

A few weeks after my arrival in Baghdad, the Prime Minister, who seemed anxious to encourage me to leave Iraq, offered me the Paris Embassy, which I declined. He then urged me to accept a Turkish invitation to visit Ankara. The Turks were very grateful for the stand I had taken on the Cyprus problem at the United Nations the previous December, and anxious to show their appreciation and to strengthen their relations with Iraq. I went to Turkey on 5 February 1966. The British Embassy in Baghdad made the following comment on this visit in its report to the Foreign Office, in dispatch no. 1038-1-66 dated 22 January 1966:

> Dr Pachachi, Minister of State for Foreign Affairs, is due to leave shortly to Ankara on a nine-day visit at the invitation of the Turkish government. He seems assured of a warm welcome if only because of the considerable help which he gave to the Turkish Delegation at the UN over the Cyprus issue. Furthermore he no doubt hopes that the Iranians will take note of this renascent friendship but more important he is undoubtedly anxious to get a clear idea of Turkish plans for the utilization of the Euphrates waters and the Pachachi mission will probably try to induce the Turks to agree on a firm date for the long promised tri-partite talks with Syria. I imagine Pachachi will need all his legendary diplomatic skills and shrewdness if he is to succeed in the tri-partite talks on the Euphrates. The rapprochement with Turkey is seen as something of a tour de force engineered by Dr Pachachi.

The Turks accepted at our urging the principle of established historical rights, which suited Iraq since the two rivers have supported the creation of great civilizations and empires and have been in constant use for over ten thousand years. The British Embassy commented as follows in a dispatch they sent to the Foreign Office on 31 May 1966, report no. 1038966:

> Turkish Agreement to abide by the provisions of International Law on the Riparian rivers has been greeted here as something of a triumph for Pachachi's painstaking diplomacy.

From Turkey I travelled directly to Cairo to attend a meeting of the Council of the Arab League. This was my first experience of inter-Arab politics, and I was appalled by the hostility and mutual suspicion dividing the Arab states. The Arab situation at that time could be summarized as follows. Egypt was deeply involved in Yemen's civil war, where it was trying to defend the republican regime against rebels financed and equipped by Saudi Arabia. The Ba'athist regime of Ameen Al-Hafez in Syria was extremely hostile to both Egypt and Iraq, while the Palestine Liberation Organization under Ahmed Shukairi was locked in endless disputes with the government of Jordan. Iraq was linked to Egypt in what was called the United Political Command, a high-sounding name with little substance, since as a forum of consultation it could not dispel the suspicions Egypt had with regard to Al-Bazzaz and what were perceived as his anti-Egyptian policies.

Although I wholeheartedly supported Al-Bazzaz's domestic policies, I was not too happy with certain aspects of his foreign policy, especially his espousal of the proposed Islamic grouping, because I feared this would further erode Arab solidarity. I believed that we should stand firmly with Egypt, which seemed to be harassed on all fronts and was suffering from an acute sense of isolation.

On 23 February 1966 an event occurred in Damascus that was to have far-reaching consequences for the Arab world. The radical wing of the Ba'ath party overthrew the regime of Ameen Al-Hafiz and installed in power a largely Alawite leadership under Salah Jadid. Nasser enthusiastically supported the new government because he hated the Ameen Al-Hafiz regime and hoped to regain his influence in Syria. We, in Iraq, were not too happy about those developments. The new Syrian government was even more hostile to President Aref than the previous one. In general, the Ba'ath party could never forgive Aref for toppling them from power in November 1963, and the new rulers of Syria wasted no time in showing their hostility to the Iraqi regime. Differences relating to the utilization of the Euphrates waters and the use of the Iraqi petroleum pipeline in Syrian territory were exacerbated by new and what seemed to us to be unreasonable demands.

On 13 April 1966, President Aref was killed in a helicopter crash. A joint meeting of the Council of Ministers and the Council of National Defence was held to elect the new President. Al-Bazzaz submitted his candidacy, but the military establishment, fearing that he would impose civilian rule, backed the Chief of Staff, General Abdul Rahman Aref, the dead President's elder brother. On the first ballot, the two candidates obtained an equal number of votes. Al-Bazzaz, realizing that the military would not tolerate a civilian President, withdrew his candidacy, and Abdul Rahman

Aref was elected unanimously. He asked Al-Bazzaz to form a new government, which I entered as Minister of Foreign Affairs, freed at last from the stifling restraints placed on a junior minister. A week after I became Foreign Minister, the British Ambassador asked for a meeting with me, which I welcomed because it gave me an opportunity to make clear my views on many issues. The following is the report of the British Ambassador to the Foreign Office on 29 April 1966:

> The Foreign Minister, Dr Pachachi, asked whether it would not be possible for the British Government to make it clear to the Iranians that H.M.G. was in favour of a reasonable settlement which gave the Kurds in Iran a certain measure of decentralization and local administrative autonomy.
>
> On <u>Aden</u> he was more forthcoming. He recalled that when he had met the Secretary of State for Colonies and Lord Caradon in New York he and the U.A.R. Ambassador had acted as intermediaries for the Adenis who were by and large very reasonable and moderate people. He deplored the breakdown of F.L.O.S.Y. (Front for the Liberation of South Yemen). It had been his hope that, as a result of those meetings, the Adeni exiles from the Colony, the Federation and the South Arabian League, would get together themselves and then in turn, associate themselves with elements in Aden to work out a positive and agreed plan for the interim period before independence. He added that H.M.G. by settling a date for independence and deciding to remove the base, had left the way clear for these people to come to an understanding. Indeed they had reached some understanding in the creation of F.L.O.S.Y. in Cairo, and he was mystified as to why they had fallen apart again. He would certainly enquire of Messrs. Makkawi and Asnag when they arrive in Baghdad (they are due today) why it appeared to have fallen apart.
>
> Pachachi suggested that Iraq, unlike U.A.R., might be able to act as an intermediary between ourselves and the Adenis, since Iraq was sufficiently far away to have no particular irons in the fire. There might be merit, he thought, in Iraq sounding out the Adenis and then making contact with H.M.G. either to

conduct talks directly on behalf of the Aden exiles or merely to fix up a meeting between a representative of the British Government and the exiles. Perhaps even a round table conference in which the various Adeni factions would participate together with a representative from for instance, Saudi Arabia, the U.A.R. and Iraq or the Arab League, rather on the lines of the 1939 Palestine Conference. In any case he would enquire of the Adenis to find out what the possibilities were.

The Gulf, the Ambassador told the Foreign Minister, as he had likewise said to the Prime Minister, that Iraq's policy towards Aden might be the touchstone for our position vis-à-vis Iraq in the Gulf. We might have to turn to Iran and Saudi Arabia if Iraq was uncooperative. Pachachi countered that the Gulf was certainly tricky and that, unlike in Aden, there was a foreign, i.e. non-Arab interest in the shape of Iran. He said that he sometimes felt that the British Government had already come to some arrangement with the Saudis in respect of the Gulf Principalities with the tacit assent of the Iranians. He hoped that this was not so since Iraq, for geographical reasons, had a definite interest in what went on in the Gulf.

On the domestic front, Pachachi told the Ambassador that it is hoped to hold elections in October or November, some three or four months after the Prime Minister's visit to Moscow, which is now scheduled for June. These elections would be on the basis of a reconstituted Arab Socialist Union. Pachachi agreed, when questioned by the Ambassador on the point, that it might have been preferable to hold municipal or liwa elections as a start and national elections at a later date. On the other hand a national election was expected by the population, was promised by the Provisional Constitution, and would therefore have to be held.

If Pachachi succeeds in convincing the F.L.O.S.Y. delegation that there is merit in the proposals outlined above, he told the Ambassador that he would get in touch with me and I shall, of course, telegraph you at once.

As Foreign Minister I was determined to pursue an independent foreign policy free from the former impediments that had been imposed upon our freedom because of our special relationship with Egypt, which made some see Iraq as a mere satellite of that country. During my years at the United Nations, I had formed friendships with the leaders and ministers of many countries. Since I had received invitations to visit many of these countries, I decided to avail myself of this opportunity to break out of Iraq's isolation.

My first visit was to Cairo, where I was anxious to renew my acquaintance with the Egyptian leaders, and especially President Jamal Abdul Nasser. Ostensibly I was in Cairo to attend the meeting of the UN Decolonization Committee, at the time discussing the question of Aden, but my real purpose was to find out where Egypt stood on certain vital issues, the most important of which were the deteriorating relations between Iraq and Syria and deciding how best to confront Israel's increasingly threatening and bellicose actions. The Foreign Minister of Syria, Dr Ibrahim Makhous, was also in Cairo, and so I had an excellent opportunity to understand Syria's policy, which seemed to me based on slogans and half-baked ideas totally divorced from reality. I met Jamal Abdul Nasser on 12 June 1966. We spent about an hour together and these, in summary, were the main points discussed during the meeting:

1. He urged Iraq to reach an understanding with Syria and said he would do everything in his power to persuade the Syrians to be reasonable, but he also made it quite clear that he considered Syria to be an important ally and would not allow any harm to come to her.
2. He expressed in a veiled and indirect way his displeasure with the politics of Al-Bazzaz, especially those concerning Iraq's relations with Saudi Arabia, which he thought were closer than they should be, in view of Saudi hostility to Egypt's defence of the Yemen Republic.
3. He assured me that Egypt had nothing to do with the coup attempt against President Aref the previous September, but he urged the nationalist elements in Iraq to get together and stop the drift towards what he called the reactionary regimes in the Arab world.
4. On Israel, he said that his policy was to avoid any armed confrontation until the Arabs were ready.

I also met Zakariya Muhieddin, the Egyptian Prime Minister, and

Mahmoud Riad, the Foreign Minister. Several senior Egyptian officials visited me in my hotel suite, among them the Egyptian Chief of Staff, General Fawzi. This parade of senior Egyptian officials to my hotel room struck me as extraordinary at the time. It was the sort of reception usually given to heads of state and I was just a foreign minister. I often wondered whether it was intended to convey some message to me and I have come to believe that the anti-Bazzaz factions were preparing a plot against him and that the Egyptians knew about it; perhaps they were anxious to tell me that I should distance myself from Al-Bazzaz, since they considered me to be one of the trustworthy nationalist elements in the country.

As an Arab nationalist, I was naturally attracted by Nasser's call for Arab unity. I admired him because, more than any other leader, he personified the idea of Arab unity and seemed the only one capable of achieving it. While Nasser himself was an ardent Arab nationalist, most of his close associates, and the Egyptian people in general, were not. He dragged a reluctant Egypt into playing a central role in Arab affairs. In so doing he was not only serving his Arab nationalist ideals but also promoting the interest of Egypt itself. He realized that Egypt by herself was no more than an over-populated, impoverished, underdeveloped Third World country, but that as leader of a united Arab world she could play a decisive role in international affairs. For Nasser, Arab solidarity was not only a step towards eventual unity but also an instrument of great potency in Egypt's external relations. For this reason he would not tolerate any Arab government breaking ranks and defying Egypt's claims to leadership of the Arab world. This in part explains his opposition to two Iraqi leaders who had nothing in common except their rejection of Egyptian claims to leadership. The first of these, Nuri Said, tried to give Iraq an independent role as member of a Western alliance, while the second, Abdul Karim Qassim, wanted to assert his independence by moving very close to the Soviet Union and the communist bloc. They were both vehemently attacked as enemies of Arab solidarity and traitors to the Arab cause. I personally was ready to follow Nasser as long as his policies seemed to advance the cause of Arab unity, which was for me the ultimate test for any Arab leader.

I started to have doubts about his ability to realize the hopes and aspirations which he himself had inspired among Arabs everywhere when he committed what were in my view two major errors. The first was his failure in 1961 to confront and destroy the secessionist conspiracy in Syria which succeeded in breaking apart the UAR and ending the first genuinely popular union between two Arab states. The second, committed in 1963, was to allow the Federal Union of Egypt, Iraq and Syria to collapse before it saw the light of day because of the mutual distrust and struggle for power to dominate the proposed union. I believe that he missed a historic opportunity, which cost the Arabs dear in the years to come.

I returned to Baghdad on 16 June 1966, worried about Nasser's support of the Syrian regime and fearing that it would bring about a calamity for the Arabs.

When I took over the Foreign Ministry in April 1966, I surveyed our relations with the West and found them to be in a very unsatisfactory state. The United States had adopted a decidedly pro-Israeli and anti-Arab stance after Lyndon B. Johnson became President in 1963. We were engaged in a continuing dispute with Britain on Southern Arabia and Oman. We had broken off diplomatic relations with West Germany because of its close ties with Israel and established diplomatic relations with East Germany. I felt that it was wrong for us to ignore Western Europe and saw a danger in depending entirely on our relations with the Soviet Union.

I decided to visit France, which, after Algerian independence in 1962, had pursued, under General de Gaulle's leadership, friendly policies towards the Arab world. I spoke to the French Ambassador in Baghdad and told him of my desire to improve relations with France and my wish to visit Paris and meet President de Gaulle. Before long I was informed that the President would meet me at the Elysée Palace in July 1966. I felt certain that my reputation in the United Nations as a strong critic of US policy in Palestine and British policy in Southern Arabia appealed to de Gaulle, as he retained a deep-rooted hostility towards the 'Anglo-Saxons'.

My visit to France was preceded by a visit to Algeria at the head of an Iraqi delegation taking part in the celebrations of Algerian independence. In Algeria I attended the very moving ceremony of the burial of the Emir Abdul Qadir Al-Jazairi, the leader of Algeria's struggle against French colonial rule during the 19th century, whose remains had been brought from Damascus. There was something poignant about this great hero coming home to a free Algeria after an absence of a hundred years. Even though I may be accused of being a romantic nationalist, I confess that the ceremony filled me with pride and joy. It was difficult to fight back my tears during the minutes of silence as the coffin was lowered into its final resting place among the martyrs and heroes of the Algerian revolution.

While I was in Algeria, I discussed with other Arab Foreign Ministers the proposed Arab summit which the 'reactionary' Arab states, like Saudi Arabia, were pressing for, but which the 'progressive' Arab states, like the UAR (as Egypt continued to be known until 1971) and Syria, were opposing. I never liked or accepted such labelling of the Arab states, because it only deepened the divisions in the Arab world and weakened our position internationally. I tried, in spite of Iraq's special relationship with Egypt, to resolve the differences between the two camps. But unfortunately I was unsuccessful and the Arab summit never took place in 1966 and did not convene until after the catastrophic military defeat of June 1967.

From Algeria I went to Geneva, where I spoke before the Economic and Social Council, and then went on to Paris. First I met M. Couve de Murville, the French Foreign Minister, and was then received by President de Gaulle at the Elysée Palace. I spoke a few words in French, which greatly pleased him, and then, through an interpreter, spoke in Arabic about Iraq's desire for close relations with France. I noticed that President de Gaulle had a dossier in front of him that must have contained a lot of information about Iraq and about me. He asked me about two events in Iraq which had occurred on the day of my departure from Baghdad. The first was the agreement that Al-Bazzaz had concluded with the Kurdish leadership and which we had approved in the Council of Ministers and announced on 30 June 1966. On that same day, yet another military coup had been attempted but had been easily put down. This one was also engineered by pro-Egyptian officers, and was directed against Al-Bazzaz rather than President Abdul Rahman Aref. I explained to President de Gaulle the reasons behind the coup and the main provisions of the agreement with the Kurds, which gave them a large measure of autonomy and recognized their distinct nationality within the Iraqi state. After we had discussed various international problems and political relations, he said that France historically enjoyed close relations with Egypt and the

Levant but not with Iraq. I said that I hoped my visit would change this and begin a period of close Franco-Iraqi relations in such fields as oil, armaments and general economic and cultural exchanges; and happily my visit did indeed launch a new era of co-operation between the two countries. These relations have become stronger over the years and have developed into a model for relations between a great industrial power and a rapidly developing third-world country.

On my return to Baghdad, I found Al-Bazzaz's government to be on the way out. The military establishment was no longer able to tolerate Al-Bazzaz's policy of civilian control or his intention to hold democratic parliamentary elections to end the interference of the army in politics. They were able to persuade the President to get rid of him, and he was forced to resign at the end of July 1966.

President Aref then called on General Naji Talib, one of the 'Free Officers' responsible for the revolution of 14 July 1958, to form a new government. He asked me to join his Cabinet as Foreign Minister, an offer that I readily accepted because I felt that my work was not finished. At the end of August 1966, we were surprised by the Syrian regime's decision to halt the pumping of Iraqi oil through the pipeline located in Syrian territory. This action was ostensibly taken because of a dispute concerning the royalties paid by the oil companies to the Syrian government, but in reality the action was politically motivated and designed to damage Iraq's economy and create problems for its government. We persuaded the oil companies to be flexible and accept some of the Syrian regime's demands, but to no avail. On my way to the United Nations early in September, I requested the Egyptian Foreign Minister to ask President Nasser to intercede personally with the Syrians. While I was at the UN, leading the Iraqi delegation to the Twenty-first Session of the General Assembly, a high-level Iraqi delegation went to Damascus but failed to change the Syrian attitude. Pumping was not resumed until March 1967. Iraq's losses were considerable and only a large loan from the oil companies enabled the government to meet its immediate financial obligations. In September 1966, during the Twenty-first Session of the General Assembly, I spoke in the general debate and, in addition to Palestine and Aden, I referred to Vietnam, strongly condemning the war being waged by the United States and demanding immediate cessation of bombing and the start of negotiations based on the 1954 agreement affirming the independence and neutralization of Vietnam. During the session I met many foreign ministers, including those of the Permanent Members of the Security Council.

For example I met with United States Secretary of State, Dean Rusk, in New York on 8 October 1966. I reiterated our view that there was a noticeable shift in US policy in favour of Israel, especially after the US became its main weapons supplier. I returned back time and again to this theme, which Rusk tried to justify as a response to increased Soviet military assistance to some Arab states. Rusk affirmed that the US would not tolerate Israeli territorial expansion. However, this policy was reversed a few months later when the US acquiesced in the occupation of Arab territories after the war of June 1967. I told Mr Rusk that we had just concluded an agreement with the Kurds and I urged the US to do whatever it could to stop Iranian military help to the Kurdish rebels, and I expressed the hope that the US would help in the reconstruction of northern Iraq.

The following excerpts are from the memorandum prepared by the Foreign Office on 28 September 1966 for the Foreign Secretary, George Brown, prior to his meeting with me on 10 October 1966:

> Her Majesty's Government has been very conscious of the constructive contribution made by Dr Pachachi in his capacity as Iraq's Permanent Representative to the work of the Economic and Social Council. The improvement which has taken place in the work of the Council as a main centre of the discussion of international economic development owes much to his influence.
>
> [Personal note:] He is clever, ambitious, polished and sophisticated and is a master of U.N. procedures.
>
> [On the Aden mission:] Although Dr Pachachi is very skilled at giving an impression of sweet reasonableness, we cannot believe that his presence on this mission would be in any way helpful to U.K. interests.

And the following is the official British record of my meeting with Mr Brown.

CONFIDENTIAL
RECORD OF A MEETING BETWEEN THE FOREIGN SECRETARY AND THE FOREIGN MINISTER OF IRAQ IN THE OFFICE OF THE PRESIDENT OF THE SECURITY COUNCIL AT THE U.N. HEADQUARTERS, NEW YORK, AT 10:20 A.M., ON MONDAY, 10 OCTOBER 1966.

PRESENT
The Rt. Hon. George Brown, M.P., Mr Adnan Al-Pachachi, The Lord Caradon, Mr D. A. Greenhill

Mr Pachachi described Anglo-Iraqi relations as good. There were certain outstanding claims by British companies which were under discussion but these ought not to give undue difficulty. Serious negotiations with British oil companies lay ahead. The Iraq Government attached the highest importance to these negotiations and hoped that Her Majesty's Government would contribute to their success both as a shareholder in the oil companies and in the interests of Anglo-Iraqi relations. Lack of a settlement would be a barrier to development of good relations. The Iraq Government depended on a substantial increase of oil revenues to carry out their programme of economic development and social welfare. Mr Pachachi then went on to speak of the United Nations Mission to Southern Arabia. He hoped very much that before the departure of the Mission, H.M.G. would issue a clarification of the reservations that had been expressed in August. Mr Pachachi said the first reservation was acceptable. The second reservation which concerned the impossibility of constitutional change without federal approval gave more trouble. He thought that the second reservation nullified the whole purpose of the United Nations resolution which was that there should be constitutional changes in Southern Arabia before independence. Lord Caradon said that H.M.G. had treaty commitments with the Federal leaders. They must stand by these commitments and the existing constitutional arrangements until these were changed with the agreement of the Federal leaders. Mr Pachachi said that the constitutional changes should be made not by mutual agreement with the sultans and the sheikhs but by mutual agreement with the whole people of South Arabia. Mr Brown said that agreements existed with the rulers which we were bound to observe. Any change made would have to take into account our commitments. It would be quite improper to ignore them. Mr Pachachi regretted that the letter of reservation had been sent to the Secretary-General in August. Could not a new letter of explanation now be sent which could eliminate misunderstanding about the implementation of the United Nations resolution? Mr Brown wondered whether any further attempt to clarify the position would not merely draw attention to differences. He would take note of what Mr Pachachi had said but he urged him not to push his objections too hard. If a mistake had been made in August it was perhaps better now to ignore the matter. Mr Pachachi said that there was already agreement on the composition of the Mission. The only obstacle lying ahead was the existence of a piece of paper. If the Mission went in the shadow of British reservations its freedom of action in South Arabia would be affected. A clarifying message to the Secretary-General was, in his view, required. Mr Brown said he would consider the matter further in the light of what the Foreign Minister had said.

2. Mr Pachachi reverted to the question of the British oil companies in Iraq and asked that the British Government should use its influence with them. Mr Brown said that H.M.G. regarded the negotiation of new agreements as a management function and did not therefore interfere on the basis of the Government's own shareholding in the companies. Mr Pachachi said that questions relating to oil had serious political implications in the Middle East. This was not just a book-keeping matter. The political implications of the negotiations ought to interest the British Government.

3. Mr Pachachi asked what were the intentions of H.M.G. in the Persian Gulf. Iraq was vitally interested in this area. Her relations with Iran were involved and there was a strong

possibility of a clash of interests in the Gulf. What had H.M.G. in mind? Mr Brown said that the British Government had treaty commitments in the Gulf and he said he had mentioned this question in his speech at the Labour Party Conference in Brighton answering those in the United Kingdom who were putting pressure on the government to withdraw from the Gulf. He said that the government would like to see people of the area able to stand on their feet and the UK in any case would not try to impose any new form of colonial rule. Mr Pachachi said the Gulf was a dangerous region to which Mr Brown replied H.M.G. will do nothing to increase such dangers and asked Mr Pachachi to inform him specifically of what he had in mind. Mr Pachachi said that the first requirement is to speed up the modernization of the Gulf taking into account the wishes of the people. Mr Brown said the record of the British Government in pushing modernization was a good one and it continues to put pressure on the Rulers to initiate meaningful reforms. Mr Pachachi indicated that the special relations Britain has with the Sheikhdoms of the Gulf should enable H.M.G. to bring about the desired changes. Mr Brown said the Labour Government is eager to see that the expected huge oil revenues will be spent to create modern societies. In the past, Mr Brown said the British Government was blamed for playing politics in the region and that is why he did not want to give credence to such accusations. He said that Britain hoped that measures be taken that will bring stability and peace to the area. Mr Brown hoped that economic and commercial cooperation in the area will be increased. By the end of the meeting, Mr Pachachi referred to suspicious Iranian activities in the Gulf states especially the increased migration of Iranians which may encourage Iran in the future to try to take over Arab lands in the name of a distorted right of self determination.

Among those I met in New York was Amintore Fanfani, the Italian Foreign Minister, who invited me to visit Italy on my way back to Baghdad. I accepted and was warmly received in Rome around the middle of October 1966. I had useful talks with Fanfani about strengthening Iraqi–

Italian relations in the petroleum and economic fields in general, and also informed him of my anxiety about the gathering storm in the Middle East. I urged him to use whatever influence Italy had with the United States to adopt a more balanced policy in the Arab–Israeli conflict. While in Rome I also had a friendly meeting with Pope Paul VI, whose UN representative had invited me to visit the Vatican.

I then convened a conference in Rome of all the Iraqi ambassadors in Europe. Our gracious host was Ali Haider Sulaiman, Iraqi Ambassador to Italy, an old and loyal friend of mine as well as of my father, in whose Cabinet he had served. I opened the conference by explaining Iraq's foreign policy and began by drawing attention to the difficulties and problems we were facing in our relations with Iran. I stated that a strong, aggressive Iran represented a great threat to Iraq, and that a cardinal principle of Iraqi foreign policy should always be to confront that ever-present peril effectively and by every means possible.

I then took up the question of Palestine and stated that Iraq supported the Palestine Liberation Organization as the representative of the Palestinian people. Regarding the tensions between Syria and Israel, I pointed out that the escalation of border clashes made war inevitable. This dangerous situation had been exacerbated by US attempts to destabilize the Syrian regime through encouraging Israeli threats and fomenting internal disturbances.

On Kuwait, I drew attention to the fact that relations between the two countries were satisfactory. Iraq had tried repeatedly to improve those relations and co-operate closely with Kuwait, but the Kuwaitis kept on asking for a final demarcation of the frontiers, which they insisted must precede any co-operation in the economic and financial fields; while Iraq wanted the two questions to be considered separately. At the same time, I declared that Iraq would encourage and facilitate the investment of Kuwaiti capital in Iraq through meaningful incentives. The Kuwaitis unfortunately did not respond favourably. I reiterated the Iraqi position on the border problem by reaffirming our legitimate right to have free access to the waters of the Gulf and to protect our rights in the oilfields within the frontier zone.

I stated that our relations with Iran had deteriorated in the last few years and that our disputes and differences with Iran were not new, having persisted even between 1955 and '58 when the two countries were close allies in the Baghdad Pact. Recently Iran had been active in supporting the Kurdish rebellion in the north of Iraq. While I was in New York, I discussed this interference in Iraq's internal affairs with the Iranian Foreign Minister. He agreed to visit Baghdad to discuss all outstanding problems, including issues centring on the Shatt al-'Arab waterway, the confluence of the Tigris and Euphrates debouching into the Gulf and forming the southernmost section of the border between Iraq and Iran. I informed my Iranian counterpart that Iraq refused to amend the treaty of 1937 fixing the frontier between the two countries, but was willing to discuss ways and means of improving navigation in the Shatt al-'Arab.

On relations with Turkey, I expressed satisfaction at their steady improvement in recent years. On the question of the utilization of the waters of the Euphrates River, I reiterated Iraq's insistence on protecting its historic and acquired rights to them. I informed our ambassadors that the Soviet Union had undertaken not to render any assistance to Syria for building the Euphrates dam without prior consultation with Iraq. Our relations with the Soviet Union and the socialist countries I described as good, and steadily improving.

As to Iraq's relations with Western countries, I stated that relations with France had significantly improved recently. The French were ready to assist Iraq in the military, economic, technical and cultural fields. The French government was also ready to enter into a special relationship with Iraq for the development of Iraq's oil resources. I stressed the importance of good relations with France and suggested that we should not criticize her over so sensitive an issue as nuclear tests.

I spoke about our relations with the United Kingdom, which were complicated by our differences on Aden, as well as Britain's apparent indifference to the increase of illegal Iranian immigration into the Gulf. I said that I had reminded the British Foreign Secretary of Britain's responsibilities in this regard and warned of serious consequences if this Iranian infiltration continued.

On our relations with the United States, I stated that Israel and the Zionist movement were the two principal factors adversely affecting Iraqi–American relations, and said that I had drawn the attention of Dean Rusk, the Secretary of State, to the fact that the US had become the main supplier of weapons to Israel and had been openly misleading Arab governments whenever they raised this issue.

I concluded my statement to the assembled ambassadors by referring to two internal questions of paramount importance to Iraq. The first related to the dispute with oil companies regarding levels of production and pricing and the utilization of areas which the oil companies had consistently refused to develop; I told them I discussed this question with the foreign ministers of the United Kingdom, the United States and France. On the second question, the Kurdish problem in northern Iraq, I said that the present Iraqi government fully supported the proposals of the previous Al-Bazzaz government. I pointed out that while there was no legally binding agreement, the Kurds had accepted the proposals in principle.

On my return to Baghdad at the end of October 1966, I was questioned by my colleagues in the Cabinet about the reasons why Iraq had not been invited to join the recently concluded military alliance between Egypt and Syria. My explanation was that Iraq was already closely linked to Egypt by the United Political Command, and that the agreement with Syria was a symbolic gesture to reaffirm Egypt's support and commitment to defend that country. I was mildly criticized by some ministers for allegedly neglecting our relations with the Arab countries for the sake of promoting our relations with the West. My reply was that there was no conflict between our desire to pursue active world diplomacy and our basic national commitments in the Arab world.

At the beginning of December 1966, I accompanied President Abdul Rahman Aref on an official visit to Kuwait. I was well known in Kuwait, because of my stout defence of Iraq's claim in the Security Council in 1961 and my successful efforts to prevent the admission of Kuwait to UN membership until 1963. I was under no illusions about the strong reservations that the rulers of Kuwait felt towards me. However, as hosts they were very correct and went out of their way to be cordial in the tradition of Arab hospitality.

I could not help detecting a certain coolness, though, in the official Egyptian attitude, in sharp contrast to the warm reception I had received in June. I concluded that this was caused mainly by my constant warnings about their close relationship with the Syrian regime of Salah Jadid, and the detrimental effect such closeness could have on Iraq.

Before the end of 1966, I received in Baghdad two foreign ministers, Fanfani of Italy and Abbas Aram of Iran. My talks with Aram concerned our perennial dispute with Iran over the Shatt al-'Arab. The Iranians wanted to scrap the 1937 treaty giving Iraq exclusive sovereignty over the Shatt, except for two small areas opposite Mohammara and Abadan. They claimed that the frontier between the two countries should be the thalweg, that is to say the deepest part of the river. We rejected this claim, which ran contrary to Iran's treaty obligations, and pointed out that, whereas the Shatt al-'Arab was Iraq's only outlet to the open seas and therefore of vital national interest, it had no such importance for Iran, which enjoyed a long coastline on the Gulf and the Arabian Sea. Moreover, navigation in the Shatt al-'Arab required continuous dredging, and Iraq could not accept that such vital work be left to the whims of a neighbour who had not always shown much concern for Iraq's interests. These discussions, as I anticipated, were inconclusive.

In December 1966, the Joint Arab Defence Council was convened in Cairo. It was composed of the Ministers of Foreign Affairs and Defence as well as the commanders of the armed forces of all member states of the Arab League, with the Defence Minister and myself representing Iraq. The Council reviewed the situation in the Middle East and the increasingly bellicose attitude of Israel, which we attributed to the growing support of the United States. We had before us a report of the Commander-in-Chief of the Unified Arab Military Command containing proposals for the specific participation of each Arab state in defensive operations against Israeli aggression, which at the end of 1966 had become a distinct threat. Unfortunately, inter-Arab relations were at that time at a low ebb. Mutual suspicions and hostility were rife, and the meetings of the Arab Defence Council degenerated into a bitter slanging match of mutual recrimination and abuse. The Egyptian Commander of the Joint Arab Command resigned, but was persuaded to withdraw his resignation. At the end of the meeting, Jordan accepted the proposals of the Commander to allow the deployment of Iraqi and Saudi troops on its territory. On the whole, I found the meeting a distressing experience. I felt the Arab governments failed sufficiently to appreciate the seriousness of the Israeli menace and allowed their bickering and petty quarrels to frustrate any meaningful common action to meet the dangerous challenge that loomed ahead.

A full year had passed since I took responsibility for Iraq's foreign relations, and the following excerpts from the annual review of the situation in Iraq, dated 9 January 1967, by the British Ambassador in Baghdad, Sir Richard Beaumont, assessed my incumbency as follows:

> Pachachi has a realization of the limits of the possible and respect for the urbanity of diplomatic intercourse. His influence was not negligible in the agreement of the United Nations General Assembly to set up a mission to advise on the independence of Aden. What is more it gives a significant glimpse of the possibility that Iraq policy may not be necessarily tied to that of the United Arab Republic.

In February 1967, I accompanied President Aref on two official visits to Turkey and Egypt, and at the beginning of March, at the invitation of their governments, I visited both Pakistan and India, where I met Mohammed Ayub Khan, the Pakistani President, and Indira Gandhi, Prime Minister of India. I made several speeches about the relations between our countries, the situation in Iraq and the Palestine issue. On the whole, these were well received. I tried to be as neutral as possible on the issue of Kashmir. This angered some Pakistanis, who thought I should support their position, and displeased some Indians, who took offence at my mentioning the Islamic ties that bind Iraq and Pakistan. While in Pakistan, I pleaded with President Ayub Khan to release from jail Zulfiqar Ali Bhutto, whom I had known as Foreign Minister of his country. He promised to look into the matter but showed his true feelings when he described Bhutto as arrogant, conceited and unworthy of help.

From 14 to 19 March I accompanied President Aref on an official visit to Tehran. As is their custom, the Iranians gave us a sumptuous reception. It was obvious that the Shah, well aware of the tensions in our relations with Egypt arising from President Nasser's all-out support for the Syrian regime, tried to distance us further from his arch enemy in Cairo by offering vague promises about the Shatt al-'Arab and Kurdistan. The Shah was a member of the Western military alliance and saw Nasser and his Arab nationalism and rejection of military alliances as a threat to Iran. The British Ambassador in Baghdad sent the following telegram to the

Foreign Office on the visit to Tehran:

> Dr Pirasteh (Iranian Ambassador in Baghdad), had been warned by a well-known Iraqi to beware of Pachachi as he was untrustworthy and pro-Egyptian. He asked what I thought; I replied that by and large I subscribed to the view that Pachachi is very clever but not entirely trustworthy. In international affairs at the U.N. he generally put the Egyptian view with more deftness and urbanity than the Egyptians themselves but there were exceptions, e.g. recently in connection with Cyprus and with the U.N. Mission to Aden.
>
> Pirasteh asked how could the untrustworthy and pro-UAR [namely Egypt] sentiment be neutralized during the visit without giving offence. I suggested a tête-à-tête meeting of the Heads of State.

The exact opposite happened. The Shah asked me to see him alone at his palace in north Tehran. Our meeting lasted more than an hour and he was not particularly worried by the fears and suspicions of his Ambassador. He was extremely cordial and friendly and declared that Iraq should distance itself from Nasser and pay more attention to its relations with Iran. I replied by saying that we valued our relations with Iran and would do everything to improve them but there was no incompatibility with good relations with Egypt, to which Iraq was closely linked by obvious strategic and national interests.

In April 1967, I paid official visits to the Soviet Union, Hungary and Romania. In Moscow I met Podgorny who, with Brezhnev and Kosygin, formed the 'troika' then ruling the Soviet Union. I also held extensive discussions with my host, Andrei Gromyko, the Foreign Minister. I raised three main points with him. The first was the Soviet Union's continued support of the rebellion in Kurdistan. The second related to the apparent reluctance of the Soviet Union to fulfil its commitment to furnish us with the military equipment needed by the armed forces. My third point related to Palestine, on which the Soviet Union had always had an ambivalent attitude, for while they supported us verbally in facing Israel's aggression, they were less keen to commit themselves on the rights of the Palestinians. It took me several days of strenuous argument to persuade the Soviets to include in the joint communiqué a paragraph supporting the right of the Palestinians to self-determination.

At the end of April 1967, a year after assuming the post of Foreign Minister, I looked back on my achievements and failures. On the whole the track record was not bad, though I could perhaps have done more. My aim was to ensure the security of Iraq and defend its national interests. There were major issues of urgent concern requiring our immediate attention: first, the qualitative improvement of Iraq's defensive capabilities; second, the protection of Iraq's vital maritime outlet via the Shatt al-'Arab to the Gulf; third, having our just share of the Euphrates and Tigris waters; and, finally, expediting the settlement of the Kurdish problem, which constituted a costly drain on our manpower and resources. The other vital issue was the improvement of our relations with Western Europe, which I found to be in a terrible state of confusion and disarray.

Now that a year had passed I was beginning to enjoy my work and was making preparations to extend the scope of my activities – which is why I did not encourage rumours that I was a candidate for the post of Secretary-General of the Arab League. In fact two of my best friends, Talib Shibib, Arab League Representative in London, and Nadim Dimichkie, Lebanese Ambassador to Britain, had indeed proposed me for that post, as was revealed in Foreign Office memoranda in 1967.

Before concluding this chapter, I would like to offer some general thoughts about Iraq's foreign policy.

There are certain geographical, economic, human, national, religious and ideological factors that will, in my opinion, always shape the foreign policy of Iraq, irrespective of personalities or regimes. Rulers and governments come and go, but Iraq's fundamental interests are constant.

To begin with, Iraq's geography and the peculiarities of its existing frontiers have to a great extent determined, and will continue to determine, the direction of its foreign policy. Practically a landlocked country whose economy depends on its ability to export large quantities of crude oil through its natural outlet, the Arabian Gulf, and various oil pipelines passing through neighbouring countries, Iraq must at all times enjoy easy access to the waters of the Gulf and ensure the unhindered flow of Iraqi oil to international markets. For this reason, it needs to maintain a strong naval presence in the Gulf to confront any threat to freedom of navigation and prevent any power from dominating its vital maritime lifeline. To protect their own interests, Iraq's Arabian Gulf neighbours would be well advised to agree to whatever territorial adjustments may be deemed necessary to improve Arab defensive capabilities in the Gulf. Iraq has unfortunately been vulnerable to blackmail by hostile regimes in Syria as far as the flow of oil through the pipeline located in that country is concerned. The same vulnerability potentially exists with regard to pipelines passing through Saudi Arabia and Turkey. The problems with Syria can be resolved by closer relations between two neighbours who have so much in common. With Saudi Arabia, no difficulties are likely to arise, and hopefully they would be permanently eliminated when Iraq joins the Gulf Co-operation Council (GCC). Relations with Turkey could be complicated by the diversion of the waters of the Euphrates and the building of dams at the source of the Tigris River. Iraq cannot afford to have a hostile neighbour in Turkey, and we should strive to maintain good and mutually beneficial relations with the Turks.

The problems arising from Iraq's landlocked position are particularly acute and dangerous with regard to the Shatt al-'Arab and the Gulf. Iraq cannot accept any threat to navigation in this vital waterway, and can ill afford to subject it to the whims of a neighbour which has never concealed its aggressive intentions and expansionist ambitions. Successive Iraqi regimes have tried in vain to come to terms with Iran. Until and unless Iran gives up its dream of becoming the superpower of the region, the question of the Shatt al-'Arab and Iraq's free and safe access to the waters of the Gulf will remain a vital concern of Iraq's foreign policy. This issue, however, is just one of the many preoccupations and challenges that have clouded Iraq's relations with its difficult and troublesome neighbour. The rulers of Iran have, over the centuries, always nurtured ambitions of dominating Iraq. The Shi'a majority in the country, and the fact that the holiest shrines of the Shi'a sect are located in Iraq, has given those ambitions a highly emotional and fanatical content that has hindered the establishment and maintenance of normal relations between the two countries. The Iranian menace is something that, unfortunately, Iraq has to live with. It could successfully confront it if a strong Arab front were to be created through the union of Iraq and Syria, and the accession of Iraq to full membership in the Gulf Co-operation Council; or alternatively, if the polyglot Iranian state broke up into its various ethnic components. Iraq has to be vigilant and must possess a credible military deterrent to discourage any adventurous and irresponsible Iranian regime from encroaching upon its sovereignty and threatening its vital interests.

The utilization of the waters of the Euphrates and Tigris Rivers is a matter of vital importance for Iraq. The livelihood of millions of Iraqi citizens and wide areas in Iraq would be affected if Syria and Turkey were allowed to divert large quantities of water from these rivers. Iraq has a strong and, in my view, unassailable position based upon the long-established practices and acquired rights sanctioned by international law. The building of dams at the source of the Tigris River has added to the problems we have had with Turkey.

The Kurdish problem meanwhile has undergone dramatic changes. Full Kurdish autonomy is now a living reality. The Kurds are also active participants in the central federal government. They have established close economic and cultural ties with Turkey. As a result there has recently been a noticeable change in Turkey's attitude vis-à-vis the Kurds of Iraq. They are no longer fearful of Kurdish autonomy or even independence. They have increased substantially their economic and commercial interests in Iraqi Kurdistan. However, there are still outstanding issues between the Kurds and the central government in Baghdad which must be resolved in order to preserve the unity and territorial integrity of Iraq.

By virtue of its natural and human resources, Iraq is qualified to play an important role in the affairs of the Arab Middle East. Its two main objectives in the area should be to preserve the Arab character of the Gulf and to confront the growing Israeli menace. In my considered opinion, the Arabs will never be able to achieve those objectives without the unity of Iraq and Syria. I am not speaking about solidarity or co-operation, but about a federal union which might then be joined by Jordan and other Arab states in the region. This, in my view, is the *sine qua non* for any effective defence of Arab interests, not only in the Middle East but throughout the world. This is why I consider the establishment of a federal union between Iraq and Syria to be a matter of supreme national importance and urgency. Such a union would give the Arabs the military capability to deny Israel easy victories and ultimately force the Israeli ruling establishment to renounce its expansionist ambitions in Palestine and the rest of the Arab world. Meanwhile Iraq should support Palestinian efforts to negotiate a peaceful settlement of the conflict with Israel.

I believe it is in the interest of all concerned that Iraq should as soon as possible join the GCC, which should eventually also include a united Yemen. Iraqi membership would greatly improve that organization's defensive capabilities and put an end to Iranian attempts to interfere in the affairs of the smaller countries of the Gulf.

As an integral part of the Arab nation, Iraq must have as one of the principal aims of its foreign policy the ending of the tragic fragmentation of the Arab world. As I have suggested above, Iraq should, in pursuance of this aim, unite with Syria and join the Gulf Co-operation Council. It should also maintain a special relationship with Egypt, which occupies a central position in the Arab world, not only geographically but also historically, culturally and politically. Egypt is a great asset to the Arab world. It carries great weight in international affairs and is capable of rendering considerable service to the Arabs. Iraq should always seek to maintain excellent relations with the Islamic countries. This includes Iran, when and if the rulers of that country face reality and give up once and for all their dreams of dominance and hegemony. Iraq's Islamic credentials need no affirmation. Baghdad was the capital of the Islamic Caliphate for more than five hundred years, and the people of Iraq were among the first to embrace the Muslim faith. Many imams, religious leaders and theologians have lived, died and been buried in Iraq. Islamic solidarity could be a great asset for Iraq and the Arab world in general and its pursuit should never be neglected.

Our relations with the rest of the world will have to be governed by mutual interests which are today mainly economic. As a major oil-producing country, Iraq is naturally interested in protecting its markets. It is therefore a matter of great urgency and importance to establish friendly relations with the European Union, China and India. Close economic co-operation often produces important and mutually beneficial results. Europeans, Chinese and Indians can make a valuable contribution to the current efforts to achieve peace and justice for the Palestinians.

Our relations with Russia have undergone significant changes. The collapse of the former Soviet Union fundamentally altered the character of Russian relations with the Arab World. The Arabs should not forget several decades of close co-operation with the Soviet Union and should maintain the best of relations with its successor, the Russian Federation, which will remain a power to be reckoned with and will continue to have a powerful influence in world affairs.

The United States poses a problem of great complexity. Its unconditional support for Israel and its failure to use effectively its enormous influence to stop Israel's expansionist building of settlements and to end the cruel oppression of the Palestinian people, have cast a dark shadow over Arab–American relations. On the other hand, it is possible for Arab and US interests to coincide at certain points, as became apparent during the final phase of the Iraq–Iran war. The United States and the Arab countries of the region have a common interest in resisting any interference with the freedom of navigation in the Gulf and in ensuring the unhindered flow of oil to world markets. The Arabs therefore need to work tirelessly to move the United States from a position of total support for Israel to one that is more moderate and even-handed. This battle, difficult as it may be, has to be waged with vigour and determination. The Arabs have certain advantages, such as oil and large investments in the United States, which may, if judiciously used, bring about a favourable change. A policy compatible with justice and fairness will, in the long run, serve the interests of the United States far better than the present policy of blind and unquestioning support for Israel.

The strategic alliance between Israel and the United States is justified on grounds of common beliefs and shared values. I can think of no two countries more dissimilar than Israel and the United States. One is an exclusivist theocratic state where religion and race play a crucial role in determining the status of those who live within its borders and whose laws and policies are openly designed to give preferential treatment to one segment of the population, while minorities are continuously harassed and intimidated. The other is an open and egalitarian society which welcomes, indeed thrives, on racial, ethnic and religious diversity and prohibits any form of institutionalized discrimination on grounds of race, religion and ethnic origin. The alliance, far from being beneficial to the United States, has seriously undermined American interests in the Arab world and delayed the settlement of a conflict which has caused so much human misery and suffering.

9

THE ARAB–ISRAELI WAR OF 1967

To understand the origins and underlying causes of the war of June 1967 it is necessary to study the tortuous developments in American–Egyptian relations from 1952 to 1967. There can be no doubt that the final breach between the United States and Egypt was a crucial element in Israel's decision to launch its attack on its Arab neighbours on 5 June 1967.

When Jamal Abdul Nasser came to power after overthrowing the Egyptian monarchy in a bloodless coup on 23 July 1952, he, like many Arabs of his generation, harboured warm feelings towards the United States. Its anti-colonial past, its apparent sympathy for the struggle of the Arabs to free themselves from European colonial rule and its egalitarian and open society appealed to many young Arabs. America's support for Israel did not at the time seem as great or as decisive as that of the Soviet Union and France. It was also felt that the tragedy of Palestine was the primary responsibility of Britain, as author of the Balfour Declaration and the mandatory power instrumental in the establishment of the Jewish national home in Palestine.

The US Ambassador in Egypt, Jefferson Caffery, showed great sympathy for the revolution, and Nasser himself established an excellent relationship with Kermit Roosevelt, the personal emissary of Allen Dulles, head of the CIA. Nasser welcomed American support, which he felt he needed to bolster his position in the negotiations with the British on the question of evacuation of their base in the Suez Canal. The Americans, for their part, were happy to deal with a young, idealistic officer bent on reform, and hoped that the new Egypt would lead the Arab countries in concluding peace with Israel and forming a solid front against communist ambitions in the region. Nasser wanted to test American sincerity by asking for assistance to supply the Egyptian army with the modern weapons it woefully lacked. The Americans responded favourably at first, and promised to allocate $100 million for that purpose. This promise, however, was not fulfilled because the British government prevailed upon the Americans to postpone any arms shipment until after the conclusion of the negotiations relating to the British base in the Suez Canal. This was Nasser's first disappointment with the Americans.

In June 1954, when the Anglo-Egyptian negotiations were nearing completion, President Eisenhower assured Egypt that the United States would provide large-scale military and economic assistance following the successful conclusion of an agreement on the Suez Canal base. When that agreement was signed, an Egyptian delegation went to Washington to discuss Egypt's military and economic requirements. For a start, the US agreed in November 1954 to furnish Egypt with $40 million in economic aid, and there was every reason to believe that military assistance would follow; the Eisenhower administration, as far as the Arab–Israeli conflict was concerned, seemed a vast improvement on its Democratic predecessor and appeared to have shown a genuine desire to pursue a more even-handed policy.

It was precisely at this moment that Israel attacked, with massive force, the weakly defended Egyptian army headquarters in the Gaza Strip, killing thirty-eight military personnel and civilians. Here was an obvious attempt by Israel to sabotage any US–Egyptian rapprochement, which it greatly feared and sought to prevent at all costs. The timing of the Gaza attack immediately after the conclusion of a defence pact between Iraq and Turkey, which was promoted by the US as a precursor to the Baghdad Pact Alliance of 1955, was calculated to place maximum strain on US–Egyptian relations.

As previously indicated, Nasser's foreign policy was built on the premise that the Arab states under Egyptian leadership should adopt a common stand in foreign affairs and negotiate as a bloc with other countries. He was therefore utterly opposed to any Arab state unilaterally joining a military alliance with others. The fact that the conclusion of a defensive alliance between Iraq and Turkey was almost immediately followed by the Israeli attack on Gaza convinced Nasser that the United States was trying to impose its will on Egypt and was not serious about its promise of arms deliveries, especially since John Foster Dulles, the US Secretary of State, had been insisting that Egypt should join the Western defence system in order to qualify for sizeable American military assistance. As a result, negotiations with the Americans dragged on inconclusively for several months and finally petered out.

As I described in Chapter 5, Nasser's decision to get weapons from the Soviet bloc in 1955 led to the withdrawal of the US guarantee for financing the Aswan High Dam project, which in turn led to the Suez crisis and a brief improvement in US–Egyptian relations, which was almost immediately undermined in 1957 by the Dulles-inspired Eisenhower Doctrine. That final initiative of Secretary of State John Foster Dulles was soon overtaken by events. The first was when the Nationalist parties in Syria, threatened by pro-Western plots and fearing growing communist influence in the country, persuaded Nasser to accept the union of Syria with Egypt, which was proclaimed as the United Arab Republic in February 1958. The second event to undermine both the Eisenhower Doctrine and Dulles's policy of creating an anti-communist coalition in the Arab world was the revolution in Iraq on 14 July 1958.

The United States blamed Nasser for the Iraqi revolution and decided to send Marines to Lebanon in an attempt to prevent further erosion of Western influence in the Near East. Nasser countered by flying to Moscow as a gesture of defiance. While he was there, he tried to persuade the Russians to intervene if the revolutionary regime in Iraq was threatened. He received no such undertaking and had to be content with a strongly worded declaration.

Eisenhower was against widening US military intervention and realized, as a prudent soldier, that the time had come for the United States to cut its losses and curtail its ambitions in the Arab Near East. The Iraqi republican government was recognized. In Lebanon a new neutral president acceptable to Nasser was elected, whereupon the US Marines were withdrawn.

Despite the failures and disappointments that had plagued US–Egyptian relations, there was still a chance to salvage something and start afresh. A new opportunity presented itself with the break between Egypt and the communist-influenced regime of Abdul Karim Qassim in Baghdad, and with the tension this break created between Egypt and the Soviet Union. The Russians enthusiastically supported Qassim and severely criticized Nasser, who rallied around him all the anti-communist elements in the Arab world. The United States, with Dulles no longer directing its foreign policy, had a chance to benefit from the rift between the Soviet Union and Egypt. The first step towards improvement was to resume US wheat shipments to Egypt in accordance with Public Law 480 under which Egypt paid for these shipments with local currency. From then on US–Egyptian relations once more steadily improved; this improvement continued when Kennedy succeeded Eisenhower, but was abruptly cut short by Kennedy's assassination.

Within a year of Johnson's accession to the presidency, relations with Egypt deteriorated rapidly. The United States considerably increased its weapons sales to Israel and in June 1965 Johnson decided not to renew the wheat shipments to Egypt. This was a serious blow to Nasser, since Egypt had become dependent on the United States for 50 percent of its wheat imports. The wheat shipments were resumed at the end of 1965 only to be stopped again in June 1966. This problem led Nasser to adopt an increasingly hostile attitude towards the United States, attacking its war in Vietnam and intensifying the pressure on its two principal allies in the Arab world, Saudi Arabia and Jordan. Johnson's response was to increase substantially military and economic aid to Israel, while denouncing Nasser as the principal enemy of American and Western interests in the region. From then on, Israel's actions were all calculated to provoke an armed confrontation in which Egypt would be defeated and humiliated. The military alliance concluded with Syria in November 1966 increased the possibilities of such a confrontation, and in the early part of 1967 all of Israel's military and verbal abuse and threats of reprisals were directed against Syria. It became clear that Israel hoped to draw Egypt into armed conflict by concentrating all its efforts against Syria, the ally Nasser could not control but was pledged to defend in the event of outside attack.

This was the situation at the end of April 1967 when I returned from my visit to the Soviet Union. During the early part of May, information reached Cairo that Israel was about to launch a large-scale attack on Syria. This information, which was relayed by the Russians, may well have been planted by Israeli intelligence.

Syria appealed to Egypt for help, and Nasser responded by ordering Egyptian troops to take up positions on the armistice line with Israel. In so doing, he faced a difficult problem. The troops of the United Nations Emergency Force (UNEF) stationed on the Egyptian side of the armistice lines since 1957 had to be withdrawn to make room for the Egyptian forces. The government of the United Arab Republic [i.e. Egypt] formally asked the Secretary-General to withdraw the UN troops from their positions on the Egyptian–Israeli border. The Secretary-General of the United Nations, U Thant, on the advice of Ralph Bunche, decided to withdraw the UN force not only from the border area but also from the Gaza Strip, where they were also stationed, and the Gulf of Aqaba. Nasser's hand was thus forced, because once the UN troops were withdrawn he could not be seen to allow the passage of Israeli and other ships destined for the Israeli port of Eilat: since 1957, under the protection of UNEF, Israel had been able to use the Gulf of Aqaba and to have its ships pass through the Straits of Tiran, which lie exclusively in Egyptian territorial waters. With the removal of UNEF, Nasser was unable to countenance Israeli ships passing through Egyptian territorial waters under the nose of his own forces. He therefore closed the Gulf of Aqaba to Israeli shipping, an act which Israel considered a *casus belli* – one justifying going to war. The closure was announced even as Secretary-General U Thant was on his way to Cairo to try to defuse the crisis. That announcement was deliberately made to preempt his mission, and when he arrived in Cairo there was really very little he could do. Nasser had been unable to resist the temptation to recover his standing and prestige in the Arab world with one bold stroke.

As the crisis intensified, I went to Egypt as a member of a large Iraqi ministerial delegation which included, besides myself, the Deputy Prime Minister and the Minister of Defence. I asked Nasser what in his opinion were the chances of war. He said, "Eighty percent". When I asked whether he was ready, he said: "We can handle the Israelis, but if the Americans intervene, then we would have to ask for Soviet help."

Secretary-General U Thant meanwhile proposed what he called a "breathing spell" to allow time for negotiations. During these negotiations, Israel would not send any of its ships through the Strait of Tiran, other countries would refrain from shipping strategic materials to Israel, and Egypt would undertake not to search any ships going to the port of Eilat. These proposals were accepted by Egypt but ignored by Israel. I was requested by the Egyptian Foreign Minister, Mahmoud Riad, to go to New York to assist in the debates taking place in the Security Council.

I instructed all our ambassadors to convey to the governments to which they were accredited our support for the Secretary-General's initiative and to warn of the imminent danger of war. A few days before my departure for New York, the Italian Ambassador in Baghdad handed me a message from the Italian Foreign Minister, Amintore Fanfani. The text of that message, as translated by the Italian Embassy in Baghdad, was as follows:

> Rome, 26 May 1967
>
> Upon request of HE Minister Al Pachachi, Ambassador Suleiman called on me in order to illustrate the position of the Iraqi government in the present crisis.
>
> In my turn, I illustrated to him the efforts made by the Italian government for a peaceful solution, and I stressed that the situation would become very serious in case of failure of the endeavours of U Thant. I had noticed myself how deeply concerned the Secretary-General was when I met him yesterday at Fiumicino.
>
> I invited therefore the Iraqi Ambassador to inform HE Dr Al Pachachi that I am personally convinced that his immediate intervention with U Thant or with other influential friends at the UN, could be extremely useful in order to facilitate not only the evaluation of the real aspects of the situation, but also the research of tentative solutions both for the Gaza question and for that, even more serious, of the navigation in Aqaba Gulf.
>
> As far as the latter is concerned, I am aware that the measures taken by the UAR are considered so far unacceptable by Israel: this might be the unfortunate cause of a clash, although incidents have been avoided up to now owing to the efforts and advice of many friends, including ourselves.
>
> I deem therefore urgent and indispensable that all those who

have a wide and deep knowledge of the problems of the area and the many facets of the issue should put their experience at the disposal of the UN in order to co-operate in finding out diplomatic alternatives to war.

The well-known competence of HE Dr Al Pachachi and the esteem and authority enjoyed by him at the UN are at this moment a most useful asset for the cause of peace.

Your Excellency is therefore kindly requested to call immediately on him to convey my personal greetings and the friendly invitation to consider the possibility of undertaking a direct step with U Thant before he presents his proposal, as well as with all those who will be requested to support his recommendations: in my opinion we should avoid a clash by adopting either a more or less definitive solution which could give enough time for negotiating and finding out an equitable settlement of the issue.

Please emphasize that more than ever I am convinced that an authoritative intervention of Dr Al Pachachi would be a decisive factor for the world peace.

Fanfani

On my way to New York, Fanfani met me at Rome airport and implored me to do everything I could to avert a war which, in his view, might not go well for the Arabs. I arrived in New York on 29 May 1967. I spoke in the Security Council two days later.

We had been assured by our military commanders and experts that we could repel any Israeli attack and that we were ready for a long war, and my speech, part of which I quote below, reflected the confidence we all felt that this time any military contest with Israel would not end in an easy Israeli victory.

> Those who think the issue will be settled by a quick lightning thrust are indulging in dangerous delusions. My friend and colleague, the Foreign Minister of Lebanon, yesterday gave the Council a moving and eloquent account of the feelings of our people and their unshakeable determination to put an end to twenty years of humiliation at the hands of the aggressor in our

midst. We shall defend ourselves whatever the cost and however long and difficult the struggle may be. We are prepared to use every tool at our disposal. The conflict will be total and uncompromising. The day before I left Baghdad, my government decided to deny our oil resources to any state which takes part in or supports the Israeli aggression against the Arab states. We have invited all the other Arab oil-producing and exporting countries to meet with us to co-ordinate our positions. This must prove that our people are prepared to beat any hardship and accept any sacrifice. But there will be no retreat. Make no mistake about that; make no miscalculations.

It was not a bad speech, I think, but it now seems hollow and full of wishful thinking in the light of the subsequent disastrous military defeat.

While the debates were proceeding in the Security Council, the United States informed Egypt that they would not tolerate hostilities started by either side and cautioned Nasser against precipitate action, strongly advising him to accept the Secretary-General's plan. At the same time, US President Lyndon Johnson met Abba Eban, the Foreign Minister of Israel, on 26 May, in secret, and assured him that the United States would not exert pressure on Israel to withdraw from any territories that might be occupied in the course of an armed conflict with Egypt and other Arab states. The Soviet Union, for its part, was completely taken in by this American deception and advised Egypt against initiating any hostile or belligerent action against Israel.

On 1 June, I was invited by Arthur Goldberg, the Permanent Representative of the United States, to have breakfast with him. He said that I should do everything I could to prevent the outbreak of war and assured me that, should Israel start the war, it would not be supported by the United States; but he warned me that, if the Arabs attacked Israel, they would be defeated, because Israel was stronger than we thought.

Goldberg informed me that President Johnson and Secretary of State Dean Rusk would welcome me in Washington later that day, provided the visit would be kept secret like the one made by Abba Eban. I went to Washington and had talks with President Johnson, Rusk, Eugene Rostow, the Deputy Under-Secretary of State, and Walter Rostow, Presidential Assistant. I assured them that the Arabs would not start any war and requested that the United States restrain Israel. The Arab position which I expounded to the President and his aides was based upon U Thant's formula that there should be a short breathing space, during which efforts would be made to settle the problem of navigation through the Strait of Tiran. Egypt had proposed that the dispute should be submitted to the International Court of Justice and that, while the matter was *sub judice*, the partial blockade would continue. It is sometimes forgotten that the blockade imposed by Egypt was a partial one applying only to strategic materials, oil, and ships flying the Israeli flag. It was pointed out at the time that, in practice, such a partial blockade did not inflict undue hardship on Israel. Very few ships flying the Israeli flag had gone through the Gulf of Aqaba during the ten years it was open to Israeli shipping. Strategic materials were never shipped to Eilat but always to Israel's Mediterranean ports, particularly Haifa. Only the embargo on oil could have conceivably caused serious inconvenience to Israel. However, during the short breathing space proposed by the Secretary-General, Israel's oil needs could easily have been shipped to Haifa, where incidentally most of the oil coming through Eilat was in any case destined to go because of the large refinery situated there. To all those who were interested in preventing war, this was an eminently fair and reasonable approach to the problem. Israel and her backers, however, were not interested in a peaceful solution but in a public humiliation of the United Arab Republic and President Nasser. They insisted that all diplomatic discussions and negotiations be preceded by an unconditional lifting of the partial blockade. The United Arab Republic government could not accede to these demands without seriously weakening its standing at home and in the Arab world, and jeopardizing its whole diplomatic and legal position. The impression which I got from my talks in Washington was that the United States felt bound by an understanding it had reached with Israel in 1957 that no unilateral change would be permitted in respect of navigation rights through the Strait of Tiran. Needless to say, the United Arab Republic was not a party to this 'understanding' and could not be bound by it. It became clear from my extensive talks with US officials that, for the United States, the point of departure for any diplomatic effort to defuse the crisis was the full restoration of Israel's freedom of navigation and the total lifting of the blockade. On the question of war and peace, President

Johnson assured me that he had repeatedly and in the strongest terms warned Israel not to initiate offensive military action against the Arab states.

The same information was given to the other Arab governments and the great powers, particularly the Soviet Union. On the strength of the assurances given by President Johnson that Israel had been warned not to start a war in the Middle East, it was decided to send Vice-President Zakariya Muhieddin of the United Arab Republic to Washington to negotiate with the United States government the details of a diplomatic solution to the crisis. The United States government was informed that the Egyptian delegation would adopt a very flexible approach and that it was authorized to make whatever concessions were necessary to reach a settlement. The date of the Vice-President's arrival in Washington was fixed for 7 June. It turned out that the assurances given by the United States to Arab leaders and diplomatic representatives had been designed primarily to ease Arab fears and apprehensions. As a result of this, the emphasis in Arab capitals shifted from war-preparedness to diplomatic activity. This gave Israel, which was bent on war, a great psychological advantage, not to mention the time it needed to complete preparations for its preemptive strike. It really seems quite extraordinary that, having realized that war was inevitable and having received intelligence information that Israel was going to launch an air attack on 5 June, Nasser did not order his armed forces to strike first. He was completely deceived by the Americans and accepted the repeated advice of the Russians not to start offensive action.

On 5 June 1967, Israel unleashed a surprise attack that, within a few hours, destroyed the Egyptian air force. I was awakened at 7 a.m. that morning in New York and informed of the Israeli attack. When I asked the Egyptian representative for more details about the situation, he assured me that everything was going well. I went to the United Nations and contacted the Egyptian Foreign Minister in Cairo by telephone; he assured me that, although they had sustained some losses in their air force, the situation was under control. Shortly thereafter, however, when the magnitude of the disaster became apparent, the friends of the Arabs in the Security Council proposed an immediate ceasefire and the withdrawal of forces behind the armistice lines. The United States rejected this proposal and submitted a draft resolution calling only for a ceasefire, which was adopted unanimously by the Security Council on the evening of 6 June. I took the floor and made a short impromptu statement in which I described the resolution as an abject surrender to Israel. The statement apparently had quite an effect since I received numerous telephone calls, telegrams and written messages of congratulations. The text of that statement can be found in the verbatim records of the 1348th meeting of the Security Council.

The following day I went back to Baghdad. In the meantime the Security Council continued its meeting and war did not end until 11 June, when a ceasefire was agreed with Syria and Jordan. The results were catastrophic for the Arabs. The West Bank, Gaza, Sinai and the Golan Heights were occupied by Israel. For me, the Arab defeat was a traumatic experience from which I have never really recovered. Looking back at all the twists and turns of Egypt's relations with the United States, the Soviet Union and other Arab countries, as well as Nasser's relations with his own subordinates in Egypt, one is left with the inescapable conclusion that the catastrophe of 1967 could have been avoided.

What were Nasser's mistakes?

First, he left Abdul Hakim Amer in charge of the armed forces in spite of his blunders during the 1956 Suez crisis. Nasser should have assumed direct control of the army himself and not have been content with the inaccurate information that Amer and his friend Shams Badran, the Defence Minister, gave him about the fighting capabilities of the Egyptian armed forces, which were inferior compared with the much better trained and equipped Israeli forces.

Second, he allied himself to the irresponsible minority faction that ruled Syria, and allowed them, by their slogans and empty gestures, to drag him into a war for which he was unprepared.

Third, he should have known from experience that he could not rely on the Soviet Union. They were anxious to avoid any confrontation with the United States and would not fight to save Egypt. In 1956 during the Suez war, as well as in 1967, they failed to give Egypt the prompt assistance it needed. He should have realized that the ties between Israel and the United States were much stronger than those between Egypt and the Soviet Union; while the US was ready to commit its military power if Israel was threatened, the Russians were not willing to do the same for Egypt.

Fourth, he sent a large part of the Egyptian army to Yemen to fight in a guerrilla war for which Egyptian soldiers were ill equipped. That operation exhausted his army and sapped its morale. While it must be acknowledged that Nasser went into Yemen from the best and most honourable of motives, namely, to save Yemen from returning to the cruel and medieval regime of the Imams, he had other more important and pressing problems to deal with.

Fifth, he expended too much time and effort in either fomenting or reacting to endless inter-Arab quarrels. He should have realized that, so long as Israel was there, he could ill-afford to dilute Arab solidarity. And, finally, he allowed himself to be deceived by American assurances and influenced by Russian faint-heartedness, and failed to take military preventive action.

Having said all the above, it must be acknowledged that Nasser leaned over backwards to improve relations with the United States. All his genuine efforts to establish friendship between the two countries were frustrated first by American insistence that Egypt should, for all practical purposes, become a client state and part of the West's grand anti-communist alliance, and, second, by the enormous power of the Zionist lobby, which sabotaged and wrecked every initiative to improve relations between the United States and the Arab world. It must also be conceded that he was wise enough to avoid any military confrontation with Israel until and unless the Arabs were fully prepared. He was able to restrain the hotheads among the Arab leaders, and believed he could end the 1967 crisis peacefully, not realizing that, by a series of avoidable miscalculations, he was giving Israel the pretext it had awaited since 1957 to inflict a decisive military defeat on the Arabs.

The Israelis themselves have acknowledged with a good deal of self-satisfaction that their sudden preemptive strike on 5 June 1967 assured their swift military victory. They contended that their attack was a justifiable response to the closing of the Strait of Tiran, which in their view constituted a legitimate *casus belli*. Under the Charter of the United Nations, defensive military measures are permissible only in case of actual outside attack. Since no such attack took place, the claim that Israel acted in self-defence is untenable. Preventive war, whatever the alleged provocation, is totally prohibited under the UN Charter. This legal technical point, important though it is, unfortunately evoked little public interest in a world in which violations of international law have become commonplace.

Soon after the 1967 war ended, it became clear to us that Israel, elated by its decisive victory, was not going to withdraw from the territories it had occupied, and since, for the time being at least, the military option was no longer possible, the Arabs would have to content themselves with a diplomatic offensive in the United Nations. I attended a meeting of Arab foreign ministers in Kuwait on 18 June to prepare for the fifth Emergency Special Session of the General Assembly, which was convened on 19 June 1967, at the request of the Soviet Union, after it became clear that the Security Council would be unable to take meaningful and effective action. I led the Iraqi delegation, in which I included the distinguished Palestinian Arab scholar and historian, Dr Walid Khalidi, who made invaluable contributions. I delivered a major address on 27 June 27, in which I dealt with every aspect of the Palestinian question and particularly the obvious responsibility of Israel for starting the war, and I demanded the immediate and total withdrawal of Israeli forces from all the territories occupied during the Six-Day War. I was deeply involved in the long and arduous meetings and consultations which took place prior to the drafting and introduction of resolutions. Our group – the Arab group – decided not to sponsor any resolution, to give ourselves greater flexibility, and instead asked their supporters to undertake this task. The following seven draft resolutions went before the General Assembly.

1. A draft resolution, sponsored by a mixed group of Asian, Latin American, African and European states, calling on all members to render assistance to the relief efforts undertaken by the United Nations and various international and intergovernmental organizations to help the victims of the war. This resolution, which was called the 'humanitarian resolution', was adopted by 116 votes to none.

2. A draft resolution, proposed by six Afro-Asian states, considered that all Israeli measures to change the status of Jerusalem were invalid and called on Israel to rescind them

and desist "from taking any action which would alter the status of Jerusalem". This resolution was adopted by 99 votes, with none against and 20 abstentions.

3. A draft resolution, submitted by the Soviet Union, condemning Israel's occupation of Arab territories and demanding the withdrawal of Israeli forces. This draft resolution, voted on in parts, failed to obtain the required two-thirds majority.

4. A draft resolution, introduced by the United States, proposing that peace in the Middle East should be achieved through negotiations based upon five principles, i.e. mutual recognition of all countries of the area within recognized boundaries, including disengagement and withdrawal; freedom of innocent maritime passage; solution of the refugee problem; limitation of arms shipments to the area; the right of every state to live in peace and security. This draft was withdrawn by its sponsor when it became clear that it did not have any chance of success, because it did not specifically call for the immediate withdrawal of Israeli forces from the occupied territories.

5. A draft resolution, submitted by Albania, condemning both Israel's aggression and incitement, and aid and direct participation in that aggression by the United States and the United Kingdom, and demanding the immediate and complete withdrawal of Israeli troops. This draft, which reflected the extreme Arab position, was rejected.

6. A draft resolution, sponsored by eighteen non-aligned countries and reflecting the moderate Arab position, calling on Israel to withdraw its forces from the occupied territories and requesting the Secretary-General to designate a personal representative "who will assist him in securing compliance with the resolution" and requesting the Security Council, after the withdrawal of Israeli forces, to seek peaceful ways and means for the solution of all outstanding problems. This draft failed to obtain the required two-thirds majority.

7. A draft resolution, submitted by twenty Latin American countries, urgently requesting Israel to withdraw its forces from the occupied territories; asking the parties to the conflict to end the state of belligerency; reaffirming that there should be no recognition of occupation or acquisition of territories through force; requesting the Security Council to ensure withdrawal, the end of belligerency, the solution of the refugee problem and the establishment of demilitarized zones; and reaffirming previous resolutions on the internationalization of Jerusalem. This draft resolution, which the Arab states and their supporters voted against, failed to obtain the required two-thirds majority.

In the meeting of the Arab group, I urged my colleagues not to vote against the Latin American draft, which called for the withdrawal of Israeli forces from all the occupied territories and, instead, recommended abstention to ensure its adoption by the General Assembly. The majority of the Arab representatives, however, ignoring strong Soviet advice not to reject the Latin American draft, would not accept the paragraph calling for an immediate end to belligerency and the right of innocent passage through Egyptian territorial waters and, therefore, voted against the Latin American draft.

The Twenty-second Session of the General Assembly opened on 19 September 1967. I again led the Iraqi delegation, this time in my capacity as Permanent Representative to the United Nations, the post to which I had been reappointed on 10 July, when the government of which I was a member had resigned, as will be described at the beginning of the next chapter.

During the session I worked tirelessly with other Arab delegations to obtain a resolution providing for the withdrawal of Israeli forces from the occupied territories. I met with the foreign ministers of the great powers as well as leaders of delegations of sixty member states, including Arthur Goldberg, with whom I had a long meeting. He was adamant: peace first, then withdrawal. Our position was withdrawal first, then peace. Egypt asked for a meeting of the Security Council, and after lengthy negotiations in which I took part, the Council adopted the famous Resolution 242 on 22 November 1967. The English text of the resolution stipulated that Israel should withdraw from territories occupied in the recent armed conflict and proclaimed the right of every state to live within secure and recognized boundaries. The Arab interpretation was that withdrawal should be from all the territories, while Israel insisted that the dropping of the word 'the' before territories was not accidental, but meant that Israel was not required to withdraw from all the territories, but some territories, provided such withdrawal did not prejudice its right to have secure boundaries. The Arabs rejected the notion that it was up to Israel alone to decide what was meant by secure boundaries and maintained that withdrawal should be complete from all the occupied territories, and that the secure boundaries referred to were those which existed on 4 June 1967, that is, the armistice lines agreed upon in 1949. Israel exploited this ambiguity in the English text to maintain its occupation and prepare for the eventual annexation of the West Bank and Gaza. Gunnar Jarring of Sweden was appointed representative of the Secretary-General to ensure the implementation of Resolution 242. After years of unstinting effort, he failed to persuade Israel to change its position. It may be useful to insert here a passage from a speech which I made as representative of the United Arab Emirates in the Security Council on 13 June 1973 concerning the alleged security requirements which Israel used to justify its continued occupation of the West Bank and Gaza.

> Let me deal with the question of secure and insecure boundaries and the meaning of Resolution 242 (1967) in this regard. A great deal has been said from the Israeli side about the vulnerability and insecurity of the armistice lines which separated Israel from its Arab neighbours until the war of June 1967. The fact of the matter is that, until the outbreak of that war, Israel had never complained about the so-called vulnerability and insecurity of the armistice lines. Quite the contrary, it considered them highly satisfactory, and its main aim for eighteen years was concerned with the transformation of those lines into permanent and recognized frontiers. Let me quote from Mr Eban's statement before the General Assembly in October 1966 – only eight months before Israel launched its war of aggression of 1967:

"Behind the armistice frontiers established by agreement between Israel and its Arab neighbours in 1949, the national life of sovereign states has become crystallized in an increasing stable mould. There is some evidence that thoughtful minds in the Middle East are becoming skeptical about threats to change the existing territorial and political structure by armed force. Such threats, and the policies concerted to support them, offend the spirit and letters of the United Nations Charter. They violate bilateral agreements freely negotiated and solemnly signed. They undermine the central principles of international civility ... for they encounter insuperable obstacles ... in the opposition of the world community to the alteration by aggressive force of legally established and internationally recognized situations." [A/PV.1428, para. 112]

He then added: "We regard the present armistice lines as immune from any change without consent." [ibid., para. 113]

Yet, as we all know, eight months later Israel did exactly what Mr Eban cautioned the Arabs against.

This demonstrates conclusively that the claim of vulnerability and insecurity of the 4 June 1967 armistice lines was only a convenient excuse to justify Israel's territorial expansionist ambitions.

That explains why in the General Assembly, when it met in an Emergency Special Session one week after the end of hostilities in June 1967 and before Israel clearly and openly declared its expansionist aims, all of Israel's staunchest supporters in the Assembly felt that what was needed was transformation of those armistice lines into permanent and recognized boundaries, thus fulfilling the hope voiced by Mr Eban eight months earlier. And that is why the Latin American draft resolution, which was supported by the United States and was unopposed by Israel, demanded the urgent withdrawal of all Israeli forces from all the territories occupied.

Arthur Goldberg, who could hardly be described as an Arab sympathizer, said the following as late as 14 July 1967, more than a month after the end of hostilities: "One immediate, obvious and imperative step is the disengagement of all forces and the withdrawal of Israeli forces to their own territory." [A/PV.1554, para. 91] He spoke not of withdrawal to recognized and secure boundaries, but of withdrawal to their own territory — meaning the territory they occupied prior to the war of 1967.

The differences of opinion separating UN members during the Emergency Special Session were related not to the question of withdrawal, on which there was unanimous agreement, but to other questions such as belligerency, freedom of navigation, mutual recognition, and so on. Those differences, as we all know, were finally resolved in Security Council Resolution 242 (1967) of 22 November 1967. When that resolution was introduced in November of that year by the British representative, Lord Caradon, he declared that the policy of his government was that enunciated by the Foreign Secretary, George Brown, in the General Assembly a few weeks earlier. And he read out that statement:

> I should like to repeat what I said when I was here before: Britain does not accept war as a means of settling disputes, nor that a state should be allowed to extend its frontiers as a result of war. This means that Israel must withdraw, but equally, Israel's neighbours must recognize its right to exist, and it must enjoy security within its frontiers. What we must work for in this area is a durable peace, the renunciation of all aggressive designs, and an end to policies which are inconsistent with peace. [A/PV. 1567, para. 91]

During 1968, the futility of UN efforts to settle the Palestine–Israel conflict became apparent. I decided that my continued presence at the United Nations would be useless and I made up my mind to resign.

10

Resignation from the Iraqi Foreign Service, 1969

As described in the last chapter, I led the Iraqi delegation to the fifth Emergency Special Session which convened on 19 June 1967, in the aftermath of the Six-Day War, and, as Foreign Minister of Iraq, was deeply involved in the deliberations and difficult negotiations between the Arab states and other groups to agree on an acceptable resolution.

On 10 July 1967, I received a cable from Baghdad informing me that a new cabinet had been formed and that I was appointed Permanent Representative of Iraq to the United Nations. My first impulse was to decline the appointment, but I realized that I could not leave the United Nations in the midst of the diplomatic struggle to secure Israel's withdrawal from the occupied territories. My colleagues, the Arab foreign ministers and their representatives, were unanimous in urging me to stay. I accepted my appointment as Permanent Representative and informed the Iraqi government that I would remain temporarily in New York, until such time as I felt that my presence there was no longer necessary. At the Twenty-second regular Session of the General Assembly, in the autumn of 1967, I presided over the Iraqi delegation, and was very active in the negotiations that led to the adoption of Resolution 242 of the Security Council. After the end of the session, during which I continued my impassioned defence of the rights of the Palestinian people, I made up my mind to resign as I stated in the last chapter. I decided, however, to postpone my decision because the Special Representative of the Secretary-General, Ambassador Gunnar Jarring, had just started his mission under Resolution 242 and was expected to report on the progress of his mediation to the Security Council in the spring.

A new regime came to power in Iraq in July 1968. I again decided to postpone my resignation, because I thought it inappropriate to leave my post just when a new government had been installed. In August I went twice before the Security Council to denounce Israel's murderous attacks against Palestinian civilian targets across the border in Jordan in reprisal for illegal incursions by Palestinian guerillas. By the end of the Twenty-third Session of the General Assembly in December 1968, I realized that Jarring's mission was doomed to failure and that the question of Israel's withdrawal from the occupied territories was going to drag on, reducing thereby the role of the United Nations and rendering it largely irrelevant. I felt that there was not much point in my staying on in New York.

At the same time I became convinced that the new Ba'athist regime was far more brutal and oppressive than anything Iraq had seen and ultimately it would be morally wrong for me to stay at my post and represent this government whose practices I was utterly opposed to. The arrest and torture of former Prime Minister Abdul Rahman Al-Bazzaz was the last straw. So for all these reasons I tendered my resignation on 10 January 1969. Unfortunately, a few weeks after I resigned, while the government in Baghdad was considering my resignation, several people, among them a number of Jews, were executed as spies and their bodies publicly exhibited. A tremendous outcry resulted and Iraq was pilloried in the world press. It was at that time that my resignation became known, and many people thought I had resigned in protest against the executions. Although I was appalled by the barbaric display of dead bodies in the streets of Baghdad, I had to state the fact that my resignation had nothing to do with the executions, quite aside from my personal opposition to capital punishment as a matter of principle.

Some Iraqi newspapers attacked me viciously, and I answered them in kind, but I also received many messages of support and encouragement, some from people I did not know. In New York, the media had a field day. I have selected a few extracts from the local newspapers. Michael J. Berlin of the *New York Post* wrote as follows on 30 January 1969:

> Pachachi, who holds a PhD from Georgetown University, served as Foreign Minister from 1965 to 1967, between his two stints as UN ambassador, stretching back to 1959. At the UN, he has won the respect of Western diplomats as by far the most eloquent and rational of the Arab ambassadors even as his country's policy has grown progressively more leftist and more vociferously anti-Israeli.

The well-known columnist Drew Middleton reported in the *New York Times* on 31 January 1969:

> IRAQ'S DELEGATE AT UN RESIGNS: DENIES ACTION WAS RELATED TO HANGINGS BY REGIME
>
> Adnan Pachachi, Iraq's permanent representative at the United Nations, disclosed today that he had resigned. He denied that his resignation was connected with the spy trials and executions in his country.
>
> The former Foreign Minister said that he submitted his resignation three weeks ago, before the trials began. He refused three times to say whether the resignation had been accepted.
>
> Mr Pachachi asserted that his reasons for resignation were personal, but he added one political reason: his disappointment with the United Nations for its failure to handle the Middle East situation, a failure he ascribed to the "obdurate attitude of one party, namely Israel".
>
> The question of the trials, he emphasized, does not arise in connection with his resignation.
>
> The diplomatic consensus is that his departure will weaken the presentation of the Arab case in the United Nations. An experienced and skilful diplomat, Mr Pachachi's command of English enabled him to make concise and telling expositions of the Arab case in both the Security Council and the General Assembly.

I left my post with a heavy heart, sad to end a career that had spanned a quarter of a century serving my beloved country. I decided not to go back, although I received many invitations from the Ba'ath government to visit Baghdad. I did not trust them and feared for my safety. I never imagined at the time, however, that it would be another thirty-four years before I would set foot in my country again, to renew my involvement with Iraq and its history.

11

SERVICE IN THE UNITED ARAB EMIRATES, 1969–93

I LEFT NEW YORK ON 6 MARCH 1969 for Geneva. Two days earlier we had been informed of the death of my father-in-law, Ali Jawdat. Selwa, who was very close to her father, was devastated – as was I, for I loved and revered that wonderful man, who was a true patriot, who fought for Arab and Iraqi independence during and immediately after the First World War. He was known for his wisdom and tolerance, and for a modern outlook far ahead of his contemporaries'.

After my resignation from the Iraqi foreign service, I was approached by the foreign minister of Kuwait, Sheikh Sabah al-Ahmad al-Jabir Al-Sabah, the current ruler of Kuwait, who informed me that he had just concluded an agreement with Fiduciary Trust International, a New York bank specializing in investment management, to set up a joint venture, the main purpose of which was to attract funds from the Gulf States. He offered me the post of principal consultant on this joint venture, which was called Akimco, at its headquarters in Geneva. I accepted this offer and went to the Gulf in May 1969. Sheikh Sabah had already sent letters of introduction to the rulers of Bahrain, Qatar, Dubai and Abu Dhabi. I soon found out that there was little interest in investing in the American stock market, which was passing through a period of decline. In Bahrain, the ruler Sheikh 'Isa bin Salman Al-Khalifa, was preoccupied with the renewed

Iranian territorial claims to his country. I advised him to refer the matter to the United Nations where he would most probably receive substantial support. That was good advice; the UN fact-finding mission decided that the majority of the people in Bahrain favoured independence. The Shah of Iran accepted this decision after a deal was struck with Britain enabling Iran to occupy the islands of Abu Musa and the two Tunb Islands belonging to the Trucial States of Sharjah and Ras al-Khaimah. In Qatar I met the ruler, Sheikh Ahmed bin Ali Al-Thani and his deputy, who later supplanted him, Sheikh Khalifa bin Hamed Al-Thani, father of the present ruler of Qatar. I expressed my fears about the growing Iranian migration to the Arabian Gulf States, which I felt might create serious problems in the future. They dismissed my concerns and said the situation was under control. In Dubai the ruler, Sheikh Rashid bin Said Al-Maktoum, received me in his modest office overlooking the busy harbour and said that he was encouraging foreign investment in Dubai and welcomed professionals, businessmen and entrepreneurs of all nationalities to help him make Dubai a great international centre.

The most important part of my Gulf visit was in Abu Dhabi, where I met Sheikh Zayed bin Sultan Al-Nahyan, an outstanding personality in the Arab world during the second half of the 20th century. When I first met him, he was in his mid-fifties. He spoke with great enthusiasm and confidence about the future of his country as a member of a federation comprising Bahrain, Qatar, and the seven Trucial States. He asked me to accompany Ahmed Al-Suwaidi, his chief adviser, on a tour of the other eight emirates, to try to resolve the differences between them and remove the obstacles delaying the establishment of the Federal Union. The Union, without Qatar and Bahrain which had in the event opted for independence, came into being as a sovereign and independent state on 2 December 1971; at that time Britain signed an agreement whereby the protectorate treaties with the various emirates dating back to 1892 were terminated.

My first task before independence was to draw up a basic law for an Abu Dhabi government organized along modern lines. I collaborated with a small group, mostly of Iraqi compatriots, to complete the task early in 1971. I was then appointed Minister of State in the first government of the Emirate of Abu Dhabi and took up office on 1 July 1971. Subsequently, in 1974, I was granted UAE citizenship and felt my presence there afforded me a tremendous privilege, opportunity and challenge to help establish a new modern Arab state in a region long neglected by the Arabs and isolated from the rest of the world.

Before independence, Sheikh Zayed wanted to assure himself of the backing of other Arab states, because he knew Saudi Arabia was withholding its support and demanding that all border disputes be settled before the proclamation of the Union. The Communist regime in South Yemen was implacably opposed to the Union, which it described as a British creation and an imperialist tool, while President Anwar Sadat, whom I went to Cairo to meet, welcomed it. On 2 December, I flew to New York and submitted the application of the United Arab Emirates for membership of the United Nations. I soon found that I had to persuade two permanent members of the Security Council – China and the Soviet Union – not to veto our application. I assured them that the new state would not be bound by any treaty obligations and would join the ranks of the non-aligned countries. Our application was approved by the Security Council and the General Assembly, and on 9 December 1971 the UAE became a member of the United Nations. I had the honour and pleasure of raising the flag of the new state beside the flags of other nations in the presence of Secretary-General U Thant, who came specially to say a few words of welcome. I spoke in the General Assembly and the Security Council affirming the sovereignty of the United Arab Emirates over the islands occupied by Iran.

After completing my task at the UN, I returned to Abu Dhabi and started working with others in laying the foundations of the new state. At first, I worked to organize the Ministry of Foreign Affairs and establish a foreign service for the new state, and took part in its early diplomatic activities. Thus, I led the UAE delegation to the conference of non-aligned countries in Georgetown, Guyana, in 1972. When war broke out between Israel, Egypt and Syria in 1973, Sheikh Zayed decided to impose an oil embargo, a move followed by other Arab oil-producing countries. In the midst of the ensuing crisis, the Arab League decided to send a high-level delegation to visit several countries in Europe and the Far East. The foreign ministers of Algeria, Tunisia, Sudan and myself, representing the United Arab Emirates, went to Copenhagen where a summit meeting of the European Economic Community was being held. We addressed the meeting and I was selected as spokesman of the group at the press conference attended by hundreds of newsmen. We stated that the embargo had been imposed in response to the large-scale military assistance given to Israel by the United States and we demanded justice for the Palestinians and the settlement of the conflict on the basis of total withdrawal of the Israeli forces from the Arab territories occupied in the 1967 war. When I complained about the freezing cold temperature in my hotel suite in Copenhagen, I was told that heating was reduced to a minimum because of the embargo! Then I went with Mansoor Khalid, the Sudanese Foreign Minister, to Bonn, where we met the German Chancellor Willy Brandt, and from there we travelled to London where we held talks at the Foreign Office. Finally, I went to Japan accompanied by the Syrian Foreign Minister, Abdul Halim Khaddam, where we had extensive talks with the Japanese Prime Minister and the Ministers of Foreign Affairs and Foreign Trade. Early in January 1974, Anwar Sadat came to Abu Dhabi to plead with Sheikh Zayed to end the embargo, because the US had informed him that it was trying its best to persuade Israel to come to terms with the neighbouring Arab states and withdraw from the occupied territories. Sheikh Zayed reluctantly lifted the embargo. This opened the way for the Camp David Egyptian–Israeli peace treaty.

I had the pleasure of accompanying Sheikh Zayed on his state visits to Morocco, Tunisia, Pakistan, India and France. And I was a member of the delegation to the Summit Conferences of Non-Aligned Countries in Algeria in 1973 and the Arab Summit of 1974 in Morocco, which decided that the Palestine Liberation Organization was the sole and legitimate representative of the Palestinian people. During that meeting, I suggested to Faruq Qadoomi, the Palestinian representative, that we should call for direct negotiations between Israel and the PLO. He did not accept the suggestion although it was supported by Mahmoud Riad, Secretary-General of the Arab League. As a result Israel was able to withhold its recognition of the Palestine Liberation Organization for many years. Later, direct negotiations became an important demand of the Palestinians and, after several years of procrastination, Israel consented to direct talks and imposed on the Palestinians the humiliating conditions of the Oslo Agreement.

In 1975, I accompanied Sheikh Zayed to the Summit Meeting of the

OPEC Countries held in Algeria, where Saddam Hussein and the Shah of Iran concluded their famous agreement whereby Iraq surrendered its full sovereignty over the Shatt al-'Arab in return for Iran's undertaking to withhold its assistance to the Kurdish rebels. Saddam Hussein explained his position to Sheikh Zayed in my presence, stating that he was unable to force Iran to relinquish its de facto control over half of the Shatt al-'Arab, which it exercised in violation of the Treaty of 1937 between the two countries. He therefore accepted a fait accompli which he could not alter, and received in return a major concession from Iran which stopped its military support of the Kurds. This enabled the Iraqi government to end the Kurdish rebellion in the north of the country.

After 1975, my work as a member of the Abu Dhabi government was concerned mainly with economic matters. I was appointed member of the Board of Directors of the Abu Dhabi National Oil Company (ADNOC), the Abu Dhabi Investment Authority (ADIA) and the Abu Dhabi Fund for Economic Development. I recall with pride my association with ADIA especially. That organization was a great success and is now considered one of the best of its kind in the world. I was also a member of the Abu Dhabi Executive Council and chairman of the General Projects Committee, whose job it was to look at proposals for projects to be implemented inside Abu Dhabi and to make recommendations to the Executive Council who had the final decision.

Abu Dhabi had money and so visitors started to beat a path to its door. Hundreds of proposals were presented to the General Projects Committee and, as its chairman, I was often approached by people asking me to speak on their behalf. One of my more bizarre encounters was with the sculptor Christo, who wanted to construct a piece of public art – a pyramid made of oil barrels. Sheikh Zayed didn't buy the idea.

Being appointed to these bodies central to the development of the country enabled me to contribute in a meaningful way to the building of a new nation on a solid economic and financial footing. I witnessed the transformation of Abu Dhabi from what was essentially a small fishing village on the edge of the desert into a modern metropolis, in a remarkably short period of time. And I feel I was fortunate to have been able to contribute to this extraordinary metamorphosis.

At the beginning Abu Dhabi, an oil-producing and exporting country, lacked the skilled human resources needed to establish the infrastructure of a modern state virtually from scratch and, at that time, there was a great reliance on foreigners, Arabs and non-Arabs, who were largely experienced and did a credible job of helping to build the foundations of the new state. Now, of course, an intensive programme of education and training has enabled young indigenous nationals to take over the entire administration of the country.

The goals that Sheikh Zayed sought to achieve can be summarized as follows. In foreign affairs, he realized from the outset that a small but immensely rich country like the United Arab Emirates, and particularly Abu Dhabi, must be able to defend itself against those who might covet its land and riches. This could be done only if the country possessed a deterrent force capable of making others think twice before embarking on any aggressive act against the Emirates. Sheikh Zayed was essentially a peaceable and tolerant man, so he went a long way to settle disputes with the neighbouring states even if such settlement entailed sacrifices. In spite of its illegal occupation of the three islands belonging to the UAE, he tried to have normal relations with Iran. He proposed that if negotiations failed the whole matter should be referred to the International Court of Justice for adjudication. Sheikh Zayed was a firm believer in Arab solidarity and co-operation and worked tirelessly to settle inter-Arab differences and disputes whether in Palestine, Lebanon, Iraq or Yemen. He was very generous and financed many social, educational and infrastructural projects in Arab and Islamic countries.

Internally, the guiding principle of Sheikh Zayed's life, which informed his every endeavour, was to ensure a life of dignity, economic security and wellbeing for every citizen of his country, and he realized that an equitable distribution of wealth was a necessary condition for this. The cornerstone was education. Sheikh Zayed himself had had no formal education, but he attached enormous importance to it; he believed it was the only way to develop the country. He settled the nomadic tribes by building them housing, medical clinics, schools for their children, mosques and shops. Education was free and people were given incentives to send their children to school. At the same time, big basic infrastructural projects were undertaken – the building of an international airport, a harbour, roads, schools, hospitals and public housing.

Sheikh Zayed also had a passion for the environment, for agriculture and the greening of the desert. He wanted to make Abu Dhabi a garden city. Experts advised him it couldn't be done in the sand, but he was undeterred. An intensive programme of desalination and well digging was undertaken. Plants were brought from all over the world – among them thousands of date palms from Iraq – and they were watered constantly. And now, indeed, Abu Dhabi is full of plants and flowers and green spaces. I have seen the climate change and at a certain point we began to notice there were birds in Abu Dhabi – which had not been the case when I first arrived.

The citizens of Abu Dhabi are fortunate in having had Sheikh Zayed as the founding ruler of their country. His commitment to their welfare means they now live in peace and prosperity to a standard surpassing that in many developed countries. I am grateful for the opportunity to have participated in Sheikh Zayed's great historic undertaking.

At the outset, life in Abu Dhabi was exciting and challenging. I lived for two years in a modest hotel, the only one in Abu Dhabi as it happened. My wife, Selwa, joined me there every few months, but it was hard for her without a home of her own. Some of my expatriate Arab friends and colleagues lived in small flats in hastily constructed buildings, others in pre-fabricated bungalows. Our life was simple and devoid of frills or luxuries. It felt like being at the frontier of civilization. The electricity was intermittent and our cars would get stuck in the sand. The lack of creature comforts, however, failed to dampen our enthusiasm and determination to ensure the success of this unique experiment in nation building.

Sheikh Zayed would frequently summon me to his presence. We would sit cross-legged on a carpet thrown down on the patch of sandy ground outside his modest house and talk. I greatly enjoyed these sessions, but I have to admit that sitting on the ground is something I have never found easy to do.

Our small group of expatriates worked hard and we used to meet daily to entertain each other in our houses. There was plenty of singing, dancing and merry-making. Once Selwa and I threw a party in the hotel for our friends, where the well-loved Iraqi singer, Afifa Skendar, performed for us deep into the night, stirring up all our nostalgia and wistful reminiscences. I cherish the memories of those days, when my life was so different to my ambassadorial life in 'the centre of the world' – in New York and the United Nations.

We eventually moved into a small house on the Corniche, where the sand had to be swept off the road every day. Selwa, with her usual flair, taste and inventiveness managed to transform this nondescript place into what our friends called an 'oasis' in the desert. And finally we began to settle and to watch and participate in the remarkable development that was taking place in the city.

While I was in Abu Dhabi, I received an invitation from the Center for Middle Eastern Studies at Harvard University to be a visiting scholar for one year. After reflection, I accepted. But unfortunately other commitments prevented me from going, and I sincerely regret having missed the opportunity to attend that great university.

12

IRAQI EXPATRIATE OPPOSITION, 1991–2003

MY SERVICE IN ABU DHABI ended when, on reaching the age of seventy in 1993, I retired. I had spent twenty exciting, fulfilling years participating in the creation and establishment of a new state. I had been warmly welcomed and embraced and I was happy to live in Abu Dhabi. It had become a home. But, during that time, my connection to Iraq had never left me and the pain that I felt at the state it now found itself in was acute. I did not know if I would ever be able to go back to my country but I now began to devote most of my time to the problems facing Iraq after Saddam Hussein's ill-conceived and criminal act of aggression against Kuwait in August 1990.

That disastrous adventure had its origins in the Iraq–Iran war of 1980–88. It should be recalled that Saddam's accession to supreme power in 1979 coincided with the Iranian Islamic revolution. While the situation in Iran was becoming increasingly chaotic, Khomeini tried to destabilize the Saddam regime by rekindling sectarian tensions. Saddam, on his part, thought that with Iran's armed forces greatly weakened by the virtual destruction of the officer corps, the time was propitious to deal a decisive blow that would rid Iraq, once and for all, of the Iranian menace which had hovered over the country for centuries. He greatly miscalculated and soon realized that war with Iran would not yield any satisfactory result.

Two things should be remembered about the Iraq–Iran war. First, Saddam was supported by every Arab state except Syria and, to a lesser extent, Libya. Second, from the end of 1982 Iraq had tried repeatedly to end the war. All its peace overtures were contemptuously rejected by Khomeini. The prolongation of that dreadful and costly conflict was due entirely to Iran's stubborn refusal to end the bloodshed. When Khomeini was forced to end the war in the summer of 1988, Iraq, though totally bankrupt, came out intact with a strong and well-equipped army and a real opportunity to achieve significant breakthroughs in weapons technology. Its relations were excellent with the Arab states of the Gulf, as well as with Egypt, Jordan, Yemen and most other Arab countries. Relations with the West, particularly the United States, had greatly improved, without diminishing its traditional ties with the Soviet bloc. Everything seemed to favour Iraq. It had a unique opportunity to enhance its position as a major regional power.

Two years before the Kuwait debacle of 1990–91, I was worried that the regime under Saddam was failing to appreciate the dangers facing Iraq. For that reason, I called the Iraqi Ambassador in Abu Dhabi to my office in 1988 and asked him to convey to his government the following observations and suggestions.

Iraq had lost hundreds of thousands of its youth, I said, but despite that the domestic front had remained firm during the war with Iran. Iraq's relations with other Arab countries except Syria were excellent and relations with the United States and the Soviet Union, which was in the process of disintegration, were greatly improved, so it was time to ease restrictions and give people more freedom and abolish the apparatus of terror and oppression from which Iraqis had suffered for far too long. I emphasized to the Ambassador the absolute necessity of refraining from any kind of provocative action and to exercise great vigilance and restraint, and above all to avoid involvement in military adventures.

I told the Ambassador that Iraq was targeted because Israel wanted to ensure that Iraq would never possess the deterrence capacity that would make Israel's frequent resort to force costly and unacceptable to Israeli society. I gave the same advice for caution and patience to Tariq Aziz, Iraqi Foreign Minister, when I met him in Geneva in the summer of 1989. Instead of heeding this advice, Iraq's president embarked on an insane and criminal adventure that had not the remotest chance of success. Neither the economic problems facing Iraq, nor its legitimate desire to have a secure outlet on the Gulf, nor the unresolved frontier dispute, could justify the invasion and annexation of Kuwait. It was simply a blatant act of aggression. The miscalculation, ineptitude and sheer stupidity of the Iraqi regime was truly mindboggling. Saddam should have realized that the strategic aim of the United States and its allies was to destroy Iraq's growing military capability, which was viewed as a potential threat to the security of Israel and the oil-producing Arab countries of the Gulf. Instead of exercising vigilant restraint he made it possible for the Western allies, with negligible cost to themselves, to achieve an important geopolitical objective with the blessing and support of the United Nations.

The severe sanctions that were imposed on Iraq destroyed its economy, obliterated its middle class, and left its social fabric in tatters and disarray. I felt I had to raise my voice, so I wrote an article which was published in *The Guardian* on 30 July 1991. The section dealing with the questionable grounds on which the war against Iraq had been justified is reproduced here:

> In my opinion Resolution 678 of the Security Council which authorized the use of force against Iraq is contrary to the Charter of the United Nations. I maintain that the conditions and procedures laid down in the Charter for the use of force have not been fully or scrupulously followed in the case of Iraq. By Resolution 660, which may be called the key document, the Security Council decided that Iraq's invasion of Kuwait was a breach of international peace and security within the meaning of Articles 39 and 40 of the Charter, and called on Iraq to withdraw immediately and unconditionally its forces to the positions they held on August 1st 1990. Four days later, on August 6th 1990, the Security Council, acting under Article 41 of the Charter, decided in Resolution 661 to impose economic sanctions. These sanctions were further extended and reinforced in Resolutions 665 and 670 of August 25 and September 13 imposing a maritime and air blockade. The next phase of United Nations action envisaged in the Charter would have been the use of force in accordance with Article 42 which

1. The author with his father, Muzahim Pachachi, in 1934.

2. The author as a boy in Geneva, 1935.

3. *Inset* The author at ten years of age.

4. *Left* The author (right) as a young diplomat in Paris with Norwegian lawyer and politician Trygve Lie (second left), first Secretary-General of the United Nations, November 1951.

5. *Below* The author (second left) greets Nikita Khrushchev, Premier of the Soviet Union, New York, 1960.

6. *Above* US President John F. Kennedy greets the author, with Adlai Stevenson, US Permanent Representative to the United Nations, New York, 1961.

7. *Below* The author (centre) presiding over the United Nations Economic and Social Council, Geneva, 1965.

8. *Above* The author with Pope Paul VI, Vatican City, October 1966.

9. *Below* Egyptian President Jamal Abdul Nasser and the author, Cairo, 1966.

10. *Above* Dr Adnan and Mrs Pachachi with Indira Ghandi, Prime Minister of India, New Delhi, March 1967.

11. *Above right* The author (right) as Foreign Minister of Iraq in discussion with Andrei Gromyko, Foreign Minister of the Soviet Union, Moscow, April 1967.

12. *Below* The author (centre) as Foreign Minister of Iraq, in discussion with the foreign ministers of Jordan and Morocco in the UN Security Council, on the eve of the adoption of Resolution 242 for the settlement of the Arab–Israeli conflict after the 1967 June war, November 1967.

13. *Above* The author makes a point to HH Sheikh Zayed bin Sultan Al Nahyan, Founder and President of the United Arab Emirates, 1971.

14. *Centre* The author with his wife and three daughters, London, 1983.

15. *Below* The author shares a joke with HM King Abdullah II of the Hashemite Kingdom of Jordan, Amman, 2003.

16. *Above* The Governing Council of Iraq in 2004: the author (second right) with Jalal Talabani (second left), Massoud Barzani (left) and Ghazi al-Yawar (right).

17. *Below* HH Sheikh Sabah al-Ahmad al-Jabr Al-Sabah, Emir of Kuwait, greets the author in 2006.

states clearly that if the Security Council considers that measures taken in accordance with Article 41 – i.e. economic sanctions and blockade – prove to be inadequate, then the Security Council may take whatever measures are necessary including the use of military force to restore international peace and security. In other words force might be used only after the Security Council had determined that the sanctions, the blockade and the embargo were inadequate to achieve their purpose of maintaining international peace and security. Such a determination never took place, either explicitly or implicitly. Resolution 678 mentions nothing about the inadequacy of sanctions, it refers merely to Iraq's refusal to withdraw. It is clear therefore that the use of force was authorized not in accordance with Article 42, which is not specifically mentioned in resolution 678, but was presumably based on Article 51, which reads as follows:

> Nothing in the present Charter shall impair the inherent right of individual or collective self-defence, if an armed attack occurs against a Member of the United Nations, until the Security Council has taken measures necessary to maintain international peace and security. Measures taken by Members in the exercise of this right of self-defence shall be immediately reported to the Security Council and shall not in any way affect the authority and responsibility of the Security Council under the present Charter to take at any time such action it deems necessary in order to maintain or restore international peace and security.

It is clear from this Article that measures of self-defence are of an urgent and provisional character, taken before and not after the Security Council has acted to maintain or restore international peace and security. Once the Security Council has acted, the exercise of the right of self-defence under article 51 can no longer be invoked, and the question becomes the exclusive concern of the Security Council, which alone has the right to order the use of force in accordance with Article 42.

Secretary-General Perez de Cuellar himself stated, on November 8th 1990, that since the Security Council was already seized of the matter, and had taken measures under Chapter VII of the Charter, any military action under Article 51 was legally questionable.

Resolution 678 merely authorizes member states co-operating with Kuwait to use all necessary means to secure the implementation of previous resolutions and restore international peace and security in the region. Such a blanket, carte blanche authorization is unprecedented in the annals of the United Nations. The war unleashed on January 17th 1991 was not a United Nations action and cannot claim international legitimacy. The right to use force can be delegated to individual countries only as an urgent and temporary measure of self-defence under Article 51 and such authorization would automatically lapse as soon as the Security Council had taken action under Chapter VII, which it did when it imposed sanctions on August 6th 1990. In other words the use of force under Article 51 is not an open-ended affair, but is restricted in its time-frame and method. The Secretary-General himself admitted as much when he said in a press interview on January 28th 1991, that the war was not a United Nations war. What was it then? A war permitted by the United Nations outside the Charter? Can the Security Council give such permission? The answer is no, since its authority to initiate or order military action is governed by the provisions of the Charter and it has no right to exceed such authority and distribute dispensations here and there for the use of force. Under the Charter there is no such thing as a war permitted by the United Nations. There is only war undertaken under the authority and supervision of the Security Council.

Prior to the publication of my article, the Iraqi regime put down with extreme brutality the revolt or *intifada* in northern and southern Iraq during March and April of 1991. I immediately contacted some Iraqi opposition figures to stress the absolute necessity of getting the sanctions lifted and to discuss with them the possibilities of regime change in Iraq.

I was deeply concerned that weakening Iraq would open the way for Iran to fill the expected power vacuum. It was evident that the real victor in the Gulf war was Iran which, at no cost to itself, was seeing the disappearance of the only real impediment to its hegemonic ambitions.

In 1993, I addressed a letter to the US State Department protesting at the views expressed by the Secretary of State, Warren Christopher, and Martin Indyk, the officer responsible for Middle Eastern Affairs at the National Security Council, that sanctions would not necessarily be lifted after the fall of the Iraqi regime. It should be noted that many dissident Iraqis in exile, belonging to or working with the Iraqi National Congress under Ahmad Chalabi, urged the Clinton Administration to intensify and strengthen the sanctions on Iraq in the mistaken belief that this would hasten the fall of Saddam, ignoring the fact that the sanctions – far from weakening the regime – had in fact strengthened it and enabled it to tighten its iron grip over the country. In May 1994, I sent a memorandum to Robert Pelletreau, US Assistant Secretary of State, warning him of the deteriorating situation in Iraq and the serious error of US policy in maintaining the sanctions.

As the expatriate Iraqi opposition was clearly divided into several factions, I decided not to get involved in their quarrels and refused to join them, preferring to work alone. In the meantime, the royalist faction working for the restoration of the monarchy convened a conference in London in which I was one of the main speakers. I urged the leaders of the various groups to work together to create a united opposition that would become a viable alternative to Saddam's regime. When this effort failed, the new US Secretary of State, Madeleine Albright, decided to play a more active and assertive role in relations with the Iraqi opposition. This apparently new development in US policy encouraged me to visit Washington where I had extensive talks with Thomas Pickering, the Under-Secretary of State. I was still unhappy about the insistence of the United States on maintaining sanctions, and in a statement that appeared in Arabic newspapers I criticized the operation called Desert Fox, which inflicted serious damage in parts of southern Iraq.

After several years of working alone, I came to the conclusion that it was important to form a new centrist secular opposition that I hoped would attract a significant number of people, including professionals and intellectuals. The initial response was encouraging and I was elected secretary-general of the new group. In this capacity, I went to Washington with other opposition figures in response to an invitation from Mrs Albright. We had lengthy talks with officials of the State Department and with Sandy Berger, the National Security Adviser, and congressional leaders from both political parties. I pushed for the immediate lifting of sanctions and explained what steps I thought should be taken to establish a democracy in Iraq. I again stressed my view that the change of regime should be achieved internally without external intervention, although we, of course, welcomed political support at the United Nations and elsewhere for our efforts. I recall our meeting with Senator Joseph Biden (now Vice President of the United States) in which he said, to our surprise and amusement, that his Senate colleagues whom we were to meet the following day were all liars and that we should believe nothing they said. We decided to form a preparatory committee to co-ordinate the activities of the entire Iraqi opposition and plan its political and public relations campaign to bring about change in Iraq. The Iraqi opposition again failed to agree on concrete and practical measures. Having despaired of any meaningful co-operation with other opposition groups, we decided to formalize our Centrist Party by holding a meeting in February 2000, which was attended by hundreds of members and sympathizers. I was confirmed as leader of the group. At our second meeting in September 2000, I announced my intention to relinquish my post as secretary-general of the Centrist Party because of persistent differences between members of the executive committee. This retirement from political activity was short-lived, and it ended when it became clear to me in 2002 that Iraq would be the next target of US military action after its success in toppling the Taliban regime in Afghanistan.

The decision to attack Iraq was very probably taken earlier. According to Secretary of Defense Donald Rumsfeld in his memoirs (*Known and Unknown*, published in 2011), immediately after the destruction of the Twin Towers of the World Trade Center in New York on 11 September 2001, his deputy Paul Wolfowitz urged the Bush administration to attack Iraq on the grounds that Saddam was developing weapons of mass destruction and had close contacts with Al-Qaida. No proof was given to substantiate these allegations but Wolfowitz, supported by such pro-Israeli stalwarts as Defense Under Secretary Douglas Feith and Department of Defense Consultant Richard Perle, was able to persuade President Bush to use force against Iraq. I often wondered why Bush went along with them knowing full well that Saddam had no weapons of mass destruction and no contacts with Al-Qaida. It is evident that Wolfowitz and his friends were determined to destroy Iraq's potential ability to develop a credible deterrent to Israel's military might. Bush on his part was eager to get the help of the pro-Israeli lobby in the presidential election of 2004. Ever since his controversial election in 2000, Bush wanted to prove to the American people that he could be elected on his own without the help of Supreme Court justices. The victory in Afghanistan and the overthrow of the Taliban regime considerably improved his standing and encouraged him to turn his attention to the easy target of Iraq. It was a pariah state, part of the "axis of evil", weakened by years of sanctions and clearly unable to withstand a military assault by the United States. Thus, Bush's decision to improve his standing and win the election coincided with Israel's desire to remove once and for all Iraq's deterrent potential. President Bush tried and failed to obtain Security Council authorization for military action against Iraq, but that did not prevent him waging an illegal war of choice in March 2003, the declared motive for the invasion being to destroy Iraq's weapons of mass destruction. This, of course, was a spurious pretext which, in the event, was proved to be unfounded when after many attempts no caches of such weapons were ever found.

In the hope of averting the approaching catastrophe and stemming the dangerous drift to war, I decided to convene an urgent meeting of all the secular and democratic forces. The meeting, held on 13 February 2003, was attended by a number of prominent Iraqis who shared my opposition to any US military intervention designed to topple the Iraqi regime. We appealed to the international community to join our efforts to prevent war. We supported Sheikh Zayed's proposal that Saddam be allowed to relinquish power voluntarily, and that then the United Nations and the Arab League would appoint a provisional Iraqi government authorized to hold elections for a Constituent Assembly that would draw up a new constitution for the country. It was at that time that a group of State Department officials led by Ambassador Ryan Crocker, Deputy Assistant Secretary of State, visited me at my home in London to discuss how they could best help us to move the country from dictatorship to democracy. I was impressed by Crocker's understanding and knowledge of the Iraqi situation; like other Arabists, he seemed sympathetic to our efforts. A few months later, Crocker would be appointed deputy to Paul Bremer, the new civilian US administrator in Iraq. From the beginning there were serious disagreements between the two men. Bremer, who received his instructions from the Defense Department, acted in an authoritarian manner while Crocker favoured consultation with Iraqis and seemed ready to do what he could to help us. I recall vividly how strongly he urged me to present our demands with more force and energy. Shortly thereafter Crocker was transferred, leaving Bremer and his Department of Defense associates to assume sole responsibility for the administration of Iraq.

Later in February 2003, just after Crocker's visit to me, Zalmay Khalilzad, the United States special representative to the Iraqi opposition, visited me at my home in Abu Dhabi and asked me to participate in the efforts to establish a democratic, pluralist government in Iraq. He said that the first step would be to entrust temporarily the administration of the country to the US military authorities aided by an Iraqi advisory council. I rejected this proposal and insisted that the Iraqi body should be given executive power. Khalilzad's visit angered the pro-Israeli neo-conservatives in the United States who supported Ahmad Chalabi. I clarified my position further in an article published by the *Financial Times* on 3 March 2003 (see Appendix 4). In the meantime, the Kurdish leader Jalal Talabani asked me to be a member of a group of six that called itself the Leadership of the Iraqi Opposition. I declined his invitation because this so-called "Leadership" had only advisory functions and in any case I had doubts about its legitimacy and representative character. On the eve of the war that the United States unleashed on Iraq on 20 March 2003, I issued an urgent and final appeal against military intervention. After the outbreak of hostilities, we hastened to convene a conference in London on 29 March 2003, to deal with the problems that would arise after the fall of Saddam's regime. Thus was born a new political group called the Independent Iraqi Democrats. I opened the conference with a detailed account of what we intended to do. These were the main points of my speech:

1. The removal of the regime which we held responsible for the catastrophe that had engulfed Iraq.

2. Ending the military occupation of the country.

3. The installation of an Iraqi authority to manage the affairs of the country during a short interim period.

4. The immediate lifting of sanctions by the Security Council.

5. The appointment of a United Nations Special Representative who would conduct extensive consultations with a view to convening a conference to elect a Council of Sovereignty, whose first task would be the appointment of ministers and heads of departments.

6. The transitional authority would be given the means to keep peace and order in the country and revive the stagnant economy.

7. The enactment of laws necessary to ensure fair and honest elections under international supervision for a Constituent Assembly that would draw up a new constitution for the country.

8. One of the main tasks of the new elected government would be to reach agreement with the representatives of the Kurdish people based on the right of self-determination.

I ended my speech by describing our group as Iraqis who believed in democratic, secular, liberal values, and who rejected sectarian divisions by affirming our national Iraqi identity and working for the establishment of a democratic, secular, liberal government.

I was elected head of the new political group and started preparations to go back to Iraq. Before my departure for Baghdad, I went with two colleagues to Egypt, Jordan and Kuwait. We met President Hosni Mubarak and the Egyptian Foreign Minister, Ahmed Maher, in Cairo. We also met King Abdullah II of Jordan and several of his ministers in Amman, and Sheikh Sabah al-Ahmad Al-Sabah, Foreign Minister (now Amir) of Kuwait. I went alone to Saudi Arabia where I met Prince Saud Al-Faisal, the Foreign Minister. We presented ourselves in these meetings as representatives of a new political force which we hoped would play a pivotal role in creating a new Iraq. It may be of interest that President Mubarak said that he believed the war on Iraq was unleashed for the sake of Israel and nothing else. The Jordanian monarch was especially supportive of our aim to establish a democratic, pluralist and secular government in Iraq. Our greatest supporter however was Sheikh Zayed bin Sultan Al-Nahyan, President of United Arab Emirates. We are deeply indebted to him for his unstinting support.

13

RETURN TO IRAQ,
2003–10

I ARRIVED IN BAGHDAD ON 6 May 2003, a week before my 80th birthday, accompanied by fifteen colleagues in our party, the Independent Iraqi Democrats. After an absence of thirty-four years, I was elated and at the same time heartbroken: elated finally to be back in the country and city of my birth, Baghdad, and heartbroken to see the chaotic and dilapidated state of the Iraqi capital. Friends and family had expressed doubts about my going back to become involved in, as I saw it, the process of reconstructing Iraq, and suggested that I wait. But, at my age, this was not a luxury I could afford. I felt I had something to offer; my experience, especially internationally, including my knowledge of treaties and constitutions, could be of use to the country. Perhaps I could even help to end the occupation of the country sooner and to establish at least a basic constitutional framework based on ideas of fundamental human rights for all Iraqis. At any rate, if I was going to be able to do anything, I had to try to do it now.

Unlike some other opposition leaders, I rented a house and did not occupy buildings and houses that had belonged to the state or leaders of the former regime. The first thing that struck me on my return was the belief of many Iraqis, especially the young, that the US presence, even as an occupying power, would benefit Iraq. They were impressed by American achievements, particularly in science and technology. There was hope that Iraq's hard-working people and the country's great natural wealth would, with American guidance and assistance, make Iraq one of the most advanced nations in the world. The miracle of the United Arab Emirates in the Gulf would be duplicated and surpassed.

All those hopes and expectations soon disappeared, to be replaced by frustration, anger and resentment. So what went wrong? This was the question asked with some emotion by Colin Powell when I saw him in Abu Dhabi in 2010. I was touched by Powell's anguished lament, which I fully shared, and asked myself time and again why Iraq's brief experiment in democracy failed.

Here are some of the reasons that may have contributed to this failure. First, change came as a result of a war of doubtful legality which the UN Security Council refused to endorse. Second, the United States came to Iraq without a clear and coherent plan to move the country from dictatorship to democracy. A third reason was that the US was unprepared to take over the administration of the country and shoulder the responsibility of maintaining peace and order in the wake of the total collapse of government structures. In these circumstances, the first responsibility of the occupying power in preventing the country from sliding into anarchy and lawlessness should have been to reinstate the police and security services. I discussed these ideas with Khalilzad when he came to see me in Abu Dhabi; unfortunately, nothing was done and the occupying troops had to act as policemen. They were neither trained nor equipped for such a task and at the slightest provocation they used excessive force against Iraqi civilians.

A fourth reason was that corruption was rife. While Iraqis had become inured to corruption after years of sanctions and administrative mismanagement, they did not expect the complicity of some American officers and officials in pushing projects of doubtful benefit and legality that cost Iraq billions of dollars, and that are still unaccounted for.

Finally, perhaps the most serious mistake the US made was to organize the new political system in Iraq on a sectarian basis. They had the preconceived idea that Iraqi society by its nature was divided along sectarian lines. That was a fallacy. As a result, the secular groups did not receive the recognition they deserved and the government fell under the influence of religious and ethnic parties. Fully exploiting their built-in advantages, they established a regime that proved over the years to be incapable of governing the country. My fear that their incompetence and corruption, and particularly their subservience to Iran, would result in Iraq becoming a failed state has unfortunately been borne out. The most tangible result of US involvement in Iraq has been the consolidation of Iran's influence and power in the country. The US had the means to prevent this but lacked the will and determination. I, like most Iraqis, am still at a loss to understand why the United States squandered the historic opportunity to make a success of democracy in Iraq.

To return to my narrative, a few days after my arrival in Baghdad, the two Kurdish leaders Massoud Barzani and Jalal Talabani urged me once again to join the political process by becoming the sixth member of the leadership group. I declined again because I had been chosen as a Sunni Arab, a sectarian description which I rejected. Khalilzad, who added his voice to that of the two Kurdish leaders, was expected to come to Baghdad to prepare for a national Iraqi conference which would include representatives of all sections of the population. I waited for him for a whole week while he continued to say that he was coming. But I soon learned that he being was replaced by a new representative, Paul Bremer, who scrapped all of Khalilzad's plans.

Meanwhile, the US State Department invited Iraqis of different backgrounds and experiences to form study groups on the future of Iraq. I nominated seventeen highly qualified individuals to take part in these studies. Unfortunately the recommendations these groups made were ignored after the occupation of Iraq. A new approach and a new policy was being prepared. The British representative in Iraq, John Sawers, showed me a draft resolution that was submitted to the Security Council that considered Iraq as enemy occupied territory, in accordance with the Geneva Conventions of 1949. A Civilian Provisional Authority linked to the coalition military command was to be established to manage the affairs of the country. Iraqi participation was limited to an advisory council. The draft was approved by the Security Council on 22 May 2003 and became Resolution 1483. I was appalled by this turn of events. I could not accept the fact that Iraq, a founding member of the United Nations and the first Arab state to gain its independence, was to be placed under what amounted to foreign trusteeship. Two days after the adoption of

Resolution 1483, on 24 May 2003, I strongly criticized American policy in an interview published in the Arabic daily, *Asharq Al-Awsat*. I said that the United States came uninvited to Iraq and took over the administration of the country without a clear policy or adequate preparation. I warned that the situation would explode into chaos and violence. I turned to the United Nations hoping that it would halt the drift towards anarchy. We were fortunate to have a UN representative who sympathized with Iraq's aspirations and resisted American pressure on him to refrain from intervening in Iraqi affairs. Sergio Vieira de Mello, Special Representative of the Secretary-General to Iraq, arrived in Baghdad at the beginning of June 2003 and immediately came over to visit me at our headquarters. We had very useful talks and to my delight I found a wide convergence of views between us. He worked hard to give Iraqis a place in the administration of the country. In a meeting I had with United Nations Secretary-General, Kofi Annan, in Jordan in June 2003, I stressed the importance of UN involvement in Iraq's transition towards democracy. He was receptive to my suggestions and said he would instruct his representative in Baghdad to do what was necessary. During June 2003, I was interviewed by two prominent journalists, Patrick Tyler and Patrick Cockburn. Their reports were published in the *New York Times* and the *Independent* on 15 and 16 June 2003 respectively. Following are the texts:

New York Times
15 June 2003

IRAQI LEADER ASKS U.S. TO STOP MILITARY SWEEPS
By Patrick Tyler

Baghdad, Iraq, June 14 – Adnan Pachachi, a respected elder Iraqi statesman encouraged by Bush administration officials to enter postwar politics here, criticized the United States military today for its increasingly aggressive operations in Iraq and said they should be suspended while an interim Iraqi government is formed over the next month.

Mr Pachachi said that military sweeps through civilian areas with mass arrests, interrogations and gun battles, intended to suppress the remnants of Saddam Hussein's Baath Party and military command, were inflaming sentiments against the

American and British occupation.

He predicted that if such sweeps continued, they would be "exploited by the Baathists," and he added, "It would be much better if we didn't have these operations."

Mr Pachachi, a former foreign minister who returned to Iraq last month after more than 30 years of exile, emphasized that he supported allied efforts to re-establish security in the country. But he expressed concern about the marked escalation of allied assaults through civilian areas, where guerilla raids have attacked troop convoys or checkpoints and left 10 American soldiers dead in the last three weeks.

"These incidents will not help to pacify the country," he said, referring to the military operations. "For now, the quieter it is, the better" for the postwar political process, he added.

Speaking in an interview, Mr Pachachi, who served as Iraq's ambassador to the United Nations during the Kennedy and Johnson administrations, called on the top American administrator, L. Paul Bremer III, to allow Iraqis to form an interim government with only "consultations" with Mr Bremer and the United Nations representative here. He said such a step would help meet the rising demands from Iraqis that they control their own political destiny during reconstruction.

The pointed remarks from the man the State Department had nudged back into Iraqi politics at the age of 80 are likely to add to the pressure on Mr Bremer to respond to Iraqi opposition groups and religious figures who want a speedy transition to substantive Iraqi control over the political process. They see such a transition as an essential step in preventing a backlash against the occupation authority.

Mr Pachachi spoke at the end of a week of major military operations in Iraq in which allied forces have laid siege to a peninsula along the Tigris River 40 miles north of Baghdad, where more than 380 arrests were made during house to house searches in civilian neighborhoods and at military roadblocks.

Northwest of Baghdad, allied strike aircraft and helicopters assaulted what the military command called a terrorist training camp, killing 70 people.

In a separate operation on Thursday near the northern city of Kirkuk, the 173rd Airborne Brigade detained 74 "suspected symphathizers" of Al Qaeda, the terrorist organization of Osama Bin Laden. There were no further details about the operation, or explanation for the basis of the suspicions about those arrested.

Today, Iraqi detainees at the Abu Ghraib prison complex west of Baghdad attacked their American guards by throwing rocks and charging them with pieces of sharpened metal during an apparent escape attempt. One American guard was wounded and other guards opened fire during the melee, in which one detainee was killed and seven were wounded, two critical.

It was the third incident in a week involving Iraqi prisoners, and the second attempted escape as allied forces were rounding up more suspected Baathists believed to be planning or inciting guerilla attacks on allied checkpoints and convoys in central Iraq. On Thursday, two prisoners were shot trying to escape from an allied camp and one died.

Mr Pachachi has been regarded by American officials as a unifying figure on Iraq's rapidly developing political landscape. He has deftly kept his distance from a group of former Iraqi opposition leaders who have formed a "leadership council" to negotiate a postwar political structure with Mr Bremer but Mr Pachachi also has stated common cause with them.

The council includes the two main Kurdish factions of Massoud Barzani and Jalal Talabani, the Iraqi National Congress of Ahmad Chalabi, the Iraqi National Accord of Iyad Allawi, the democratic movement of Nasir Chadirchy, the Shiite Dawa Party represented by Ibrahim Al-Jaafari, and the Supreme Council for the Islamic Revolution of Iraq under Ayatollah Muhammad Bakr Al-Hakim.

Mr Bremer has ultimate authority in Iraq under a United Nations resolution that recognizes the United States and Britain as occupation powers. He has said that he intends to appoint a 25 to 30 member "political council" of Iraqis. Some Iraqi political figures have criticized this model for forming a transitional administration, and a prominent Shiite Muslim political organization said it would not be able to take part in any administration appointed directly by Mr Bremer.

Mr Bremer has said that any Iraqi political group is free to boycott the selection process for his political council if it chooses to do so. But he has been working assiduously and diplomatically behind the scenes to ensure the broadest participation possible in the postwar political process.

Mr Pachachi said he was working to bridge the differences between the American administrator and Iraq's emerging political forces.

"Why would Bremer want to dictate to the Iraqis whom he wants?" Mr Pachachi said. "I don't think he knows Iraq better than the Iraqis."

Mr Pachachi said he was going to press this view in a meeting with Ryan Crocker, the State Department official assigned to Mr Bremer's administration and a likely choice to serve as the first United States ambassador to Iraq when a government is formed.

"The people of Iraq want a government," Mr Pachachi said, "and we could easily say this political council is a true government of Iraq" if Mr Bremer essentially turned over the authority to choose such a body to a large group of Iraqi political figures.

Instead of a decree from Mr Bremer, a decision to invite the selected Iraqis to serve on the political council of the interim government could be announced, Mr Pachachi said, "as the result of extensive consultations" with the Iraqis assembled from all parts of the political, religious and economic spectrum.

Their task, once seated as an interim government, would be to make policy on economic recovery, a new currency, a new judiciary, a census and electoral law to guide the first democratic elections in about a year's time.

The interim administration would have the authority to appoint ministers and carry out Iraq's foreign relations during the occupation period "by appointing and receiving ambassadors," he said.

"I think for us, speed is of the essence," he said. "We want to have a government as soon as possible."

The negotiations with Mr Bremer are set to continue this week.

Independent
16 June 2003

Iraq 'has three weeks to avoid falling into chaos'
By Patrick Cockburn

Iraq needs a transitional administration within three weeks if it is to avoid a descent into chaos, the most prominent Iraqi leader acceptable to all sides told *The Independent* last night.

Adnan Pachachi, a highly regarded former Iraqi foreign minister who is expected to play a big role in a transitional Iraqi administration, criticized the heavy-handed US sweeps that have cost more than 100 Iraqi lives, calling them "an overreaction". He said the Americans felt "very vulnerable and afraid".

Mr Pachachi, 80, may be the only prominent opponent of Saddam Hussein who all sides are prepared to work with. He said the Americans were coming round to the idea of an Iraqi transitional administration with real authority but with the US and Britain as occupying powers. "The Iraqi people are impatient," he said. "They want an Iraqi government as soon as possible. The Americans can shift responsibility to it." Given the embarrassing failure of the US authorities in Baghdad to restore living conditions even to the low level enjoyed by Iraqis under Saddam Hussein, the option of giving some power to Iraqis is one that clearly has its attractions for the US.

Mr Pachachi wants an interim administration to be set up within three weeks to prepare the way for elections and to draw up a constitution.

He believes that the transitional period would last for about two years before a freely elected government could be in place. He said: "The Americans want to withdraw the bulk of their army within a year."

Asked about the danger that any Iraqi administration under US occupation would be seen as an American pawn, Mr Pachachi said: "This might happen if it is perceived as a rubber stamp, but if it takes a strong stand then people will say this is as good an administration as we could get under the circumstances."

He does not think there will be a general uprising against the US. He said: "There are sporadic attacks which are not coordinated. It wouldn't be easy to organize a countrywide revolt. I don't think that the people are ready for an uprising because they are dealing with an enemy which does not hesitate to use its massive fire-power."

Mr Pachachi is probably right about the mood among Iraqis. But given the degree of force being used by the US Army after a few small attacks, it might easily overreact to more serious losses, making the stabilization of Iraq under its control extremely difficult.

The main issue at that time was the formation of a representative Iraqi body and deciding what powers and responsibilities it would have. The occupation authorities proposed an advisory or consultative body to help the Civilian Provisional Authority. I and other leaders of the opposition flatly rejected this proposal and insisted that the Iraqi body should have executive powers, such as the appointment of ministers and senior officials and be given exclusive responsibility for Iraq's external relations. Those demands were granted and it was agreed to call the new Iraqi body the "Governing Council". We had serious problems choosing its members. The Americans were determined to organize the Governing Council on a sectarian basis.

When I was nominated to be a member of the Governing Council, I hesitated at first. I had to decide whether it would be better to remain outside the political process as a voice for the opposition or to try as a member to improve things from the inside and stop the dangerous slide towards political religious fundamentalism. I decided in favour of the more difficult option – that of fighting within the process rather than outside it. I was eighty years old and did not have the luxury of waiting for another ten years for things to settle, so I became a member of the Governing Council that was formed after extensive consultations among ourselves, the leaders of Iraqi political groups and with the United Nations representative and the occupation authorities. Some of my closest friends disagreed with me accepting membership in the Governing Council while the country was under foreign military occupation. But my participation was a result of my belief that we should try to improve things from within, rather than being content to remain observers and critics from the outside.

A week after its formation, the Governing Council decided to send a delegation under my chairmanship to take part in the Security Council discussions on the report of the United Nations special representative. I went to New York with two members of the Governing Council, Ahmad Chalabi and Aqila Al-Hashimi. I spoke before the Security Council on 22 July 2003. It was the first time since the fall of Saddam's regime that Iraq's voice had been heard in the highest organ of the United Nations. I said in my speech that my appearance in the Council marked the recognition by the international community of the new Iraq. I had extensive talks with members of the Security Council and others reaffirming our demand that Iraq regain fully its sovereignty. On my return trip from New York, I stopped briefly in London to speak with Prime Minister Tony Blair at No. 10 Downing Street. I urged him to use whatever influence he had with the Americans to persuade them to pursue a more moderate and balanced policy in Iraq. I found out later that Mr Blair was not prepared to argue and was content to follow President Bush's policy without objection. This was evident when Sir Jeremy Greenstock, Mr Blair's representative in Iraq, asked to be relieved of his duties after several months of bickering and arguing with Bremer. He intended to publish a memoir on his brief stay in Iraq but was prevented by the British Foreign Office from doing so in order to avoid embarrassing the Bush administration.

At the same time, the Governing Council decided to form a nine-member Presidency in which I was included. In August 2003, as a member of an Iraqi delegation, I visited several neighbouring Arab states. We were on the whole cordially received, but some Arab leaders expressed serious doubts about the legitimacy of the Governing Council. We tried to dispel these doubts and assure our critics of our firm intention to end foreign occupation and regain fully our sovereignty and authority.

In September 2003, I had an excellent opportunity to expound my views when Kofi Annan invited me to Geneva to meet him and the foreign ministers of the five permanent members of the Security Council. I went there accompanied by my trusted public relations assistant, Fareed Yasseen. The ministers and Secretary-General were discussing a new American draft resolution on Iraq. There were various amendments introduced by France which were similar to our position. On my part, I proposed several amendments to both the American and French drafts. In addition to the Secretary-General, I met the foreign ministers of the United States, France, China and Russia. The British Foreign Secretary, Jack Straw, was absent. My meeting with Colin Powell, the US Secretary of State, was stormy and acrimonious. He rejected my proposal to expand the Governing Council and transfer full powers to it and abolish the Civilian Provisional Authority, and he insisted that the transfer of power should occur only after the formation of a government elected constitutionally. My answer was that elections for a constituent assembly, the drawing up of a new constitution which would have to be approved by the Iraqi people in a referendum, and subsequent elections for a legislative body that would choose the constitutional government, would all take a long time; the Iraqi people were impatient and wanted to end the occupation and have in place an Iraqi government as soon as possible. Even Ahmad Chalabi – an implacable foe – praised my efforts to expedite the transfer of power.

At the same time, the Governing Council appointed the first cabinet, which included my nominee for Minister of Planning, Mahdi Al-Hafez. During the regular session of the UN General Assembly in September and October 2003, I resumed my talks with Colin Powell, who informed me that they were amending the draft resolution to meet some of the points I had raised with him; but I felt that this was not enough because the transfer of power would have to wait for a constitution. In late October, I was a member of an Iraqi delegation to the Conference of Donor Countries in Madrid. I made an impassioned speech which I concluded by saying:

> I believe that, in spite of all the problems that seem to overwhelm Iraq, the Iraqi people have the resilience and the

determination to ensure the success of this unique experiment, this vast undertaking to lift the country from the depths of misery and despair to a future of peace, freedom and prosperity. Ours is an ancient land, with a young and vigorous population. Our people want to leave the years of pain and suffering behind them. What is going on in Iraq today may go down in history as one of the great acts of national revival and regeneration. Failure is not an option. We cannot, will not and dare not fail.

With time my relationship with Colin Powell became closer, because I realized he was sincere in his desire to help Iraq. On returning to Baghdad, I was informed by Paul Bremer that the United States had reviewed its policy in Iraq and had come to the conclusion that an early transfer of power to an Iraqi government was necessary and feasible. This was quite an unexpected change. Bremer asked the Governing Council to endorse the new American policy, the main features of which were the termination of the military occupation and Civilian Provisional Authority by 30 June 2004 and the transfer of power to an interim Iraqi government.

However, it was not clear how this interim government was going to be formed. The Americans proposed a complicated system of local caucuses, a method widely used in the United States but completely unknown in Iraq. At the same time Ayatollah Ali Sistani insisted that elections be held before the formation of a new government that would be chosen by the elected representatives of the Iraqi people. It was the right approach but because of the short time available we were faced with a dilemma: should we postpone the date of the transfer of power beyond 30 June in order to give us enough time to organize proper elections or should we stick to the 30 June date and hold elections after the appointment of the interim government? The Americans adamantly refused any postponement of the transfer of power. President Bush was preparing his re-election campaign and did not want anything to affect what he thought to be his perfect record in Iraq. The Iraqis were divided: the Shi'a religious parties naturally supported Sistani's point of view; others, while eager to end the occupation, feared that hasty and badly organized elections would not reflect the true will of the people. As a compromise, it was decided to ask the United Nations to resolve the issue. I spoke to Secretary-General Kofi Annan, who said he was ready to dispatch a fact-finding mission to

Iraq to study the possibility of holding elections before June 2004. I agreed to meet with Annan in mid-January 2004 in New York to discuss the details of such a mission.

While we were preparing for the New York and Washington visits, I was informed by Bremer that Saddam Hussein had been captured and brought back to Baghdad. Although I was ill and bedridden on that day, 13 December 2003, I immediately joined Bremer at a press conference in my capacity as acting President of the Governing Council – the President for December, Abdul Aziz Al-Hakim, being absent on an official visit to France. I spoke briefly, saying that we should look forward to the future and leave the Saddam era behind, and I called on all Iraqis to unite and work together. Bremer asked whether I wanted to see Saddam in his captivity. I accepted his invitation and asked some colleagues in the Governing Council to accompany me. They could not come, but three uninvited members appeared suddenly at the heliport and took one of the helicopters that followed us: they were Ahmad Chalabi, Adel Abdul Mahdi and Muwaffak Rubai'i, all members of the Governing Council. Bremer, General Sanchez, Commander of US Forces in Iraq, and other senior diplomatic and military officers accompanied us to the US military base near Baghdad. There we were taken to a small room where we saw Saddam, clean-shaven, sitting on a simple small bed and looking rather dazed. As we sat down, Rubai'i began by hurling insults and threats, followed by Adel Abdul Mahdi who did the same. Saddam answered in kind and enquired from the Americans who we were. Immediately and without waiting for an answer, Ahmad Chalabi pointed at me, saying, "This is Adnan Pachachi". These were the only words Chalabi uttered during the entire meeting. Saddam turned towards me and said, "We knew you; whatever brought you with these people?" I replied, "I have come on my own to help establish real democracy in Iraq." He said that his regime was democratic and freely elected by the people. I replied that this was not the case, that his regime was an oppressive dictatorship. He said that Iraq needed a strong but just ruler. I replied that he was not just, but a brutal dictator responsible for the deaths of thousands of Iraqis. Then I asked him a question that had been troubling me for years: Why had he not withdrawn from Kuwait to spare the Iraqi people the terrible suffering that followed? He replied by saying that he had been prepared to withdraw provided all other outstanding issues in the region were resolved. I said that he should have known this was not possible and it gave the Americans the excuse they had been waiting for to attack Iraq. He replied by saying that history would be the judge. At the end of the meeting with Saddam, I received a telephone call from President Bush congratulating the Iraqi people on this occasion. While I had expected the abusive and shrill behaviour of Rubai'i and Adel Abdul Mahdi, both of whom were close to the Shi'a religious parties, I could not understand the total silence of Ahmad Chalabi, who had presented himself as a secularist. I asked him about it, saying that I had expected him – showman that he is – to exploit this historic opportunity to the full. I am still none the wiser about why he failed to speak out.

To this day, I am unable to fathom Saddam's thoughts and calculations when he refused to heed the advice of numerous heads of state and governments to withdraw from Kuwait. He seemed convinced that the United States would not attack him despite the presence of half a million US soldiers, three thousand military aircraft and several carriers. He also believed that the Americans had no stomach for a long and costly war, with which he expected to confront them. This mistaken idea of American passivity and unwillingness to suffer casualties was widespread in the Arab world. A former French Minister, Charles de Chambrun, who had close relations with Saddam's regime, said that he believed that the Americans had thoroughly studied Saddam's personality and psychology, and that a double agent in Washington had fed him with inaccurate information that led him to fall into the carefully prepared trap.

On 1 January 2004, I assumed the presidency of the Governing Council and immediately raised two issues with the US occupation authorities. The first was that of reinstating army officers who had not been implicated directly in acts of violence against the civilian population. These officers, who had been so thoughtlessly disbanded by Bremer, would play a crucial role in rebuilding the country's armed forces. The Americans were lukewarm on the subject. However, the Kurds, and particularly the Shiites, were strongly opposed to bringing some of the officers back to service, as they could not overcome their fear of a strong Iraqi army; they continued to behave like an opposition minority, although at the time they were in the majority and controlled every aspect of government.

The second issue concerned the release of prisoners who had not been charged with any specific offence. This was necessary in order to undo the harm of Bremer's catastrophic decision to dismiss thousands of government officials under the de-Ba'athification programme, which was directed by Ahmad Chalabi, who I considered the principal ally of Iran in Iraq. On this matter the Americans responded favourably, while some representatives of sectarian Shi'a parties and Kurds were not happy. They warned that freeing the prisoners would lead to the release of many individuals who had had close relation with the defunct regime.

My attitude on this and other issues antagonized the pro-Iranian elements in Iraq. Iranian antipathy towards me took a dangerous turn. Two senior intelligence officers warned me that they had found an assassination list on which my name appeared. An Iranian 'hit squad' was entrusted with the task of liquidating me. I wanted to be sure of the accuracy of this information, so I asked Bremer to verify it. He did so and a few days later confirmed the existence of such an assassination group, which was targeting me because they considered me a secular Sunni Arab. Four months later I escaped death by a few seconds when the car behind me was blown up. I was shaken but unhurt. Unfortunately the President of the Governing Council was killed. I believe the bomb was meant for me and not for him.

Despite such an unwelcome revelation, I was determined to make a success of our mission to the United Nations and the United States. I spoke before the Governing Council and outlined the mission's aims and purposes. The main issue to be discussed with Kofi Annan was whether the UN was prepared to play an important role in helping Iraq move quickly towards full sovereignty and authority and, to that end, to send a fact-finding mission to Iraq to establish whether or not it was possible to hold elections before the installation of the interim government on 30 June 2004. The delegation accompanying me to New York and Washington included three members of the Governing Council: Abdul Aziz Al-Hakim, leader of the Supreme Council of the Islamic Revolution in Iraq, Mohsen Abdul Hamid, leader of the Islamic Party (Sunni), and Ahmad Chalabi, whom I reluctantly included in the delegation at the request of Adel Abdul Mahdi, whom I trusted and respected at the time. I also included the Ministers of Foreign Affairs and Development and my deputy on the Governing Council, Ata Abdul Wahhab. We left for New York on 18 January 2004, on a plane placed at our disposal by the United Arab Emirates. Our meeting with Kofi Annan the following day was successful. He promised to send a special representative to Iraq, Lakhdar Ibrahimi. I fully supported the Secretary-General's choice because Ibrahimi was a friend whom I had known since the late '50s when he worked for the Algerian Front of National Liberation and, after independence, when he served as Foreign Minister and as Ambassador to Egypt and the United Kingdom. He was highly successful as a representative of his country and as an international civil servant. He had been assigned to many difficult missions in South Africa, Lebanon, Afghanistan and now Iraq. While in New York, I spoke before the Security Council and had talks with many representatives of UN member states, in which I expressed my optimism and hope that with UN assistance Iraq would be able to establish a truly democratic government.

In Washington, we had a meeting with President Bush and held talks with the Secretaries of State and Defense as well as the senior Security Adviser Condoleezza Rice. We had excellent media coverage, which gave us the opportunity to expound our intentions and hopes for a new Iraq. My public relations assistant, Fareed Yasseen, was a great help. Later that year at my suggestion he was given the rank of ambassador and is now Iraq's ambassador in Paris. The high point of the visit was an invitation from President Bush to attend a joint session of the United States Congress on the occasion of his State of the Union speech. I was warmly greeted with applause from members of Congress.

My presidency of the Governing Council ended on 31 January 2004 and in the following weeks I was fully occupied in drafting the interim constitution. I was helped by two of my colleagues, Ata Abdul Wahhab and Feisal Al-Istrabadi. I nominated both of them to be ambassadors. Ata Abdul Wahhab became a highly successful ambassador to Jordan and Feisal Al-Istrabadi became a distinguished, capable and greatly admired Deputy Permanent Representative to the United Nations. My main contribution was the inclusion of a Bill of Rights, which I consider to be my principal legacy to Iraq. It went further than anything in our region and was the cornerstone of the new Iraq we were trying to build. After intensive negotiations, horse-trading and compromises the interim constitution was finally unanimously adopted by the Governing Council; I spoke on the day of the signing, 8 March 2004, extolling the Bill of Rights, which I said must be preserved and protected. I answered those expressing doubts about the ability of Arab and Muslim societies to absorb the essential values of democracy by saying that those values were universal, and stressing that they were as pertinent and necessary in the Arab and Islamic countries as they were elsewhere.

Lakhdar Ibrahimi came to Iraq in February 2004, met members of the Governing Council and many political and religious leaders, and travelled all over the country. His report to the Secretary-General concluded that free and fair elections could not be held before 30 June 2004. He also referred to the fact – hardly unfamiliar to political circles in Iraq – that there were sectarian tensions in the country. The sectarian Shi'a parties who had hoped that Ibrahimi would recommend the holding of elections before 30 June were deeply disappointed and used his reference to sectarian tensions to attack him viciously as an Arab nationalist Sunni bigot bent on depriving the Shi'a majority of their rights. This attack angered me and I vigorously defended Ibrahimi, further antagonizing the Shi'a political parties.

In April 2004, serious fighting broke out between the Americans and the resistance forces in Fallujah. I threatened to resign from the Governing Council if the Americans did not stop their military campaign. Although hostilities came to an end, many problems remained unsolved. At the same time, fighting broke out between the American forces and the Mahdi Army of Muqtada Al-Sadr after a warrant for his arrest was issued implicating him in the murder of a Shi'a cleric, Abdul Majeed Khoi, who had been killed in April 2003 near the Shrine of Imam Ali in Najaf. Most Governing Council members who are now allied to the Sadris openly supported the strong measures taken against Muqtada Al-Sadr and his army at the time.

Lakhdar Ibrahimi returned to Iraq with full powers to appoint an interim government. In a significant reversal of US policy, the Bush administration had decided to give greater responsibilities to the United Nations. Ibrahimi held extensive talks with the leaders of the various political groups. After several weeks of intense consultations, Ibrahimi chose Ayad Allawi, a member of the Governing Council, former Ba'athist and founder of the National Accord, a broad-based secular party, to be

Prime Minister. This choice was unanimously endorsed by the Governing Council. I was able to include in the new Cabinet two ministers: Mahdi Al-Hafez for Planning and Omar Damluji for Housing and Construction. There was general agreement at first that I would be the interim President. When Ibrahimi discussed the matter with me I was hesitant for two reasons. The interim President had no real authority; the post was largely symbolic, and the real power devolved upon the Prime Minister. The second reason was that the interim government was going to be short-lived and organized along sectarian lines. Ibrahimi tried to persuade me to accept the post. When I indicated that I would consider the matter, the US seemed to be less than enthusiastic about offering me the Presidency. Ambassador Blackwill, who had been sent as a Special US Envoy, then asked me to accept the post of ambassador in Washington, which he said would be more powerful than that of the interim President because I would be one of a select group of ambassadors who had direct and immediate access to the President of the United States. I declined this offer, and now I heard he was supporting the nomination of Ghazi Al-Yawar, a member of the ruling clan of the Shammar tribe in northern Iraq and also member of the Governing Council, for the Presidency.

At this point Al-Yawar's candidacy received a boost by the support of the so-called "Shi'a House" in the Governing Council. The Kurds were subsequently won over to their side, but I was not worried by the hostility of some members of the Council because I knew I enjoyed wide support among the Iraqi public. Ibrahimi after extensive consultations throughout the country came to the conclusion that I was in fact the most widely supported and best-qualified candidate for the post of interim President. But then a vicious campaign of falsehoods and distortions was waged against me accusing me of being the candidate and stooge of the United States, while the truth was the exact opposite. Sadly Al-Yawar joined the conspiracy against me. This was the unkindest cut of all; I had been his mentor and had supported his membership in the Governing Council and nominated him for its Presidency. He himself always said that he looked up to me as his uncle and teacher, yet he became the tool of those who were determined to deny me the Presidency.

In view of what had transpired, I decided to decline the nomination. Ibrahimi would not hear of it and issued an announcement that I was to be the interim President. This was broadcast and I received several calls of congratulation. But I insisted on refusing the appointment. Ahmad Chalabi, who had headed the conspiracy, was elated by his victory. I was the man who had fought hard against his divisive sectarianism, which I had been warning would ruin Iraq and destroy its fragile democracy.

After the abolition of the Governing Council, I became a member of the Interim National Council, which had only advisory functions. The interim government had the task of organizing elections for a National Assembly before the end of January 2005. The elections soon became highly controversial when the Sunni political groups threatened to boycott them unless they were delayed for a few months. I supported this demand to ensure that the Assembly, whose job was to draft the permanent constitution, would be fully representative under the prevailing system of proportional representation. Iraq was treated as a single electoral district, so that a low voter turnout in some parts of the country and a heavy turnout in others would leave a large segment of the population disenfranchised and many regions under-represented.

The Shi'a and Kurdish parties rejected any postponement and so did the Americans and Iranians; it was ironic that with all their differences they should agree on this one issue. I believe the Iranians knew what they were doing – but not so the Americans. I warned the Sunni leaders that they would be making a disastrous mistake if they boycotted the elections. They would not listen and the result of the January 2005 election was catastrophic, leaving the National Assembly to be completely dominated by the Shi'a and Kurdish parties, who succeeded in producing a constitution heavily in their favour. Thus devolved federalism was given a boost, substantial power was given to the regions and provinces, and the management of the vital oil industry was left vague – a recipe for future disputes and conflicts. The problem of Kirkuk was left unsolved, a time bomb that could explode any moment. The Kurds wanted to annex the city to their region. This was opposed by the Turcoman and Arab inhabitants of Kirkuk who were content to stay within the Iraqi state and were apprehensive about Kurdish nationalism.

The constitution in its present form is not a sound document except for the Bill of Rights, which was taken in its entirety from the interim constitution. It is full of loopholes and vague about the division of responsibility between the regions, provinces and the central government. Within that constitution, the powers of the executive, the legislature and the judiciary overlapped and were not clearly defined. It is obvious that the constitution has to be amended sooner or later but this is not likely to happen in the foreseeable future.

In spite of our misgivings about the elections, our party, the Independent Iraqi Democrats, took part in them and failed to gain a single seat in the National Assembly. It was a bitter blow from which the secular cause has not yet recovered. Unfortunately, I let myself be persuaded to stand for election to one of the Vice Presidential positions. I was confronted by the strong opposition of the Shi'a religious parties who once again were able to get help from Ghazi Al-Yawar, who ran against me. Although I had the support of the majority of the Sunni political groups we were unable to overcome the large Shi'a majority and Al-Yawar was elected Vice President. This time the Kurds wanted to support me but were unable to persuade the Shi'a parties to accept my candidacy. In retrospect I think I made a mistake in running to fill a post reserved for the Sunni Arabs under a system of sectarian apportionment of senior posts, a policy I have opposed all my life. I compromised in the mistaken belief that I would be able to change the sectarian direction of politics, which I believed would inevitably lead to the dismemberment of the Iraqi state. The transitional government of Ibrahim Al-Jaafari came to power in May 2005; it was perhaps the worst government in the history of Iraq. It allowed large-scale infiltration of the police and security forces by members and supporters of the militias. During its short tenure of office, sectarian killings and corruption reached catastrophic proportions. For this reason, we opposed the re-appointment of Al-Jaafari as Prime Minister in 2006.

In October 2005, in the midst of our preparations to contest the elections scheduled for December 2005, I was interviewed by John Burns of the *New York Times* in the house of my close friend, Omar Damluji, where I was staying as his guest. The following are some excerpts from his report on that interview, which was published on 30 October 2005:

> For those exhausted by Iraq's relentless violence and sectarianism there is no better tonic like a conversation with Adnan Pachachi. At 82, Mr Pachachi is an Iraqi patrician who

began his diplomatic career in Washington on the day in April 1945 when Franklin D. Roosevelt's coffin arrived at Union Station from Warm Springs, Ga. A fugitive from Saddam Hussein's brutality, he returned to Iraq 30 months ago in the hope of restoring the political civilities many Iraqis say were swept away with the assassination of King Faisal II in 1958.

Mr Pachachi is a Sunni, but he believes that Sunnis and Shiites, Kurds and Arabs, and Iraq's minorities, are not by nature disposed to the current politics of religious and ethnic division. He regards the years of repression under Mr Hussein, a Sunni whose main victims were Shiites and Kurds, as less a matter of Sunnis bludgeoning others to gain minority privilege than the work of a tyrant who betrayed Sunnis' instincts for a common life. Although seething mosques and insurgents dominate the Sunni heartland now, he says, most Sunnis, at heart, would prefer an inclusive, secular Iraq.

Toward that end, he is preparing to campaign with Ayad Allawi, a secular Shiite who was Iraq's provisional prime minister until last spring, in a centrist, non-sectarian alliance in parliamentary elections for a full five-year government that are set for Dec. 15. The alliance will offer an alternative to boldly sectarian platforms of the main Sunni, Shiite and Kurdish parties, but its prospects, many Iraqis believe, are not that strong. Even Mr Pachachi's wife, Selwa, watching warily from the couple's home in London, "keeps telling me it's a pipe dream, and it could be," he says. "But we have to try and realize our dreams, because what is the option? Should we give up?"

In a Baghdad garden in the glow of a setting autumn sun, Mr Pachachi discusses ideas that seem as appealing as the man himself. But events of the last 15 days seem, in crucial ways, to contradict him. The opening of Mr Hussein's trial showed how strongly attached many Sunni Arabs still feel to the ousted dictator, regardless of his record of mass killing, and the final count last week of the votes in the Oct. 15 constitutional referendum underlined how much Sunnis disagree with Shiites and Kurds on how to decide the future Iraq.

Still, principles like Mr Pachachi's go to the heart of what many American officials here regard as the best and perhaps last hope of rescuing Iraq from sectarian civil war. That hope rests, ultimately, on core components of the Sunni insurgency, and their rivals in Shiite religious militias, laying down their arms to build a common life.

But at an age when many men would let history take care of itself, he is pressing ahead, and casting his net for fresh partners in the new alliance who, like him, believe that the country's destiny lies in the universal values trampled under Mr Hussein.

"It's going to be quite an extraordinary coalition," he said, showing his visitors out.

"There'll be Communists and people who believe in the free market, Arab nationalists and social democrats, Sunnis and Shiites and Kurds. There'll be many people who, to be very frank, I hardly know. But somehow, we have to persuade the silent majority to vote."

In December 2005, I was elected Member of Parliament on the Iraqiya list. I had joined the Iraqiya Party, a secular alliance led by Ayad Allawi, because its aims were broadly in line with my own and it was clear that it had a much wider electoral appeal than the Independent Iraqi Democrats, which had failed to win any seats in the first election. Being the oldest member, I presided over the first session of Parliament and delivered a speech, excerpted as follows, warning against sectarianism and offering a programme for the next government to follow.

> I open in the name of God and the people of Iraq the first meeting of the Council of Representatives. Nearly a month has passed since the outrageous crime perpetrated in the shrine of Imams Ali Al-Hadi and Hassan Al-Askari, and the violence that followed, in which hundreds of innocent lives were lost. It appeared that our country was sliding towards civil war. This did not happen because Iraqis of all sects and political persuasions joined in averting such a national catastrophe. Dangers still persist. There are internal and external enemies who do not wish to see a strong and united Iraq. To confront

them we must not allow narrow sectarian and ethnic loyalties to divide us and weaken our resolve to create a truly democratic Iraq. The people of Iraq have elected us. Let us be worthy of their trust. Our principal aim from which we should never deviate is to protect the security and territorial integrity of Iraq, united and indivisible. We are the conscience and hope of the nation. Great responsibilities have been thrust upon us. We will not be able to satisfy the people's aspirations if we continue to be uncompromising and intolerant and seclude ourselves in our sectarian trenches. One of our first tasks is to form a committee to consider necessary amendments to the constitution in accordance with Article 142. Parliament is also required to enact scores of new laws, to implement various constitutional provisions. We should, as a matter of urgency, enact a new law of executive authority which would clearly define the functions of governmental bodies, and establish the norms of fiscal responsibility. Our most important task, however, is to help in the formation of a national unity government in response to the overwhelming desire of the people. All the principal political parties and groups in Parliament would be represented in this government and participate in decisions on major political and economic matters affecting the vital interests of the country. Regarding the principal governmental and ministerial posts, the main criteria should be competence, integrity, and experience, and not party loyalty or sectarian and ethnic affiliations. We should not repeat past mistakes. The people demand practical and quick solutions to their problems. Their patience is running out.

Security must remain our top priority. This requires the reorganization of the armed forces and security services to ensure their independence. These forces with their undivided loyalty to the nation and the state shall protect Iraq against external threats, extremist fanatics, and militias that terrorize the population. It is necessary to implement soon the constitutional provision which prohibits military militias outside the armed forces. The security situation will improve if arbitrary arrests are stopped and thousand of detainees who have not been charged with any specific crime are released.

A great deal has been said about shortages and the absence of essential services which persist after all these years of suffering and privation. Neither the Civilian Provisional Authority, nor the Governing Council, nor the succeeding governments, were able to stop the deterioration in living and social conditions. Unemployment is still high and the level of corruption unacceptable. Serious shortages in essential services remain, and the infrastructure is in a bad state. The next government must give special attention to the development and modernization of the oil industry. Parliament has a duty to oversee this vital sector of the national economy and ensure transparency in its management.

When I was young I asked God to prolong my life so that I could see a free and democratic Iraq whose people enjoy their fundamental rights and freedoms, protected by an independent judiciary administering impartial justice to all irrespective of gender and religious, ethnic and confessional affiliations. This dream has not been realized. Our nascent democracy faces numerous challenges. We have to be vigilant and defend our precious liberties against internal and external enemies. Ultimately it is the people and not the constitution that will protect and preserve democratic institutions. So many constitutions have been used to entrench dictatorial and oppressive regimes. I am certain that the Iraqi people after all the bitter trials they have gone through will not allow anyone under whatever pretext to undermine and usurp their rights and freedoms.

The Shi'a religious parties could not agree on a candidate for Prime Minister. The two candidates, Ibrahim Al-Jaafari and Adel Abdul Mahdi, after several ballots obtained the same number of votes. Finally they agreed on a compromise candidate, Nuri Al-Maliki, a member of the Dawa party. The Shi'a leadership thought he would be very easy to handle but they soon found otherwise. Al-Maliki, with strong American support, asserted himself and was able to replace Al-Jaafari as leader of the Dawa party, and took strong action against the Mahdi army with American military help. He proved himself to be a deft, shrewd and at the same time ruthless manipulator in the game of Iraqi politics, completely outmanoeuvring his foes. I wanted to hear firsthand from the US administration of their attitude towards Al-Maliki who seemed to have America's unqualified support. The US Secretary of State, Condoleezza Rice, had invited me to meet her in Washington. I accepted this invitation and sent the following letter to Zalmay Khalilzad, the US Ambassador to Iraq, informing him of my intention to visit the United States.

> Dear Zal,
> As you know, we are in the process of forming a broadly based non-sectarian, political front, to uphold and defend the values of liberalism, equality and the rule of law, which are presently under threat. Our voice, which I believe is that of the silent majority of Iraqis, has been submerged in the chaotic sectarian violence which threatens to break up the country, and plunge it into lawlessness and anarchy. I believe the American people who are being asked to accept more sacrifices are entitled to know that there is another alternative to the rule of religious parties and their militias and armed supporters. We share with the American people their beliefs and values and it is time for Iraqis who have proven their unwavering attachment to the ideals of secular democracy to articulate them. I appreciate the gracious invitation of the Secretary of State to visit the United States. I hope I will be able to meet the President, the Secretaries of State and Defense, National Security Advisor Hadley and Deputy Secretary of State Negroponte. It would be useful to meet with the chairmen and members of the Foreign Affairs and Armed Services Committees of both Houses of Congress. We expect to be invited to leading think tanks and media outlets.
> Any help you can render will be highly appreciated.
>
> Adnan Pachachi

During my visit to Washington in May and June 2008, I found that the Americans not only supported Al-Maliki but accepted many of his conditions that in the past they had resolutely refused, such as fixing a date for the withdrawal of US troops from Iraq. The Secretary of State, Condoleezza Rice, urged me to support Al-Maliki because in her view he was honest, firm and stood up to Iran and its surrogates, specifically the Mahdi army of Muqtada Al-Sadr. I reminded her that he was the head of the Dawa, an avowedly sectarian party founded to promote Shi'a interests and in receipt of substantial financial support from Iran. Al-Maliki was also complacent about the rampant corruption in his administration. In my meeting with Ms Rice and other American officials and legislators, I stressed the following points:

1. Elections are the only way to bring about change.

2. There is a great deal that is wrong in Iraqi society, politically, economically and socially. Urgent measures are needed to undo the effects of years of mismanagement, incompetence, and corruption.

3. A new non-sectarian political front will hopefully be the engine for change.

4. The crucial importance of purging the security system and armed forces from remaining militia and sectarian influences and infiltration, to ensure their undivided loyalty, and allegiance to the Iraqi state.

5. The proposed Iraq–US agreement should not be entered into with undue haste.

6. The presence of multinational forces is necessary in the near and intermediate term because violence has not ended and it may erupt on a larger scale at any moment.

In November 2008, the Iraqi Parliament considered two draft agreements with the United States, one for the status of American troops and the other for long-term strategic co-operation between the two countries. I stated in Parliament that the time was not appropriate for such agreements because we had to consider carefully the implications of a precipitate US troop withdrawal while Iraqi security forces were clearly incapable of coping with the security situation on their own. We had lengthy discussions with Ryan Crocker, the US Ambassador in Baghdad, and the team of experts sent by the Bush administration to persuade us to conclude these agreements without delay. Our group – the Iraqiya – was divided but the majority voted in favour of the agreements, although Allawi and myself, in contrast, were in favour of renewing the United Nations mandate.

Provincial elections took place in January 2009 and revealed a noticeable shift away from the major Shi'a religious parties. The main beneficiary was Al-Maliki, who was supported by the Shi'a electorate at the expense of the Islamic Supreme Council, headed by Abdul Aziz Al-Hakim. Our group did reasonably well but the result fell short of expectations. So we decided to enter the general election a year later as part of a large coalition. The Iraqiya under Ayad Allawi won 91 seats, two more than Al-Maliki's State and Law group. I advised Allawi to join Maliki in an alliance that would be able to form a strong government without the participation of either the Kurds or the Shi'a political groups. Unfortunately personal antagonisms between the two men and conflicting programmes, agendas, loyalties and beliefs frustrated all attempts to bring them together. Al-Maliki sought the help of Iran to put pressure on the Sadri group to reverse its strong opposition to him and join in a grand Shi'a coalition. The ensuing stalemate, which continued for nine months, was further proof that the present political class in Iraq was unfit to govern.

While the political and security situation was rapidly deteriorating, the United States decided to end its military presence in the country. There was no longer any appetite among the American public for continued involvement in Iraq. Also, once the invasion's original, declared mission of rooting out Iraq's weapons of mass destruction had proved to be based on lies and misinformation, the US administration announced that its purpose now was to rid Iraq of the effects of the remnants of the old regime and to establish democracy in the country. It is also true, however, that they hoped to make space for US business. There are many lucrative contracts with US firms for projects, paid for with Iraqi money. This has largely been unaccounted for. However, the US occupation and subsequent military presence in Iraq failed to create the security conditions and stability in which business could flourish. This is perhaps another reason for the decision to pull their troops out of Iraq. President Obama assured other world leaders and the American public that democracy was firmly established and flourishing and that the Iraqi security forces were fully able to maintain law and order on their own.

Sadly, this is not the case. Many Iraqis fear that hostile neighbouring states like Iran or local armed militias will fill the vacuum left by US withdrawal. Most Iraqis believe that the United States should not evade its responsibility and hide behind the fiction of a flourishing and secure Iraqi democracy. Sooner or later they will have to face the reality of the Iraqi situation and stop indulging in delusional wishful thinking. The American people should be told that vital American interests are jeopardized, and that inaction and neglect will have catastrophic consequences for regional and world peace and security.

The main US effort has now shifted from Iraq to Afghanistan, and this will probably remain the focus of American diplomatic and military action for the foreseeable future. In my opinion this policy is wrong because it abandons a pivotal country in a region which is of vital interest to the United States, for the sake of a country with little strategic importance. The explanation we often hear is that fighting the Taliban in Afghanistan would make it easier for the United States to combat terrorism at home. In my view, this is a fallacious argument. The reason that terrorist activities have virtually stopped in the United States since 11 September 2001 is the success of the security agencies in the US, and not the futile and costly fighting in Afghanistan. The war in Afghanistan began as a project for regime change and continues to be so, and has had little impact on terrorist activities in the United States. This is a truth that no amount of obfuscation can hide.

14

Epilogue

THE YEAR 2011 WILL BE REMEMBERED as the *annus mirabilis* of the Arabs. In one country after another people have risen up to put an end to brutal dictatorial regimes. The movement for change is now unstoppable, despite the lethal means at the disposal of tyrannical regimes to stem the tide of protest and discontent. The young who launched the Arab spring need the help of educated and experienced professionals in order to translate their idealism and aspirations into reality. The failure so far of the older generation to participate in a meaningful way in the movement renders the future uncertain and difficult to predict, especially in Iraq where the young have not risen in sufficient numbers against a government that is perhaps the most incompetent and corrupt in the region. Iraq today is a failed state, unable to provide security and the minimum requirements for a decent life for its citizens.

Iraq faces two major challenges. The first emanates from Iran, which is using the Shi'a political parties in Iraq and elsewhere in the Arab world as tools in its grand design to dominate the region. The second challenge comes from the religious political parties, both Shi'a and Sunni, which are trying to establish various forms of theocracy and to halt the drive for modernity. The only way for Iraq to resist this dual challenge is by creating a strong and determined opposition combining the younger generation with all the liberal, secular democratic and non-sectarian elements and educated elite of the country. All this will depend on the ability of Iraqis to overcome their sectarian prejudices. The religious and ethnic political parties, which thrive on such divisions, will do everything in their power to keep communal and confessional antagonisms alive.

There are no magic solutions to the complex problems facing Iraq. The first step, it seems to me, must be the removal of the corrupt and incompetent rulers who have shown over the years their total unfitness for government. The change must come by peaceful means, following the example of Tunisia and Egypt. I believe the young in Iraq will eventually force their sectarian rulers to relinquish power and set about the gigantic task of rebuilding their country.

***

Now, approaching the age of ninety, I have decided to retire. My political activity is limited to a few TV and radio interviews. I have been spending most of my time finishing this personal memoir, as well as a detailed autobiography in Arabic – both of which I hope to complete before my ninetieth birthday on 14 May 2013.

APPENDICES

1

Arab–American Relations

Memorandum submitted to the Deputy Minister of Foreign Affairs of Iraq, for transmittal to the leaders of the Iraqi government on the occasion of the visit to Baghdad of US Secretary of State, John Foster Dulles, in June 1953

THE FORTHCOMING VISIT of Mr John Foster Dulles to some Arab countries is awaited with keen interest and lively though restrained optimism. While it is premature and indeed unwise to hail the visit as the beginning of a new era of friendship and understanding between the Arab people and the United States, it nevertheless provides unmistakable indications of a modification in the attitude of the US Government towards the Arab world. It is encouraging that Mr Dulles in the midst of his worldwide responsibilities will devote some of his time and attention to an area of the world which, hitherto, has been granted only secondary importance by American leaders. The fact that he is the first Secretary of State of the United States to visit the Middle East is in itself a source of some satisfaction and hope. Moreover the visit coincides with a momentous change of government in the United States.

The recent election in the United States meant, if anything, a vote of protest against the foreign policies of the Democratic Administrations during the last two decades. While the previous government has been successful to some extent in its policies in Europe, it has notably failed in other equally important areas of the world such as the Middle East, where

American influence and prestige has dwindled to a degree that has endangered the interests of the United States and threatened to undo the whole system of security which the US has patiently and laboriously constructed in other parts of the world. President Eisenhower, recognizing this, has declared that one of the first tasks of his Government would be to improve Arab–American relations, which have deteriorated over the last few years.

Amidst all these encouraging indications and in view of the imminent visit of Mr Dulles it seems appropriate to review Arab–American relations, analysing the points of conflict and seeking to find solutions that would be, as far as possible, consistent with the basic rights and aspirations of the Arab people and fully compatible with the fundamental aims and purposes of American foreign policy.

Although the Arab countries have reached varying degrees of political and economic development, and despite the obvious differences in their social and cultural conditions, they all have some basic common problems which give them an undoubted unity of purpose. This unity is greatly enhanced and considerably strengthened by their indissoluble ties of language, history, religion and a common cultural heritage. The Arab countries have at the present time three principal aims. They are:

1. Political freedom and liberation from foreign rule
2. Unity
3. Economic, social and cultural advancement

It is natural that the first aim has precedence over all others for the countries which have not attained a full measure of self-government, while others who are more fortunate direct their energies towards achieving a fuller and more lasting union with their Arab neighbours and improving the economic and social conditions of their peoples.

These are then the three fundamental aspirations of the Arab peoples: independence, unity and economic and social progress. Arab governments, no matter how different they may be, seek the same aims and work for the same purposes.

American policy, in the Middle East and elsewhere in the world, seems to have the three following basic aims:

1. To stop the spread of Communism.

2. To build up the military and economic strength of the free world, and to resist and deter Communist aggression from without and within.
3. To raise the standard of living of economically underdeveloped countries by providing financial and technical assistance.

These three aims of American policy do not conflict in any way with Arab aspirations; on the contrary, they envisage the same kind of world and move in similar directions. The Arabs oppose the spread of Communism and their governments are energetically combating subversive activities in their countries. Communist parties are outlawed and their members are kept under constant surveillance. The only communist party able to operate freely and of any consequence in the Near East is the Communist Party in Israel.

Regarding the second aim of American policy, the Arabs are very anxious to build up their military and economic strength. The Arab world, in view of its rich oil resources and strategic importance, is enormously attractive to potential aggressors especially when such aggressors are in their neighbourhood. The third aim of American policy, namely the development of underdeveloped countries, is fully in conformity with the aspirations of the Arab people.

This identity of interests and aspirations has been cemented by a tradition of friendship and mutual understanding which developed gradually and steadily over the decades until it was interrupted and almost destroyed in the tragic years of the post-war period.

Arab–American friendship dates back to the very first days of the existence of the United States as a free and sovereign nation. It is well known that the first state to recognize the independence of the United States was Arab Morocco, which was at the time a fully sovereign nation. During the 19th century, Arab–American relations were further strengthened by the indefatigable work of various American centres of learning established in the Arab world. Those educational institutions brought to the Arabs the best of American civilization and culture. The missionaries, educators and other men of goodwill who dedicated themselves to a lifetime of zealous and unflinching work for the betterment of the Arab peoples, had ingrained in their hearts and minds the true image of America as the bastion of freedom and haven of the oppressed.

The graduates of those institutions have played a leading part in the regeneration of the Arab world and have exerted a decisive influence in the political and cultural renaissance of the Arab nation.

Then there were the thousands of Arab immigrants who left their homes and went out to seek a new life in America. Many have played their part alongside peoples of different origins in building up the United States. They are loyal citizens of their new country and have played a great role in consolidating the traditional friendship between the two peoples.

After the First World War, when the Mandate system was established in the Arab world, the people signified by overwhelming majorities their desire to be placed under the mandate of the United States. This spontaneous and genuine desire stemmed from the deep conviction of many thinking Arabs that the logical friend and ally of the Arab peoples was America. To these and to so many others in the world, the United States stood alone among the great powers as the true champion of liberty and progress. Many had implicit faith in the intentions of the United States, which to them seemed a new phenomenon in international relations: a great power without imperialist ambitions; a victorious power which was the vigorous advocate of the right of self-determination of peoples.

The faith and confidence remained intact throughout the vicissitudes and upheavals of the inter-war period when the Arab peoples were deeply engulfed in their struggle for national liberation. With the end of the Second World War a new phase in Arab–American relations began. The Arabs believe, with much justification, that the United States has discarded its traditional policy and adopted a new one reminiscent of the imperialistic policies of some of the European powers. The United States, while succeeding in confronting the challenge to the free world posed by Communist aggression in Europe and the Far East, pursued a policy unworthy of a great power with worldwide responsibilities and allowed its decisions to be influenced by expediency rather than principle, completely ignoring its traditional role as the champion of the weak and the defender of the oppressed.

The present crisis in Arab–American relations can be traced to the policies pursued by the United States in two parts of the world, Palestine and North Africa.

Within a few years, and as a result of these policies, the reservoir of goodwill that America was able to draw on in the Arab world was all but exhausted. A feeling of resentment and suspicion has replaced the confidence, admiration and deep understanding which the Arabs had for America.

It is, therefore, inescapable that any improvement in Arab–American relations must be preceded by a change of American policy in Palestine and North Africa.

Palestine

Since the end of the war the Zionist pressure groups have been successful in bringing about a complete reversal of American policy towards the Arabs. It has often been said that considerations of internal politics were mainly responsible for the attitude taken by the United States government on the Palestine question. It is hoped that the new Administration would find it possible to resist such pressures and look at foreign questions primarily from the viewpoint of American interests.

The Arabs are not likely to forget that the United States, instigated by Zionist pressure, was instrumental in creating the State of Israel and was thus indirectly responsible for making a million Palestine Arabs homeless refugees.

It would be useful to remind Mr Dulles of the actions of his government from 1945 onwards, because Americans are sometimes inclined to forget the facts and express surprise at the vehemence of Arab feeling against the United States.

The following is a short survey of the policy of the US Government on the Palestine question:

1. August 1945: Mr Truman publicly asked for the immediate admission of 100,000 Jews into Palestine in violation of the British White Paper of 1939.
2. November 1945: the British Government abrogated the White Paper. It is generally believed this was done in response to strong American pressure during the British Loan negotiations.
3. 1946: The Anglo-American Committee of Inquiry included two avowed American Zionist sympathizers (Bartley Crum and James MacDonald), thus throwing doubt on the impartiality of the Committee whose report was an undisguised affirmation of the Zionist viewpoint.

4. November 1947: the United States Government and its delegation to the United Nations exerted unprecedented pressure to pass the partition resolution.
5. 15 May 1948: the recognition of Israel just a few hours after its proclamation. This unfriendly act was singularly provocative and was rightly considered to be an arrogant disregard of Arab feelings.

Ever since 1949, the United States through its official agencies and private donations has poured hundreds of millions of dollars into Israel. Mr Dulles must know that Israel has so far received more than a billion dollars, half of which came from the US Government and the rest from private sources. During this same period the seven Arab States received not more than $100 million, most of which was to the United Nations Relief & Works Agency for Palestine Refugees.

The Arab position on Palestine is simple. The partition plan adopted by the UN General Assembly in 1947 has divided Palestine into two states, one Jewish and the other Arab. It also provided for the establishment of Jerusalem as a "Corpus Separatum" under international authority. In subsequent resolutions passed in 1948, 1949, 1950 and 1952 the General Assembly has reaffirmed its 1947 partition resolution and accepted the principle of voluntary repatriation of Palestine refugees and of adequate compensation to those not wishing to return.

It must be remembered that Mr Dulles, who was a member of the US delegation during the third session of the General Assembly in Paris, played a leading part in securing the adoption of Resolution 194 concerning the Palestine Question and the rights of the refugees.

None of these resolutions has been implemented, but instead they have been violated time and again by Israel.

Israeli authorities have annexed substantial areas not allotted to them under the 1947 partition plan. They have consistently refused to accept the internationalization of Jerusalem and violated it in the most flagrant manner by transferring to it the seat of their parliament and government offices from Tel Aviv. Regarding the Arab refugees, not a single one of them has been allowed to return and none have been compensated. Many are still living as they have lived since 1948, in camps. This callous disregard of the authority of the United Nations has not once been challenged but instead some powers, most prominent among them the

United States, tried in the recent session of the General Assembly to absolve Israel of the responsibility of not abiding by UN decisions and sought to set aside those resolutions by urging a wholly unacceptable scheme of direct negotiations.

The Arabs feel that Israel must not be encouraged in maintaining this attitude and should be compelled to accept the resolutions of the United Nations.

The United States is in a position to take a firm stand on this matter. Israel, in view of its great economic difficulties and its complete dependence on American generosity, is obliged to respond to the desires and inclinations of the US. In view of this the Arabs have reached the inescapable conclusion that the key to an equitable solution of the Palestine problem lies with the United States.

The US can contribute substantially towards such a solution by taking the following measures:

1. To declare firmly and unequivocally that the United States stands by the United Nations resolutions on Palestine.
2. To strongly urge Israel to take the necessary action to implement these resolutions by withdrawing from areas not allotted to it by the resolution of 1947, and by accepting the internationalization of Jerusalem and facilitating the repatriation and just compensation of the refugees.
3. To treat Israel on a basis of equality with other Arab states and to refrain from perpetually singling it out for favours and lavish economic and military assistance.

Mr Dulles must be reminded, however, that the Arab states will never recognize Israel, and it must be stressed that while the Arabs might differ on many things they will never differ on the question of Palestine. No Arab government will ever dare to compromise on Palestine. Therefore any arrangement made conditional on peace with Israel must be definitely excluded. Mr Dulles must understand this.

North Africa

French rule in North Africa is maintained by force. It must be clear by now that the majority of the people want independence and will not accept any form of French tutelage. To say that the people are not ready for self-rule is absurd because countries far less advanced have long since been given their independence. The Arabs see no moral justification for continuing foreign rule over a country whose people want to be free. The French claim that their presence in North Africa is necessary to preserve and continue the valuable work they have done during the last half-century or so is open to question. It must be stressed that this argument, however valid and truthful it may be (and in this case it is not), cannot be used as a hindrance to the progress of a people towards self-government.

American policy has unfortunately tended to support the French view. This was not dictated by the merits of the French position but rather by other considerations having no direct relation to the question of independence. It is feared that France, an important European ally of the United States, would be considerably weakened by the loss of Tunisia and Morocco.

This argument if followed to its logical conclusion would make the United States the defender of every colonial empire in the world and the enemy of every movement of national liberation. This is a policy that entirely disregards the basic concepts of American democracy and is a complete antithesis of the traditional policy of the United States.

The Arab states together with other Asian and African members of the United Nations brought the question of Morocco before the UN General Assembly during its sixth session in Paris, but these efforts were frustrated by the alignment of the United States and other Western powers with France in rejecting its inclusion in the agenda. In April 1952, in the Security Council, the United States again supported the plea of France in objecting to the discussion of the Tunisian question in the Council. During the recent session of the General Assembly the two questions were included in the agenda over the objections of France, but the United States took a position which was hardly calculated to satisfy the just aspirations of the peoples of Tunisia and Morocco. It supported the so-called reforms that the French imposed upon the rulers of these countries. These "reforms" contemplated the establishment of municipal bodies where the French colonists would have equal representation with indigenous inhabitants who outnumber the French by 20 to 1. (It is an eloquent commentary on the oppressive character of French rule that only now after forty years in Morocco and seventy years in Tunisia are the French willing to introduce representative institutions, and this only under the strongest of pressure). The Arabs expect the United States to intervene energetically and effectively on behalf of Tunisia and Morocco. The following means could go a long way towards defusing the situation:

1. Release of all nationalist leaders detained by the French authorities and restoration of civil liberties.
2. Abolition of martial law and other repressive measures.
3. Immediate negotiations with the lawful and recognized representatives of the people for the settlement of the conflict.

These three initial steps would considerably improve matters and would undoubtedly open a new era in Arab–French relations. France would benefit a great deal from the amelioration of conditions in North Africa. It would relieve her of the political and economic strains with which she is now faced and would pave the way for fruitful co-operation between the two countries and France.

Political and economic co-operation

Political co-operation between the Arab world and the United States would become feasible if and when the questions of Palestine and North Africa are settled on the basis indicated above. It would then become possible to discuss details of mutual security arrangements for the Middle East. Such arrangements could never be effectively made without the prior consent and goodwill of the Arabs. Any Middle East defence organization must of necessity be established with the concurrence of the Arabs and their approval. Without their participation, there can be no effective collective defence of the Middle East. Strategically, geographically and economically the Arab countries are the heart of the Middle East. If the United States is really and sincerely contemplating the creation of a defensive system in the area, then she will have to come to an understanding with the Arabs.

Economically the Arab countries need the financial and technical assistance of the United States on a much longer scale than has hitherto been furnished. Point Four assistance has been on a very meagre scale and cannot be compared to the help given to Israel and some other countries. A substantial increase in technical assistance would be a very welcome indication of American readiness to extend its hand of friendship to the Arab world.

Financial assistance, though not needed in some Arab countries, would be of great value in others whose limited resources are inadequate to meet the costs of economic and social reforms.

2

The Gulf War of 1990–91

Article submitted to the *Guardian*, and published in that newspaper on 30 July 1991 in a heavily abridged form, under the title "The Healing Hope of Iraq" and under the pseudonym Mohammed Rashed, "a former high-ranking Iraqi official now living in exile".

THE CONSEQUENCES of the Gulf war of 1990–1991 are still unfolding, and it would be premature to arrive at any definitive conclusions in a situation of such volatility. There are however certain aspects of this unique conflict which can no longer be ignored. The Gulf war was truly an extraordinary spectacle: a superpower, two major military powers and a host of large, medium and small states waging war against a small Third World country about the size of California, with a population of not more than one-fifteenth that of the United States.

Iraq, whose military capability was intentionally and grossly exaggerated, was portrayed as a major threat to world peace. In spite of wide support from Arab and Islamic masses, Iraq, besieged and isolated, had to fight alone against overwhelming odds. Never has there been such an unequal contest. Iraq, totally defenceless, was pounded mercilessly for several weeks in the greatest air assault in history, its military installations pulverized, its industry and infrastructure destroyed, many of its cities reduced to rubble and its population terrorized.

To ensure continued public support, the conflict in the Gulf was personalized as a struggle between Saddam Hussein, devil incarnate, and a law-abiding world led by the saintly George Bush. The Iraqi people were totally dehumanized; all the carnage, the indiscriminate slaughter of soldiers and civilians and the destruction of a whole country were done in the name of a 'just war'.

The way the war was conducted leaves no room for doubt that the premeditated and irreversible decision to eliminate Iraq's military and industrial capability, and destroy its advanced infrastructure, was not dictated by the requirements of war but was a long-range geopolitical objective. For Arabs it was a nightmare, as we watched in horrified disbelief the systematic destruction of a precious part of the Arab homeland and the elimination of the one credible deterrent the Arabs had in their conflict with Israel.

It is impossible to fathom the full dimensions of this immense tragedy, for which the Iraqi regime must bear a major share of responsibility. I do not know whether Iraq's leaders realized that they had fallen into a trap and had played right into the hands of their enemies. In the well-orchestrated campaign against Iraq which started immediately after the end of the Iraq–Iran war in 1988, Saddam was singled out for ferocious vilification in the Western media, especially in the United States and Britain. False and exaggerated reports about Iraq's alleged nuclear weapons program were published and repeated *ad nauseam* day after day. Stories about a 'supergun' and Iraq's use of chemical weapons were taken up with great relish and enthusiasm. Saddam was called the Butcher of Baghdad and described as bloodthirsty tyrant, a successor of Hitler and Stalin.

The US halted food shipments and imposed restrictions on the export of certain goods and materials. It put pressure on private banks and financial institutions to stop Iraq's credit facilities. Many European countries followed suit. The cry went out loud and clear that Iraq's military arsenal was a threat to the stability and security of the Middle East and had to be eliminated without delay.

This relentless campaign, which continued unabated for more than two years, should have given the Iraqi leadership ample warning. Instead of exercising vigilant restraint, they allowed themselves to be provoked into actions which gave their enemies just the pretext they had been waiting for, to launch their well-prepared campaign to destroy Iraq.

Saddam's anger and frustration at Kuwait's apparent lack of understanding and sympathy for Iraq's severe economic difficulties clouded his judgment and drove him to commit the monumental blunder of invading and annexing Kuwait. I am still at a loss to understand his motives and calculations. He should have known that he could not possibly get away with such a blatant act of aggression against an independent state, a member of the United Nations, and a major oil producer with enormous investments all over the world. Iraq's historic claims lapsed when the first Ba'ath government recognized the independence of Kuwait in 1963. In spite of unresolved frontier disputes between the two countries, their relations were on the whole friendly, and became very close during the Iraq–Iran war because the Kuwaitis realized, like others in the Gulf, that Iraq's army was their shield against Iranian ambitions. Had it not been for Iraq's stout defence, the whole area would have fallen under the domination of Khomeini's Iran. Now that same army, which protected the Gulf at a tremendous cost in blood and treasure to the people of Iraq, has been destroyed.

The American decision to obliterate Iraq's military capability must have been taken very early, perhaps even before the occupation of Kuwait. The friends of Israel in the United States put great pressure on Bush to take an uncompromisingly hostile stand. Mrs Margaret Thatcher, a great friend of Israel, used her considerable prestige and influence to persuade Bush to use military force against Iraq. Bush may have been influenced also by the powerful military-industrial establishment in the United States, which viewed with apprehension and alarm the prospect of drastic cuts in defence spending as a result of the end of the Cold War.

The invasion of Kuwait was a god-sent gift to the war party in Washington. The temptation to attack Iraq became irresistible, and Bush swung into action with great zeal and determination. He obtained from the Security Council several resolutions imposing on Iraq the most comprehensive sanctions in history. He stated repeatedly that American forces were sent to Saudi Arabia for defensive purposes only, and that the liberation of Kuwait would be achieved through the rigorous enforcement of sanctions. This charade continued for three months. When American and allied forces reached a sufficient level of strength, the emphasis was shifted from defence to offence. The liberation of Kuwait became the stated military objective, still concealing the real aim which was the destruction of Iraq's military capability. Bush and the American military establishment never really wanted Saddam to withdraw from Kuwait because that "nightmare option", as it was called, would have spoilt their plans to disarm Iraq.

This unequal, devastating and unnecessary war should have been avoided. I blame Saddam Hussein for his unforgivable crime of invading and annexing Kuwait and then his refusal to show any flexibility. At the same time I cannot absolve the United States and its allies of responsibility for their wanton and totally unjustified destruction of Iraq's economy and infrastructure. The air onslaught went far beyond the provisions of Security Council resolutions and could not be explained away by alleged military requirements. This tendency to punish the Iraqi people continues with the retention of sanctions even after the acceptance by Iraq of the harsh conditions contained in the ceasefire resolution of the Security Council. There can be no justification for inflicting further suffering on the people of Iraq, who never wanted this war and were opposed to Saddam's Kuwaiti adventure from the very beginning.

Could war have been avoided? I believe it could have. Sanctions rigorously enforced and accompanied by serious diplomatic efforts could have spared the region this terrible tragedy. A dynamic, resourceful and imaginative leadership at the United Nations could have achieved a breakthrough in the diplomatic stalemate. But unfortunately Perez de Cuellar is no Hammarskjold. He did not lead, but simply followed, and was unscrupulously used by the United States to further its war aims.

In my opinion Resolution 678 of the Security Council which authorized the use of force against Iraq is contrary to the Charter of the United Nations. I maintain that the conditions and procedures laid down in the Charter for the use of force have not been fully or scrupulously followed in the case of Iraq. By Resolution 660, which may be called the key document, the Security Council decided that Iraq's invasion of Kuwait was a breach of international peace and security within the meaning of articles 39 and 40 of the Charter, and called on Iraq to withdraw immediately and unconditionally its forces to the positions they held on 1 August 1990. Four days later, on 6 August 1990, the Security Council, acting under Article 41 of the Charter, decided in Resolution 661 to impose economic sanctions.

These sanctions were further extended and reinforced in Resolutions 665 and 670 of August 25 and September 13 imposing a maritime and air blockade. The next phase of United Nations action envisaged in the Charter would have been the use of force in accordance with Article 42 which states clearly that if the Security Council considers that the measures taken in accordance with Article 41, i.e. economic sanctions and blockade, proved to be inadequate, then the Security Council may take whatever measures are necessary including the use of military force to restore international peace and security. In other words the use of force may be used only after the Security Council had determined that the sanctions, the blockade and the embargo were inadequate to achieve its purpose of maintaining international peace and security. Such a determination had never taken place, neither explicitly nor implicitly. Resolution 678 mentions nothing about the inadequacy of sanctions, it refers merely to Iraq's refusal to withdraw. It is clear therefore that the use of force was authorized not in accordance with Article 42 which is not specifically mentioned in Resolution 678, but presumably based on Article 51, which reads as follows:

> Nothing in the present Charter shall impair the inherent right of individual or collective self-defence, if an armed attack occurs against a Member of the United Nations, until the Security Council has taken measures necessary to maintain international peace and security. Measures taken by Members in the exercise of this right of self-defence shall be immediately reported to the Security Council and shall not in any way affect the authority and responsibility of the Security Council under the present Charter to take at anytime such action it deems necessary in order to maintain or restore international peace and security.

It is clear from this article that measures of self-defence are of an urgent and provisional character, taken before and not after the Security Council has acted to maintain or restore international peace and security. Once the Security Council has acted, the exercise of the right of self-defence under Article 51 can no longer be invoked, and the question becomes the exclusive concern of the Security Council, which alone has the right to order the use of force in accordance with Article 42. Secretary

General Perez de Cuellar himself stated on 8 November 1990, that since the Security Council was already seized of the matter, and had taken measures under Chapter VII of the Charter, any military action under Article 51 was legally questionable.

Resolution 678 merely authorizes member states co-operating with Kuwait to use all necessary means to secure the implementation of previous resolutions and restore international peace and security in the region. Such a blanket, carte blanche authorization is unprecedented in the annals of the United Nations. The war unleashed on 17 January 1991 was not a United Nations action and cannot claim international legitimacy. The right to use force can be delegated to individual countries only as an urgent and temporary measure of self-defence under Article 51 and, as such, authorization would automatically lapse as soon as the Security Council had taken action under Chapter VII, which it did when it imposed sanctions on 6 August 1990. In other words the use of force under Article 51 is not an open-ended affair, but is restricted in its time frame and method. The Secretary General himself admitted as much when he said in a press interview on 28 January 1991, that the war was not a United Nations war. What was it then? A war permitted by the United Nations outside the Charter? Can the Security Council give such permission? The answer is no, since its authority to initiate or order military action is governed by the provisions of the Charter and it has no right to exceed such authority and distribute dispensations here and there for the use of force. Under the Charter there is no such thing as a war permitted by the United Nations. There is only war undertaken under the authority and supervision of the Security Council.

What does the future hold for Iraq? A devastating war followed by bloody civil strife has all but destroyed this once prosperous country, the cradle of human civilization. In spite of the appalling situation prevailing in Iraq today, exacerbated by the punitive conditions imposed by the Security Council which are hindering and delaying the vital work of rehabilitation and reconstruction, the long-suffering people of Iraq cling to the hope that eventually a democratic government will emerge to guide them towards a better future.

The massive military defeat brought about by gross miscalculations, ineptitude and sheer stupidity should have been enough to bring down the regime. This did not happen because human rights and the welfare of the Iraqi people were not uppermost in the minds of those who have the power to influence the course of events. Iraqis want to make it so that never again will they submit to the rule of dictators or military adventurers. Sooner or later a democratically elected government will be installed. There is no other way if Iraq is to survive.

Such a government will have to give priority to the Kurdish question and the establishment of an autonomous Kurdish region in northern Iraq. The government will then have to turn to the herculean task of rebuilding the country. A Marshall Plan for Iraq will be needed, with the rich Arab countries as well as the major industrialized countries invited to participate. A large transfer of capital will be required at the beginning but in the end it will be the Iraqi people who will have to shoulder the main burden. Only their sacrifices, hard work and discipline will see the country through the difficult post-war years. I am confident they will be equal to the tremendous challenges awaiting them.

I hope that the new Iraq will take its rightful place as a free, democratic and progressive member of the family of nations. It will, I am certain, become a full partner in any security arrangements in the region. After this catastrophic war, Iraqis and Kuwaitis should learn to live in peace as good neighbours and resolve their differences in a manner that will satisfy the legitimate interests of both countries. Tolerance, understanding and forgiveness will be required to heal the wounds of the tragic past.

In this war there have been two principal victims, the peoples of Kuwait and Iraq. The Kuwaiti people have suffered much and I understand their feelings of anger and outrage. Their natural desire for revenge, however, should be controlled for the sake of their own future. They and the Iraqis should learn from the example of the peoples of Europe who have shed the bitterness and enmity of past centuries and are now forging a new destiny for themselves and future generations founded on shared values and common interests. The Iraqis and Kuwaitis can do no less.

The people of Iraq cannot be held responsible or accountable for the crimes of the regime in charge. If the United States can help in establishing democracy in Iraq and in restoring to the Palestinians their basic rights, then all will be forgotten and forgiven. Otherwise the hostility most Arabs feel towards the US will continue to fester with incalculable consequences for the stability and security of the region.

Arab members of the coalition must spare no effort to persuade their US allies to deal seriously and without delay with the Iraqi situation and the Arab–Israeli conflict. The US is indebted to them for their support and active participation in the war against Iraq and they should use the reservoir of goodwill they have accumulated to advance the cause of justice and peace in Iraq and in the Holy Land.

They should also remember that, with the elimination of Iraq's deterrent power, they must create a new Arab military capability to ensure the peace and security of the region and defend the Arab homeland against any potential aggressor.

In spite of repeated US and Allied statements that the quarrel was not with the Iraqi people but with Saddam Hussein, the war resulted in the destruction of Iraq while the regime remained intact. Neither the liberation of Kuwait, nor the protection of US interests in the region, can ever justify the scale and brutality of the onslaught on Iraq.

When Bush was elected to the presidency, many Arabs were happy to see the end of the virulently anti-Arab Reagan–Schultz administration. We were hopeful that the new team of Bush and Baker would seriously tackle the Arab–Israeli conflict in an impartial, even-handed manner. Whatever goodwill the administration had enjoyed in the Arab world quickly disappeared as a result of the Gulf war. If the US wishes to protect its long-term interests in the region, it will have to regain the trust of the Arab people. The first important test will be the speed and manner with which the Bush administration deals with the Iraqi and Palestinian situations.

3

Human Rights, the United Nations, and Weapons of Mass Destruction

Excerpts from a speech delivered in May 1993 at the Rajiv Gandhi Foundation in New Delhi

WE LIVE IN A WORLD characterized by abject poverty of the many and unbridled consumerism by the few. A world which is being strangled by overpopulation and ecological disasters. A world where rampant and resurgent tribalism is getting out of control, manifesting itself in nationalistic delusions of grandeur, racism and religious zealotry. In pursuit of ambitious and misguided self-interest, wars are unleashed, murders are committed, genocidal acts are perpetrated, ethnic cleansing is practised and collective punishment is used as a means to oppress and intimidate millions of human beings. Hovering above all the carnage and brutality engulfing the world is the ever-present threat of a nuclear holocaust made more menacing by the danger of uncontrollable proliferation of weapons of mass destruction. The twin objectives of elimination and non-proliferation of nuclear weapons must be pursued simultaneously. One cannot come before the other. They must proceed closely together. It is no use insisting on practical and concrete measures in dealing with one and being satisfied with exhortations and expressions of hope in dealing with the other. As long as some states wish to maintain their nuclear arsenal and improve their ability to produce, stockpile and further develop nuclear technology, other states will go on trying to acquire weapons of mass destruction, especially those who do not enjoy the protection of a great power nuclear umbrella. Non-proliferation without real progress in total elimination is not feasible.

Central to any new world order is a strengthened and revitalized United Nations. The present Charter is based on certain assumptions which sadly have proven to be illusory. Member states have undertaken to faithfully fulfil their obligations and abide by the principles enshrined in the Charter and refrain from any actions incompatible therewith. But the record shows that over the years there have been serious, continuous and systematic violations of these obligations which have gone unheeded and unpunished. When the Cold War ended there was renewed hope that at long last the Security Council would act with speed and vigour. That hope has been dashed. The performance of the Security Council, so far, has been erratic and uninspiring. At times it has acted boldly but often it has seemed squeamish and hesitant. It has been, on many occasions, uneven and selective in its response to violations of the Charter. In its haste it has sometimes adopted decisions of doubtful legal validity while at other times it has procrastinated and delayed when speedy action was required. The Security Council has also been used as a cover to attain geopolitical objectives which had nothing to do with the Charter. As a result, demands for Charter revision are growing. It is felt that such revisions, in the light of the experiences acquired during the sixty-five years of trial and error, are long overdue. Revision, however, is a long, laborious process. For the time being we have to manage with what we have. Fortunately the Charter is not a rigid document; it is flexible enough to enable the United Nations to act as a dynamic instrument of peaceful change. Nowhere has this been more evident than in the way the UN became actively engaged in the fight against colonialism and apartheid. This historic endeavour was crowned with success in spite of the fierce and stubborn opposition of some powerful UN members, especially in the early years.

What has been achieved in accelerating the process of national liberation and independence can be duplicated in the field of human rights. The time has come to make human rights a central concern of the UN, on a par with the preservation of international peace and security. There is no greater danger to world peace and stability now than the continued violation of human rights. For far too long the denial of human rights has been justified on the grounds that priority should be given to combating poverty, disease and illiteracy, as though economic and social reform is incompatible with freedom and the scrupulous respect for fundamental human rights. Recent changes in the world have shown that, far from impeding economic and social progress, respect for human rights provides the impetus for advancement.

I propose that the Charter provisions dealing with threats to peace and acts of aggression should be used to confront gross violations of human rights. The Security Council should use whenever necessary the coercive and enforcement measures envisaged in Chapter VII of the Charter. It goes without saying that this should be done with fairness and evenhandedness. Playing politics with human rights and using different criteria and scales in dealing with similar problems will erode whatever credibility the United Nations still has. The Security Council should entrust the Secretary General with the task of monitoring and reporting on serious infringements of human rights anywhere in the world. Authority should be given to him to send fact-finding missions. Any state refusing to co-operate with such missions would face punitive action. Non-compliance with Security Council decisions to put an end to human rights abuses would lead to the imposition of sanctions and other measures which might include, if necessary, the use of force. Thus Chapter VII with its elaborate procedures would become an instrument not only for ending threats to peace and resisting aggression but also for eliminating serious abuses of human rights wherever and whenever they occur. We have seen what tragic consequences the endless delays and prevarications have had in Bosnia. This must not happen again.

If what is being proposed is considered an infringement of national sovereignty, then well and good. Countless crimes have been committed and are still being committed in the name of sovereignty. No state should be allowed to use sovereignty as a shield to prevent and frustrate international efforts to alleviate the suffering of millions of victims of crimes against human rights.

Regarding the peace-keeping functions of the United Nations, the Secretary General should have at his disposal adequate forces able to be speedily deployed in any trouble-spot in the world. This can be done by implementing Article 43 of the Charter, which calls for the conclusion of special agreements for making available, on call, armed forces to implement Security Council decisions.

While the conclusion of such agreements would be a step forward and might conceivably deter potential aggressors, it would not be entirely satisfactory. The ideal solution would be for the UN to have a fully equipped standing army manned by volunteers from all over the world. The problems will be enormous and the financial burdens great. For the time being we will have to be content with the resurrection of the military staff committee provided for in Article 47 of the Charter, and proceed step by step towards the goal of creating what would be an international police force or a fire brigade able to be speedily deployed without dependence on the goodwill of this or that great power. The Secretary General is faced with the dilemma of rising expectations which he cannot satisfy with the means at his disposal. He is alternately praised and blamed, but unless he is given the authority and the means, he will not be able to discharge his duties properly.

4

Iraq's Route to a Democratic Future

Article published in the *Financial Times*, 3 March 2003

POST-CONFLICT IRAQ, rather than the conflict itself, has become the focus of global attention. Two options dominate current thinking: US military rule, or a government in exile. Both are flawed and counter-productive. The former is oblivious to a vibrant Iraqi nationalism; the latter ignores the aspirations of massive anti-Ba'athist forces inside the country.

This is the reason I have rejected offers to take a leading part in the arrangements for the post-Saddam era. Last week, Jalal Talabani, leader of the Patriotic Union of Kurdistan, invited me to join the leadership of the Iraqi opposition. I declined for three reasons. First, I have serious doubts about the legitimacy of such a group or its representative nature. Second, any body formed by such a group would have only advisory responsibilities during the transitional period, not executive ones. Serving as an advisory body attached to a US military administration would be damaging and unacceptable. Third, I have reservations about the group's structure and membership. Hence my surprise to learn on Friday that I had been elected to the six-man leadership committee. This is a portent of how selection may go through without due process of information and consultation.

Together with a group of prominent liberal, secular Iraqi figures, I issued an appeal last month urging Saddam Hussein to relinquish power in order to avert a catastrophic armed conflict and spare the Iraqi people the ravages of war. We called for the removal of the authoritarian regime and its replacement with an Iraqi civilian administration, not military rule, to manage the affairs of the nation during a transitional period, hoped to be no more than two years. This provisional government of qualified technocrats should work under the guidance of a sovereign council whose members would be chosen after consultations conducted by the United Nations with Iraqis of all political persuasions.

Most Iraqis reject the imposition of a government from outside. Iraqi nationalism is still a vibrant force to reckon with. A vast majority inside the country, which has borne the brunt of Mr Hussein's oppression, must and can be consulted before any authority is installed in Baghdad. A narrow-based government in exile would be disruptive. Reliable surveys indicate strong antipathy towards a government "parachuted" in from abroad.

The principal tasks of the interim administration should be to maintain law and order, defend the unity and territorial integrity of Iraq, provide essential services, revive the economy, and prepare for elections. Immediate steps would be required to enable the people to engage freely in political activity, such as the formation of political parties. The interim administration should enact an electoral law based on universal adult suffrage for the election, under international supervision, of a constituent assembly to draft a constitution. The constitution should contain guarantees for fundamental human rights, provide for periodic elections and the peaceful transfer of power, and ensure the subordination of the military to civilian government. The rule of law must be guaranteed under an independent judicial system. It must prohibit torture and summary execution, degrading or inhuman punishment, arbitrary arrest and other atrocities from which the Iraqi people have suffered for many decades.

The draft constitution should be submitted to a referendum under international supervision. Only then could elections be held for the first genuinely democratic government in Iraq's modern history. This government would have to deal with many problems, such as reversing the effects of political, ethnic and sectarian oppression and upholding the principle of Iraqi identity and citizenship. Pluralism and tolerance rather than segmentation are the answer. The government would have to agree with the representatives of the Kurdish people about the system under which the Kurds would live in a united Iraq. Indeed, it should endeavour to satisfy the legitimate aspirations of all ethnic and religious groups.

Gradually, the government would deal with debts and reparations so that Iraq could rebuild its free-market economy, providing the incentives, security and confidence for investors. It would have to pursue a sound oil policy, one that contributed to the reconstruction of Iraq, and co-operate with other, especially oil-producing, nations to minimize the fluctuation of oil prices. The government would also have to take a forthright stand in supporting the aspirations of the Palestinians to establish an independent and viable state in the West Bank and Gaza.

I am optimistic about the future. Although some regimes have oppressed sections of the population, the peoples of Iraq have always lived in peace and harmony. What differentiates them is not ethnic origins, or their religious or sectarian affiliations, but their political beliefs and aspirations. Among the Shi'ites, Sunnis and Kurds one will find socialists, capitalists, communists, nationalists, religious fundamentalists and secularists. With the spread of modern education and intermarriage, Iraqis have learnt the virtue of tolerance without which no democratic system can survive.

The writer was foreign minister in the government deposed by Saddam Hussein in 1968

5

An Essay on Palestine

Written in 1994 and brought up to date

Introduction

THE CONFLICT IN PALESTINE arose because the Zionist movement sought to establish by force a predominantly, if not an exclusively, Jewish state in a country overwhelmingly Arab in population, land ownership, language and culture. For a better part of the 20th century the Arab people of Palestine, Muslims and Christians alike, tried desperately to save their country from this Zionist onslaught. Thousands lost their lives and millions have been made refugees. The conquest of Palestine was completed in 1967 but the conflict has continued because of the refusal of the Palestinian people to surrender their right to their ancestral homeland. Their struggle for survival will continue and will not fade away.

For years, successive Israeli governments refused to negotiate with the Palestinians or recognize them. When at long last, thanks to the Intifada, the Israelis agreed to face the Palestinians at the negotiation table, they imposed the stiffest conditions and demanded sweeping concessions. Most of the Israeli demands were met and an agreement was concluded between Israel and the Palestinian leadership which was formally ratified by the Israeli Parliament. This agreement is now in jeopardy because the present Israeli government is reneging on the commitments made and is trying to establish new facts on the ground that will effectively pre-empt future negotiations.

The people of Palestine are now ready to live in peace with their Israeli neighbours in an independent state of their own, in a small area of Palestine where they make up 95 percent of the population. They cannot and will not accept anything less.

One of the main reasons this conflict has persisted for so long is the almost blind and unquestioning support Israel has received from the United States over the years. The alliance between Israel and the United States is justified on grounds of strategic interests, common beliefs and shared values. I can think of no two countries more dissimilar than Israel and the United States. One is an exclusivist theocratic state where religion and race play a crucial role in determining the status of those who live within its borders, and whose laws and policies are openly designed to give preferential treatment to one segment of the population, while minorities are continuously harassed and intimidated. The other is an open and egalitarian society which welcomes, indeed thrives, on racial, ethnic and religious diversity, whose constitution explicitly prohibits the establishment of an official religion and any form of institutionalized discrimination on grounds of race, religion and ethnic origin. The alliance, far from being beneficial to the United States, has seriously undermined American interests in the Arab World and delayed the settlement of a conflict which has caused so much misery and suffering.

My purpose in writing this paper is to recall for non-Arab readers the basic facts of this historic conflict, which are in danger of being lost or forgotten in the flood of distortions and misrepresentations that portray the Palestinians as the aggressors, and the Zionist invaders as the innocent victims.

The Conquest of Palestine: First Phase, 1897–1948

1. Historical and Legal Claims

The conquest of Palestine began at the first Zionist congress which was convened in Basle, Switzerland, in August 1897 by Theodor Herzl, the founder of Zionism. A programme was adopted advocating the building of Jewish settlements in Palestine, the mobilization of Jewish support all over the world and the strengthening of Jewish national consciousness, with the ultimate aim of establishing a Jewish state in Palestine. The whole Zionist doctrine is based upon the Jewish historical connection with

Palestine. What are the facts of this historical connection? The first fact to emerge from an objective study of history is that Palestine has never been an exclusively Jewish country. There were people inhabiting that country long before the Jews set foot in it and the same people remained in the country after the destruction of the Jewish state, which was established only in a small part of Palestine. It is not as though the ancient Hebrew patriarchs led their people into an empty and desolate land. There is nothing unique or special about the connection existing between the Jews and Palestine. Other peoples, mainly of Semitic stock, lived for a much longer period of time in Palestine. Far from being an unbroken connection, the physical relationship of the Jews with Palestine has been sporadic and fragmentary and was of insignificant duration in the long history of that country. Zionism draws its inspiration from a belief in the exclusiveness and separateness of the Jews, "the chosen people". In the words of Arnold Toynbee in his address to the American Council for Judaism, Philadelphia, in May 1961:

> At bottom, Zionism and anti-Semitism are expressions of an identical point of view. The assumption underlying both ideologies is that it is impossible for Jews and non-Jews to grow together into a single community, and that therefore a physical separation is the only practical way out. The watchword of anti-Semitism is "Back to medieval apartheid"; the watchword of Zionism is "Back to the medieval ghetto". All the far-flung ghettos in the world are to be gathered into one patch of soil in Palestine to create a single consolidated ghetto there.

There is undoubtedly a strong spiritual relationship between Palestine and the Jewish faith, but such a relationship – which exists in equal if not greater measure for Christianity and Islam – is not a valid basis for political or territorial claims.

Initially the Zionists had to be content with settlement and land purchase. Then came many abortive attempts to enlist the support of the Ottoman government, the sovereign power in Palestine, for the establishment of a Jewish National Home. Their great opportunity came with the outbreak of the First World War, when the Ottoman Empire entered it on the side of the Central Powers (Germany, Austria and

Bulgaria). Chaim Weizman, who assumed the leadership of the Zionist movement in Britain, was an eminent scientist who had migrated from his native Russia at the turn of the century. He was able to obtain from the British Government in 1917 the famous Balfour Declaration, which was issued after lengthy negotiations on 2 November 1917 in the form of a letter from the British Foreign Secretary, Arthur Balfour to Lord Rothschild. The text read:

> His Majesty's Government view with favour the establishment in Palestine of a national home for the Jewish people, and will use their best endeavours to facilitate the achievement of this object, it being clearly understood that nothing shall be done which may prejudice the civil and religious rights of existing non-Jewish communities in Palestine, or the rights and political status enjoyed by Jews in any other country.

The Balfour Declaration ignored the fact that Palestine had at the time an overwhelming Arab majority. In the numerous memoranda which Dr Weizman presented to the British Government prior to the issuance of the Declaration, no mention whatever was made of the Arabs of Palestine who, at the time, made up about 93 percent of the total population. The distinguished Irish author and journalist, Mr Erskine Childers, commented as follows on the negotiations that eventually led to the issuance of the Balfour Declaration:

> Only because of the insistence of influential non-Zionist British Jews, and the prophetic anxieties of a few British officials, did the final Declaration even refer invisibly to the Arabs. Its references in all their breathtaking euphemism are well known. The phrase was "the existing non-Jewish communities in Palestine". The word "Arab" did not appear. The "non-Jewish" suggested that whoever these people were, they must be an insignificant number relative to the Jews; they could in no way be homogeneous communities (in the plural); and must have no distinct cultural or national character by which to be named. No Westerner reading the Balfour Declaration, and ignorant of the facts about Palestine, could possibly have gathered that a National Home was being promised to Zionism in a land

already inhabited by a distinctively Arab, historically rooted, overwhelming majority of human beings.

The Balfour Declaration ran contrary to previous promises given to Sharif Hussein of Mecca by the British Government. In 1915 the British Government had, through its representative in Cairo, promised complete independence with few exceptions for the Arab territories under Ottoman rule, including Palestine. These promises led to the Arab Revolt against Turkey in 1916, which contributed greatly to Britain's military victory in the Near East. Once the war had ended it became clear that the Allies had no intention of fulfilling their promises to the Arabs. They proceeded to implement the Sykes–Picot agreement of 1916, which divided the Arab provinces of the Ottoman Empire into British and French spheres of influence. Before the end of the war the new Bolshevik rulers of Russia had published the secret documents of the Tsarist Foreign Office, among which were the Sykes–Picot agreement as well as the Balfour Declaration. When Sharif Hussein, at the head of the Arab Revolt, inquired about these documents from his British allies, they denied their existence and dismissed the whole thing as German war propaganda.

At the Peace Conference in Paris in 1919, in order to meet the objections of President Wilson of the United States, whose famous Fourteen Points included the right of self-determination and independence of all the subject peoples of the defeated powers, a refined version of the "White Man's Burden" called the Mandate system was incorporated in Article 22 of the Covenant of the League of Nations, which contained the following paragraph:

> ... that certain communities formerly belonging to the Turkish Empire had reached a stage of development where their existence as independent nations could be provisionally recognized, subject to the rendering of administrative advice and assistance by a Mandatory until such time as they are able to stand alone, and that the wishes of these communities must be a principal consideration in the selection of the Mandatory.

The Mandate for Palestine which was given to Britain included in its text the Balfour Declaration. This in itself was a clear violation of Article 22 cited above. Balfour himself admitted the incompatibility of his declaration with the Covenant of the League of Nations. This is what he said in 1922:

> The contradiction between the letter of the Covenant and the policy of the Allies is even more flagrant in the case of the independent nation of Syria. For in Palestine we do not propose even to go through the form of consulting the wishes of the present inhabitants of the country. ... The four great powers are committed to Zionism and Zionism, be it right or wrong, good or bad, is of far profounder importance than the desires and prejudices of the 700,000 Arabs who now inhabit that ancient land. In my opinion that is right.
>
> What I have never been able to understand is how it can be harmonized with the Covenant. ... In fact, so far as Palestine is concerned the Powers have made no statement of fact that is not admitted wrong, and no declaration of policy which, at least in the letter, they have not always intended to violate.

Also, Winston Churchill as Colonial Secretary admitted that the Balfour Declaration was incompatible with the spirit of the Mandate system, when he said in Parliament in 1921:

> The cause of unrest in Palestine and the only cause, arises from the Zionist movement and from our promises and pledges to it. ... The difficulty about this promise of a National Home for the Jews in Palestine is that it conflicts with our regular policy of consulting the wishes of the people in the Mandated territories and of giving them representative institutions as soon as they are fitted for them.

Lord Grey (Foreign Secretary 1908–16) was even more frank when he said in the House of Lords in 1923:

> A Zionist home undoubtedly means or implies a Zionist Government over the district in which the home is placed, and if ninety-three percent of the population are Palestine Arabs, I do not see how you can establish other than an Arab Government without prejudice to their civil rights. That one sentence of the Balfour Declaration seems to me to involve,

without overstating the case, very great difficulty of fulfilment.

From the outset the Arab inhabitants of Palestine rejected the Mandate and realized the dangerous implications of unrestricted Jewish immigration. They had no illusions about the ultimate aim of the Zionist movement, which was to establish an exclusively Jewish State in the whole of Palestine. From 1920 to 1948, while Britain governed Palestine as mandatory power, the Jewish population of Palestine rose from 7 percent to more than 30 percent. For thirty years the Arabs of Palestine waged a heroic but unequal fight against Britain. It is difficult to describe the anguish and fear under which the Arabs of Palestine lived during the period of the Mandate. They saw before their own eyes the character of their country transformed beyond recognition and their existence as a separate and distinct community threatened by an overwhelming tide that was inexorably advancing to engulf them and destroy their national life. They repeatedly asked the British Government, as well as the League of Nations, that a plebiscite be held in Palestine under effective international guarantees to determine the wishes of the people. But, throughout the whole period of the Mandate, the people of Palestine were never once allowed to express, in freedom and security, their desires as to their future destiny. The British Government tried to achieve the impossible, to allow unrestricted Jewish immigration and facilitate the establishment of a Jewish National Home in Palestine and at the same time to ensure "that nothing shall be done which may prejudice the civil rights" of the Arabs. In 1939, on the eve of the Second World War, the British Government came closest to recognizing the justice of the Palestinian cause by issuing a White Paper providing for the establishment of an independent state in Palestine where both Arabs and Jews would share authority. Immigration was limited to 75,000 during the subsequent five years, after which no further Jewish immigration would be allowed without the acquiescence of the Arabs.

The Second World War began soon thereafter and the full implementation of the White Paper was postponed. During the war the Zionists were active and exploited to the full the emotional impact that the persecution of the Jews by Nazi Germany had in the West and especially in the United States. They adopted a resolution in May 1942 that for the first time openly called for the establishment of a Jewish State in Palestine. When the

German threat to the Middle East receded after 1942, the Zionists began to wage guerilla warfare against the British in Palestine. Numerous murders and acts of terrorism were committed by terrorist gangs led by Begin, Shamir and others. When the war ended in 1945, the situation seemed ripe to fulfil the Zionist dream. In the United States, Congress and the new President, Harry Truman, were strongly sympathetic to the Zionists. In Britain, Prime Minister Winston Churchill, an ardent Zionist supporter, was determined to help in the establishment of a Jewish State in Palestine, although many of his Conservative colleagues adhered strictly to the White Paper policy of non-partition. The Labour Party, avidly pro-Zionist, had supported at its conference at the end of 1944 the creation of a Jewish State in Palestine.

At the end of July 1945, the Labour Party came to power in Britain, and the new Foreign Secretary, Ernest Bevin, was entrusted with the task of dealing with the Palestine problem. He was a man of great integrity and vision and he soon realized that the unqualified support of his party for Zionist aims was wrong. He tried to be even-handed and fair, and was as a result vehemently attacked by the Zionists and their supporters. Withstanding these attacks, he came under great pressure from the United States. Britain emerged from the war weak and almost bankrupt. It needed American assistance and was in no position to deal alone with such an intractable problem as that of Palestine. The British Government therefore decided to refer the whole matter to the General Assembly of the United Nations.

When the Palestine Question was discussed for the first time in the General Assembly in 1947, the Arab delegations declared that Palestine was ready for independence and that, if independence was not immediately granted, the people should be asked to determine their future in a free and internationally supervised plebiscite. The General Assembly failed to approve that proposal thanks to the combined pressure and influence of the United States and the Soviet Union which, at that time, was an enthusiastic supporter of Zionism.

Later that year, a proposal to refer the matter to the International Court of Justice for an advisory opinion on whether the partitioning of a country against the will of its people was compatible with the United Nations Charter and the Covenant of the League of Nations, under which Palestine was administered as a Mandate Territory, was similarly turned down. The General Assembly created a Special Committee with the task of recommending a solution to the problem. After visiting the area the Committee presented majority and minority reports. The majority report proposed the partition of Palestine into an Arab and a Jewish State with Jerusalem and its suburbs as a "Corpus Separatum" under international authority. The minority report proposed granting independence to an undivided Palestine. Tremendous pressure was exerted on some small countries by the United States to ensure the adoption of the partition plan by the General Assembly, on 29 November 1947. The Arabs rejected the partition resolution, which gave more than half the land of Palestine to the Jews despite the Arabs outnumbering them by a ratio of 2 to 1. The Zionists on the other hand declared with a great deal of fanfare their acceptance of partition, but proceeded immediately to nullify it in accordance with a plan drawn up from the earliest days of Zionism and perfected and brought up to date over the years.

From the very beginning, the Zionists had to face the dilemma of the existence of a sizeable Arab population in Palestine. They had to resolve the problem of what to do with the Arab inhabitants when the time came for the complete occupation of the country, because they realized that as long as the Palestine Arab community remained intact and in possession of its land, the Zionist programme could not be implemented. The only way was to uproot the inhabitants and forcibly transfer them to other places.

After the Mandate, various schemes of population exchange were proposed by the Zionists and their supporters. It was clear, however, that schemes for compelling the transfer of the Arab population outside Palestine could not be implemented without force. As a prerequisite for the eventual expulsion of the Arab inhabitants of Palestine, the Zionists had to prevent at all costs the establishment of an independent Arab state in the country. This explains why to this day neither Labour nor Likud have accepted the idea of a viable and fully independent Palestine.

As a first step numerous Jewish settlements were strategically established in the midst of predominantly Arab areas. Although these settlements were ostensibly devoted to agriculture and farming, they were in fact formidable defensive and offensive bastions which played an important role in 1967 and 1947 in preventing the Arabs of Palestine from establishing themselves in a contiguous and unified area, and in helping the Zionist offensive, in April and May 1948, to dislodge the Arabs from territories which under the partition plan were allotted to them. Thirty-three such Jewish settlements were located in the area that was to form part of the Arab state under partition, and as early as October 1947, that is, while the Partition Plan was still being debated in the General Assembly, it was decided to hold on to them. The implication of this decision was that the Zionists had decided, beforehand, and while the outcome of the debate on the partition plan was still in doubt, to prevent the creation of an Arab state in Palestine by holding on to these thirty-three strategic settlements all over the area which was to be part of the Arab state under the partition plan.

2. The war of 1948

During the Second World War the Zionists prepared for the military offensive they planned to launch at the termination of the British mandate over Palestine. They stored large amounts of weapons, trained thousands of their youth and, with their vast and unlimited financial resources, were able to equip a powerful army in Palestine and a large and effective propaganda machine outside. When the partition resolution was adopted the Zionist armed forces in Palestine swung into action, in accordance with a well-prepared plan. The plan had two phases: the first was to consolidate immediate control over the area allotted by the partition plan to the Jews and, when that was done, to occupy as much territory as they could lay their hands on in the areas allotted to the Arabs. The Zionists had no intention whatever to abide loyally by the partition plan. Thus the large Arab city of Jaffa was occupied as well as the whole of western Galilee during April and early May 1948. By that time the Zionist offensive was gathering momentum and it became clear that the Arab inhabitants of Palestine were no match for the highly organized, well-financed, well-armed and well-equipped Zionist forces.

The intervention of the Arab states was in response to the repeated appeals of the Arab inhabitants of Palestine. It became clear by the time the British completed their withdrawal from Palestine on 14 May 1948 that without outright military intervention the Arab population was threatened with annihilation and the whole of Palestine was in danger of falling under Zionist occupation. The intervention of the forces of the Arab states in Palestine on 15 May 1948, therefore, should be looked upon as a salvage operation rather than a military offensive. It helped to stem the tide of Zionist advance in many areas and saved what remained of Palestine. The defensive character of the military operations carried out by the forces of the Arab states can be seen from the fact that all of them took place in the area originally allotted to the Arabs under the partition plan, and they were undertaken solely for the purpose of defending the population of this area from the advancing Zionist armies.

At first the armies of the Arab states were moderately successful, and so in order to avert a possible Israeli defeat, the two superpowers were able to obtain a resolution from the Security Council calling for an immediate ceasefire. The Arabs accepted the resolution in good faith but the Israelis seized the opportunity to replenish their army and gain massive military help from the Communist countries. When fighting was resumed four weeks after the ceasefire, the Security Council adopted a resolution under Chapter VII of the Charter on 15 July, affirming the fundamental principle on which the truce in Palestine rested, that no military or political advantage should accrue to either side and that no party was permitted to violate the truce on the grounds of undertaking reprisals. Israel however repeatedly violated the ceasefire and occupied large areas of Arab land. In response to their repeated violations, the Security Council adopted three further Resolutions on 19 October, 4 November and 29 December 1948, calling upon Israel to withdraw from the conquered areas, but these were disregarded and Israel has kept its conquests to this day. When it is realized that these resolutions were adopted under Chapter VII of the Charter with its elaborate coercive and punitive provisions, one must marvel at the influence and sway Israel exercised in the United Nations and over the great powers in particular.

While the fighting was going on, hundreds of thousands of Palestinians left their homes for fear of atrocities, or were physically driven out. Their right to repatriation or compensation was clearly upheld in General Assembly Resolution 194 (III) 1948, which was adopted by an overwhelming majority of the members of the United Nations and has been reaffirmed numerous times since. Perhaps the best defence of that

Appendix 5

resolution was made by Mr Dean Rusk, former Secretary of State, who was a member of the United States delegation, in a meeting of the First Committee of the United Nations General Assembly at its 3rd session in Paris in December 1948, when he said:

> We could not accept the proclamation of peace as a prerequisite for the return of the refugees and [we] hope the assembly would not make the condition. ... They [the refugees] need not wait for a proclamation of peace. ... These unhappy people should not be made a pawn in the negotiations for a final settlement.

Needless to say, that resolution remains unimplemented. Israel has openly stated on numerous occasions that it has no intention of readmitting any Palestinians to their homeland. The expulsion of the Arab population of Palestine, which had been envisaged from the earliest days of Zionism and planned throughout the period of the Mandate, was thus partially achieved in 1948 through outright military action.

In 1948 the General Assembly established the "Palestine Conciliation Commission", consisting of three members, France, Turkey and the United States. The Commission convened a conference in Lausanne and at first achieved moderate success by inducing the Arab and Israeli delegations to sign a Protocol on 12 May 1949, by which both parties accepted the partition plan of 1947 as the basis for discussion leading to a peaceful resolution of the conflict. Israel of course had no intention of relinquishing any territory conquered in 1948 and the Protocol remained a dead letter. The Conciliation Commission, favouring Israel by the very nature of its composition, made only half-hearted efforts to urge Israel to abide by its commitments. In 1950 the United States, Britain and France issued a statement which became known as the Tripartite Declaration, in which the three powers pledged themselves to act jointly to prevent any attempt to change the armistice lines by force. That declaration proved to be a grotesque fraud when, in 1956, two of its signatories, France and Britain, attacked Egypt in collusion with Israel.

From 1949 to 1967 the shaky peace between Israel and its Arab neighbours, which was governed by the Armistice Agreements, was characterized by violent and frequent Israeli incursions and attacks, against Syria, Jordan and Egypt across the armistice lines. Many of these attacks were condemned by the Security Council but to no avail.

These Armistice Agreements, signed after the end of hostilities in 1949, imposed upon the signatories certain obligations, and established demilitarized zones on which no military forces might be stationed, and in respect of which the question of sovereignty was held in abeyance. Moreover, Mixed Armistice Commissions were established to deal with any complaints or infringements of the provisions of the Armistice Agreements. The Israeli authorities from the very beginning systematically absorbed the demilitarized zones. So-called agricultural settlements which were in fact military outposts manned and commanded by officers and soldiers of the Israeli armed forces, were established in the demilitarized zones, in clear violation of the Armistice Agreements. Fortifications and military installations were constructed and Israeli military and paramilitary units have frequently entered these areas contrary to the provisions of the Armistice Agreements. Israel consistently refused to cooperate with the United Nations to implement these agreements. The Mixed Armistice Commissions were boycotted by the Israeli authorities and the local machinery established to deal with violations of the Armistice Agreements was paralyzed as a result.

The Conquest of Palestine: Second Phase, 1967

1. Background

The accession of Lyndon Johnson, an avowed Zionist sympathizer, to the Presidency of the United States in November 1963 dealt a severe blow to Arab–American relations. Among the first acts of the new Administration were a considerable increase in weapons sales to Israel and a suspension of wheat shipments to Egypt which for many years had been dependent on the US for 50 percent of its wheat imports. This led Nasser to adopt an increasingly hostile attitude towards the United States, attacking its involvement in Vietnam and intensifying pressure on the two principal US allies in the Arab World, Saudi Arabia and Jordan. Johnson's response was to increase substantially military and economic aid to Israel as he denounced Nasser as the principal enemy of American and Western interests in the region. From then on, Israel's actions were all calculated to provoke an armed confrontation in which Egypt would be defeated and humiliated. The military alliance Nasser concluded with Syria in

November 1966 increased the possibilities of such a confrontation and, in the early part of 1967, all of Israel's verbal abuse and threats of military reprisals were directed against Syria. It became clear that Israel hoped to draw Egypt into armed conflict by concentrating all its efforts against Syria, the ally that Nasser could not control but was pledged to defend in the event of outside attack.

During the early part of May 1967, information reached Cairo that Israel was about to launch a large-scale attack on Syria. This information, which was relayed by the Russians, may well have been planted deliberately by Israeli intelligence. Syria appealed to Egypt for help and Nasser responded by ordering Egyptian troops to take up positions on the armistice lines with Israel. In so doing he had to face a difficult problem. The United Nations Emergency Force (UNEF) troops stationed on the Egyptian side of the armistice lines since 1957 had to be withdrawn to make room for the Egyptian forces. This action gave rise to a widespread assumption in the West that the Arabs and particularly President Nasser were responsible for starting the Arab–Israeli War of 1967. This is not so. It was Israel which planned and deliberately unleashed that war, as can be shown by the following facts.

When UNEF was created in 1957, in the aftermath of the Suez War, it was on the understanding that UN troops would be deployed with the approval of the nations concerned on both sides of the armistice lines separating Egypt and Israel. Israel refused to have any troops stationed on its side, invoking the right of sovereignty. Egypt, on the other hand, accepted the presence of UNEF on its soil, but in so doing did not surrender its sovereign rights over its own territories. In 1967 President Nasser, invoking the right of sovereignty as Israel had done ten years earlier, requested the removal of UNEF from Egyptian territory. The legal right of Egypt to make such a request was incontestable, and was upheld by Secretary General U Thant and the overwhelming majority of UN members. President Nasser sent Egyptian troops to take up positions previously held by UNEF. As he believed that the security of his country was threatened by Israel, he closed the straits of Tiran, which lay exclusively in Egyptian waters, as a necessary precautionary measure. Under international law and the UN Charter, Egypt was fully justified in taking this action. Israel found in Nasser's action the pretext and

Appendix 5

opportunity it had been waiting for to launch an attack on Egypt and put into effect a meticulously planned military operation which had been refined and brought up to date over the years with the object of inflicting a decisive defeat on the Arabs and occupying what was left of Palestine. As a first step Israel declared that the closing of the straits of Tiran was a *casus belli* and threatened to go to war to uphold the right of Israeli ships to sail unhindered in Egyptian territorial waters. Secretary General U Thant, in an effort to defuse the crisis, proposed what he called a breathing spell to give time for the mediatory efforts undertaken by many countries. During that breathing spell, Egypt would undertake not to search non-Israeli ships going to Israel provided they did not carry oil or strategic materials. Egypt and the Arab states accepted the Secretary General's proposal, and gave him assurances that they had no desire to go to war or initiate any kind of hostile military action against Israel unless they were attacked first. Israel on the other hand demanded complete surrender by Egypt of its sovereign rights in its territorial waters. The Israeli government based its position on a promise given by the US and others in 1957 that the free passage of Israeli ships through the Gulf of Aqaba would be guaranteed. Egypt was not party to this undertaking and was never consulted when it was given. Obviously Egypt could not be bound by an understanding between two foreign powers regarding navigation in its own territorial waters.

The dispute was brought before the United Nations Security Council, and while the debates were going on the United States informed Egypt that they would not tolerate any side starting hostilities and cautioned Abdul Nasser against precipitate action, strongly advising him to accept the Secretary General's plan. At the same time, on 26 May, Lyndon Johnson met Abba Eban, the Israeli Foreign Minister, in secret, and implicitly gave the green light for military action by assuring him that the US would not exert pressure on Israel to withdraw from any territories that might be occupied in the course of an armed conflict with Egypt and other Arab states. The Soviet Union on its part was completely misled by this American deception and advised Egypt against initiating any hostile or belligerent action against Israel. The American assurances given to Egypt were designed to give the Egyptians a false sense of security and prevent them from launching a pre-emptive strike and to give Israel time to complete its military preparations. It was revealed later that the United States gave the Israelis logistical support and supplied them with intelligence information before and during the war.

2. The war of June 1967 and its consequences

After the destruction of the Egyptian Air Force on 5 June 1967, the non-aligned members of the Security Council proposed an immediate ceasefire and the withdrawal of forces behind the Armistice lines. The United States rejected this proposal and submitted a draft resolution calling for a ceasefire only, which was adopted by the Security Council the evening of 6 June. This resolution was a serious departure from United Nations usage. Normally the Security Council determines first the responsibility for the breach of peace and orders the withdrawal of forces back to the point from which hostilities started. That was not done, because the United States refused to link the ceasefire with withdrawal, thereby enabling Israel to keep control of territories which it had been able to occupy. The Security Council continued its meetings and the war did not end until 11 June, when a ceasefire was agreed with Syria and Jordan. The results were catastrophic for the Arabs. The West Bank, Gaza, Sinai and the Golan Heights were occupied by Israel.

Israel has claimed and still claims that its attack on Egypt on the morning of 5 June was an act of self-defence. Preventive war is prohibited under the UN Charter and international law, for the obvious reason that, if allowed, it would give licence to any state to commit aggression. Individual and collective self-defence under Article 51 of the Charter is permitted only to repel an actual outside attack. No such attack occurred against Israel and none was contemplated. So the attack on Egypt on 5 June 1967 which started the Six-Day War could not, by any stretch of the imagination, be regarded as a spontaneous act of self-defence. It was simply and clearly an act of premeditated aggression.

Soon after the war ended it became clear that Israel, elated by its decisive victory, was not going to withdraw from the territories it had occupied, and since the military option was no longer possible, the Arabs had to content themselves with a diplomatic offensive in the United Nations. The Fifth Emergency Special Session of the General Assembly was convened on 19 June 1967, at the request of the Soviet Union, after it became clear that the Security Council would be unable to take meaningful and effective action. Unfortunately the Arab delegations were unsuccessful in their efforts to get a resolution providing for the unconditional withdrawal of Israeli forces from the occupied territories.

Israel contended that such withdrawal would endanger its security, claiming that the Armistice lines separating Israel from its Arab neighbours until the war of 1967 were vulnerable and insecure. The fact of the matter is that until the outbreak of that war Israel had never complained about the vulnerability and insecurity of the Armistice lines. Quite the contrary, it considered them highly satisfactory, and its main aim for eighteen years had been to transform those lines into permanent and recognized frontiers. The Israeli Foreign Minister, Mr Abba Eban, stated the following at the 1428th Meeting of the General Assembly of the United Nations in October 1966 – just eight months before Israel launched its war of aggression in 1967:

> Behind the armistice frontiers established by agreement between Israel and its Arab neighbours in 1949, the national life of sovereign states has become crystallized in an increasingly stable mould. There is some evidence that thoughtful minds in the Middle East are becoming skeptical about threats to change the existing territorial and political structure by armed force. Such threats and the policies concocted to support them, offend the spirit and the letter of the United Nations Charter. They violate bilateral agreements freely negotiated and solemnly signed. Many undermine the central principles of international civility ... for they encounter insuperable obstacles ... in the opposition of the world community to the alteration by aggressive force of legally established and internationally recognized situations. ... We regard the present armistice lines as immune from change without consent.

That policy, so clearly and eloquently stated, was completely reversed a few months later, after Israel attacked Egypt and forced the Arabs to enter a war they were not ready to fight and tried their best to avoid.

During the debates in the General Assembly and the Security Council during the second half of 1967, the overwhelming majority of member states, including Israel's staunchest friends, demanded the withdrawal of Israeli forces from the occupied territories. It was felt that what was needed was the transformation of the armistice lines, of which Mr Eban had spoken with such fondness, into permanent and recognized boundaries. That is why the Latin American draft resolution submitted to the General Assembly, which was supported by the United States and was unopposed by Israel, demanded the urgent withdrawal of all Israeli forces from all the territories occupied during the War of June 1967. The late Mr Arthur Goldberg, representative of the United States, said the following at the 1534th plenary meeting of the General Assembly of 14 July 1967: "One immediate, obvious and imperative step is the disengagement of all forces and the withdrawal of Israeli forces to their own territory" – meaning the territory they held prior to the War of 1967.

The differences of opinion separating members of the United Nations during the General Assembly session in June and July 1967 were not related to the question of withdrawal, on which there was unanimous agreement, but to the other questions dealing with such issues as the end of belligerency, freedom of navigation and mutual recognition. Those differences were finally resolved in Security Council Resolution 242 adopted on 22 November 1967, which flatly rejected Israel's territorial demands and emphasized instead the inadmissibility of territorial acquisition by war. What was the original intent of the framers of the resolution? Such original intent can be found in the statement of the author of the resolution, the late Lord Caradon, British representative, when he said that the resolution reflected fully the policy of his government as clearly enunciated a few weeks earlier by the British Foreign Secretary, the late Mr George Brown, who had stated the following at the 1567th meeting of the General Assembly:

> I should like to repeat what I said when I was here before: Britain does not accept war as a means of settling disputes, nor that a state should be allowed to extend its frontiers as a result of war. This means that Israel must withdraw but equally Israel's neighbours must recognize its right to exist, and it must enjoy security within its frontiers. What we must work for in this area is durable peace, the renunciation of all aggressive designs and an end of all policies which are inconsistent with peace.

Gunnar Jarring, ambassador of Sweden, was appointed a representative of the Secretary General to ensure the implementation of the Resolution. After years of untiring efforts, he failed to persuade Israel to withdraw from the occupied territories.

Besides distorting the meaning and intent of Resolution 242, Israel has completely disregarded two General Assembly resolutions on Jerusalem. It has refused to implement the Security Council resolution on the 1967 refugees, twice affirmed by the General Assembly. It has refused to apply the Geneva Conventions to the inhabitants of the occupied territories in Palestine. It has built hundreds of settlements in the occupied territories in clear violation of international law, and openly annexed Jerusalem and the Golan Heights.

After all these years it is clear that Israel's intransigence and reliance on force and its continual flouting of UN resolutions has paid handsome dividends, while the people of Palestine will be required to pay for years to come the price of their naive belief in justice and fairness and their trust in the United Nations.

Conclusions

In the forty-four years that have elapsed since the conquest of Palestine the Arab position has steadily deteriorated. The Arab–Israeli war of October 1973 had restored to some extent Arab and especially Egyptian self-confidence, but whatever gains were achieved were later squandered by the conclusion of a separate peace between Egypt and Israel. By neutralizing Egypt, Israel was able with impunity to consolidate its control of the West Bank.

Another development which had serious consequences for the Arabs was the emergence of Israel as the only nuclear power in the region. This, in addition to the continued military assistance of the United States, made Israel by far the strongest power in the area. It has become obvious that the Arabs in their present situation would be unable effectively to confront Israel should it revert to its expansionist ambitions. The United States still seems reluctant to exert any real pressure on Israel, and Russia is no longer a serious factor in the Arab–Israeli conflict. Finally, the Arab position was seriously undermined by the elimination of Iraq as a principal regional power and an active player in Middle Eastern affairs. During the long war with Iran, Iraq was able to build, at tremendous cost to its people, a strong military capability that was probably the most credible military deterrent to Israel's crushing military superiority. The elimination of the Iraqi deterrent compelled Jordan to conclude a separate peace treaty, and the Palestinian leadership had to accept the humiliating conditions of the Oslo Agreements.

The fundamental stumbling block to peace, however, has been the stance of successive Israeli governments in according a higher priority to the acquisition of land than to reaching a reasonable accommodation with the Palestinians.

Israel's position could change should a greater number of Israelis awake to the realization that the security of their country cannot be guaranteed by permanently controlling territories inhabited by a hostile population, and that there can be no future for their country without peace with the Arabs – a genuine peace that would enable the Palestinians to live in a viable and fully independent sovereign state.

I am not optimistic about the future. The Arabs and especially the Palestinians are ready for peace but not at any price. It all depends on whether Israel is prepared to relinquish the occupied territories, dismantle the settlements and accept an independent Palestinian state. The conflict of the Arabs with Israel has been and continues to be about territory and nothing else. It is not economic rivalry, nor religious antagonism, nor a clash of ideologies. It certainly is not about Israeli security. I am really astonished that there are still people who believe that Israel's security is threatened by the Arabs. The reverse is true. It is the Arabs who should fear Israel's mighty war machine. Militarily the most powerful state in the region, Israel is the only nuclear power in the Middle East, and enjoys almost unlimited economic, military and political support from the only remaining superpower in the world. How can the Arabs in their present state of weakness and fragmentation ever pose a threat to Israel?

Only time will show whether Israel is more interested in peace than in acquiring territory, and whether Israelis are prepared to live as equal and peaceful neighbours with the Palestinians. The prospects are not very encouraging.

6

Islam and Modernity

Speech delivered in November 2005 to an international conference in Vienna on the theme "Islam in a Pluralistic World", to which the author was invited by the Austrian Foreign Ministry

THIS IS A TOPIC of great international interest and concern. There is widespread apprehension about the future of more than a billion human beings who profess the Islamic faith. Those millions, as Secretary General Kofi Annan has pointed out, do not form one monolithic group or entity. They are of different nationalities and speak different languages, and they adhere to different political ideologies and beliefs. In religious matters they have different sects and schools of theology. In other words, diversity has always been a distinguishing feature of Islam.

But one thing unites all Muslims, and that is their quest for a better life and desire to be effective players in this rapidly changing and shrinking world. In my view this can only be achieved through modernization in all fields. The drive to modernity in the Islamic world is not of recent origin. It began two hundred years ago in Egypt. Let us not forget that what we may call the dark ages of the Muslim world coincided with the Renaissance, the great scientific and cultural revolution in Western Europe. While the European countries made great advances in all fields, the Muslim world fell into a long period of decay and decline. The Muslims needed a shock to wake them up from their long slumber.

This shock was provided by Napoleon's conquest of Egypt in 1798. That confrontation between Europe and the Orient demonstrated the overwhelming superiority of a modern European state and the vulnerability and weakness of the Muslims. It became clear to Mohammed Ali Pasha, the new ruler of Egypt, and to a lesser extent to the Ottoman Sultan, Mahmoud II, that modernization was essential to survival. Modernize or perish. This was the challenge two hundred years ago and it is the challenge today. It is noteworthy that under Mohammed Ali Pasha and his successors and concurrently with the drive to modernity, there arose in Egypt a religious movement led by Jamaluddin Afghani and Mohammed Abduh which proclaimed that modernization was not incompatible with religion, and they offered a more liberal interpretation of the Qur'an and Shari'a law. This quest for modernity spread from Egypt and to a lesser extent Turkey and other Muslim countries, and gradually Muslim societies were being transformed and this drive towards modernity seemed unstoppable.

Unfortunately while this was going on European colonial expansion dominated large parts of the Islamic world, so that by the end of the 19th and beginning of the 20th century almost the entire Muslim world was either directly ruled by European colonial powers or under their influence and tutelage. To many in the Muslim world modernity became synonymous with foreign domination. For some, religion provided an effective instrument in the struggle against colonial rule. Political Islam challenged the secular, nationalist, modernizing and reform-minded governments. Some of these governments were becoming increasingly autocratic and dictatorial and that strengthened the appeal of the religious political parties. The Palestine tragedy further exacerbated the situation. The religious political movements became more radical and were determined to restore Islam in its purest form as an alternative to reformist secular governments, shunning any meaningful contact and dialogue with the rest of the world. These neo-isolationists attracted more attention than the unspectacular and sometimes frustrating effort to move the Muslim world into the 21st century.

I am certain this convergence between religious fanaticism and political isolationism cannot and will not prevail. It is a temporary aberration that will disappear. If we are able to satisfy the legitimate yearning of the Palestinian people for an independent and viable state of their own, and

Appendix 6

when democracy becomes a reality and fundamental human rights are accepted as part of life, then the future will not be as sombre as it now seems.

7

A Lecture on Iraq

Given at St Antony's College, Oxford, November 2005

A GREAT DEAL has been said and written about the conflict in Iraq. The debate will go on for years about the reasons and motives for the invasion of Iraq in 2003, and the subsequent unravelling of the Iraqi state. This is not the subject of my talk today. I leave the past to historians and will confine my remarks to the present and future.

The situation in Iraq is catastrophic. How else can we describe the unprecedented lawlessness and the pervasive sectarian violence which has cost hundreds of thousands of Iraqi lives? The security forces, which have been heavily infiltrated by the militias, armed gangs and death squads, are clearly incapable of restoring peace and order. They are in fact part of the problem. We had further proof of the complicity of the security forces with the militias in the invasion and occupation yesterday of the Ministry of Higher Education and the abduction of scores of academics, government officials and students. Those who are not linked to the militias lack motivation and discipline. Their poor training and inadequate weapons make them easy and frequent targets of the terrorists. It will take time to reorganize them professionally and ensure their undivided loyalty to the Iraqi state.

The government which took office six months ago was hailed as a government of national unity. It is in fact a government of sectarian disunity, racked by suspicion and mistrust among its members. Even within the same groups, there are serious disagreements and occasional armed clashes, as we have seen in Amara recently after the withdrawal of British troops. The government has failed to deal with any of the pressing problems facing the country. The security situation has deteriorated, the shortages in essential services continue, corruption is still rampant, national reconciliation which was the centrepiece of the government's programmes has been frustrated by the uncompromising and maximalist demands of the various political parties and groups. It is doubtful that Prime Minister Nuri Al-Maliki will be able to deliver on his oft-repeated pledge to disarm the militias, since many of his colleagues and supporters in the government have close links with militias and other armed groups including the notorious death squads.

In these, circumstances, the multinational forces will have to bear the primary responsibility for the maintenance of order. Giving the Multinational Force (MNF) a bigger role is opposed, for obvious reasons, by some regional powers, particularly the Iranians, who objected from the beginning to its presence in Iraq because they viewed it as an obstacle to their hegemonic ambitions. This is perfectly understandable from Iran's standpoint. But what is inexplicable is the opposition of some insurgent groups who, while proclaiming that they are fighting against Iranian interference in Iraq, have been pressing for the removal of the only credible barrier to the spread of Iranian influence in the country. Do they not realize that until we have more dependable and better-trained and better-equipped national security forces, the MNF will provide the only guarantee for the preservation of the unity and territorial integrity of Iraq?

When Iraq was officially under occupation in 2003–04, the occupation army was the main problem, but the situation changed under the transitional government of Dr Ibrahim Al-Jaafari. When the sectarian militias were allowed to infiltrate the security services, the main problem was no longer the army of occupation, but the sectarian killing and collapse of law and order. People became aware that a precipitate withdrawal of the MNF would plunge the country into total chaos and anarchy. I realize US and British public opinion will find it difficult to accept more sacrifices, in what seems to be a conflict with no end in sight. I sympathize with their concerns and fears. But what is the alternative? A fragmented Iraq divided into feuding fiefdoms under warlords fighting each other for control of areas rich in natural resources, and supported by neighbours eager to fill the power vacuum created by the withdrawal of the MNF? You can imagine the turmoil that would engulf the whole region. The task of stabilizing Iraq should be an international responsibility and not merely an American one. That is why I believe the time has come to invite other nations from Europe, Asia and the Arab world, with the exception of Iraq's immediate neighbours, to participate in a restructured multinational force, under UN authority.

This suggestion may not appeal to the Bush administration because of their deep-rooted mistrust of the United Nations and refusal to place American troops under an international command. They may soften their attitude after the electoral defeat of the Republicans in the mid-term elections last week. The moderates in the State Department will be in a stronger position to influence US foreign policy. From what we know, they favour closer co-operation with the United Nations and with America's European, Arab and Muslim allies and friends. They are also willing to engage Iran and Syria in serious discussions and hold direct talks with representatives of the Iraqi insurgency. They believe too that a greater and more active involvement by the US in the Palestine–Israel conflict may help to defuse the crisis in Iraq, and persuade reluctant Arab and Muslim countries to participate in the MNF.

The new direction of American policy in Iraq will no doubt be influenced by the findings of the Baker–Hamilton Study Group. While it may be too early to forecast their final recommendations, it is certain they will not call for the immediate withdrawal or scaling-down of American forces in Iraq. They may propose instead to transfer some troops from various regions to Baghdad. Contrary to some reports, I do not expect them to advocate the division of Iraq along ethnic or sectarian lines, but would recommend instead greater decentralization and devolution of power to the provinces.

Let me say a few words about the proposal of some influential academics, former diplomats and politicians to partition Iraq. They presume that Iraq can be neatly divided into clearly defined areas, Kurdish, Sunni, and Shi'a. The fact is that with the exception of the three northern provinces which are predominantly Kurdish, the Arab population of Iraq is mixed, especially in the cities where most Iraqis live. Partition would encourage the militias and death squads to intensify their systematic campaign of sectarian cleansing. Hundreds of thousands of Iraqis, among them highly qualified professionals, have been forced to leave their homes and some have emigrated to neighbouring countries. The Iraqi brain drain that began in Saddam's time has now reached alarming proportions. The idea that the Shi'as and Sunnis of Iraq each act like united and disciplined monolithic entities is of course utter nonsense. Among the Shi'a Arab tribes of the south there is strong opposition to the attempts by some Iraqi politicians to create a sectarian federal region with close links to Iran. There are also bitter feuds among the Shi'a militias and sectarian parties in the south and among the various sectarian Sunni groups in the west. Partition would not lead to peace but to more violence and chaos.

If we must have federalism then it should be based on geography and not ethnicity or sectarian and religious affiliations, and above all it should provide for a strong federal government with exclusive authority over defence and foreign relations and the management of the country's wealth and natural resources.

The present political situation is not promising. The sectarian parties, both Shi'a and Sunni, have the upper hand. In the election last December, they exploited the fears, prejudices and superstitions of the voters, and with the help of their militias and armed supporters were able to gain a large number of seats in parliament at the expense of the non-sectarian liberal and secular parties. I am not casting any doubts on the legitimacy of the elections; we have accepted the results, in spite of many well-documented instances of violence, intimidation, serious irregularities and fraud. The sectarian government elected by Parliament last May has so far been a dismal failure. Only a competent government untainted by militia connections and enjoying the people's trust will be able to clean up the security forces and start negotiations with insurgent groups that are willing to be integrated into the political process if their concerns are addressed in a fair manner. Such a government would be in a strong position to engage Iran, Syria and other neighbours with a view to ending their interference in Iraq's affairs. It would also deal more effectively with security problems, combat corruption, end the serious shortages in essential services, revive the economy, and take Iraq on the road to a better future. I am talking about a government of competent, experienced technocrats, known for their integrity and independence, to manage the affairs of the country during this period of crisis. Prime Minister Al-Maliki seems to have come to the same conclusion. He has announced his intention to reshuffle his government because of the poor showing of many of his ministers. I do not know whether this is a tactical move to ease the pressure on him to deliver on his promises. I hope he will be able to disengage himself from the sectarian groups that helped him to become PM.

Looking towards the future, the Iraqis will realize sooner or later that democracy and theocracy are incompatible. Theocratic regimes derive their ideology from a twisted view of religion. They are by nature autocratic and oppressive, because they perceive themselves as the embodiment of God's will. I am sure that after the terrible experience of sectarian governments during the last two years, the Iraqi people will return to the secularism under which their country developed and prospered. I hope that the liberal parties will achieve better results in the next elections. It is only through democratic means that change will come. In the past some political parties allowed themselves to be used as a front to justify the seizure of power by the military, with disastrous consequences for the country. This should never happen again.

To recapitulate, I am suggesting the following:

1. The MNF, with additional troops if necessary, to launch without delay a determined campaign to disarm the militias and all other illegal armed groups.
2. A new resolution by the United Nations Security Council to restructure the MNF under UN authority, with a significant participation of Arab, Asian, Muslim and European countries.
3. A new government, mainly of technocrats, which will begin as a matter of high priority the reorganization of the Iraq security forces and negotiate with the insurgents and neighbouring countries.
4. An effective effort to deal with the shortages in services, corruption, unemployment, and management of the oil sector, and to revive the economy.
5. New elections, to be held under peaceful conditions at the time prescribed in the Constitution, i.e. in late 2009 or early 2010.

The time needed for the completion of the tasks enumerated above is three years.

Let me say a few words in conclusion about what has been described as a civil war in Iraq. There is no such thing. The vast majority of Sunnis and Shi'is are not involved in the daily sectarian killing and are opposed to the present senseless violence. The various militias and armed groups rarely fight each other. Their crimes and atrocities are directed mainly against innocent civilians of all sects. What most Iraqis want is life without fear, and the opportunity to enjoy their fundamental freedoms and rights in a democratic and egalitarian society. That is why I believe that the conflict in Iraq is not between Sunnis and Shi'is but between those who want to modernize and those who reject modernity in favour of a narrow interpretation of the Qur'an and Hadith. The extremist, fundamentalist, inward-looking isolationist groups gained in strength and offered a disillusioned people an alternative to modernity. Political Islam became more radicalized, shunning any meaningful contact and dialogue with the rest of the world. A highly restrictive interpretation of the Qur'an and Shari'a based on a selective choice of texts gradually gained acceptance in some sections of Arab and Muslim societies. I believe this is temporary. It is in fact an aberration because it goes against the yearning of the people for change and freedom from the shackles of the past.

Sooner or later, Arabs and Muslims will realize that if their countries are going to play a constructive role in today's world they have to modernize. We are facing the same challenge that our forebears faced two hundred years ago – modernize or perish.

8

The Situation in Iraq at the Height of Sectarian Strife

Excerpts from an article published in the *Financial Times*,
October 2006

SECTARIAN VIOLENCE perpetrated by militias, death squads and armed gangs continues unabated in Baghdad and other areas of Iraq. Two-thirds of the nearly 300,000 people killed so far during the conflict have been victims of sectarian violence. The Iraqi security forces are incapable of restoring peace and order. They have been heavily infiltrated by the militias they are supposed to fight. They lack motivation and discipline. The inadequacy of their training and insufficiency of their equipment make them easy and frequent targets of the militias and terrorists. It will take time to reorganize them professionally and ensure their undivided loyalty to the Iraqi state.

Meanwhile, to prevent the country descending into chaos, the multinational forces will have to get involved deeply in security operations. This may require an increase in their numbers. I realize US and British public opinion will find it difficult to accept more sacrifices in what seems a conflict with no end in sight. In any event an abrupt withdrawal of the multinational forces would lead to a total breakdown of law and order and the break-up of Iraq into feuding fiefdoms under warlords, with their militias fighting each other for control of areas rich in natural resources. Such a situation would engulf the whole region in turmoil.

Perhaps the time has come to review the composition and mandate of the multinational forces. Participation of troops from Asian, European,

Arab and Muslim countries – provided they were not immediate neighbours of Iraq – alongside reduced contingents of US and British forces might improve the security situation and diminish sectarian violence. There will be an opportunity to deal with this matter when the United Nations Security Council reviews the multinational force's mandate before the end of this year.

The current political situation in Iraq is extremely confusing. The so-called government of national unity is in fact a government of sectarian disunity. There is mutual suspicion and mistrust among its members. Even within the same groups there are serious disagreements and occasional armed clashes, as we have seen recently in Amara after the withdrawal of British troops.

In the election last December, religious identity replaced political identity. The sectarian parties, both Shi'a and Sunni, exploited the fears, prejudices and superstitions of the voters and with the help of their militias and armed supporters were able to gain a large number of seats in parliament. I am not casting any doubts on the legitimacy of the elections; they were on the whole free and fair, in spite of many instances of violence, intimidation, serious irregularities and fraud.

Looking towards the future, the Iraqi people will realize sooner or later that democracy and theocracy are incompatible. Theocratic regimes derive their ideology from a twisted view of religion. They are by nature autocratic and oppressive, because they perceive themselves as the embodiment of God's will. At present, most Iraqis support Nuri Al-Maliki, the Prime Minister, because of his genuine belief in national reconciliation, his pledge to preserve the unity and territorial integrity of Iraq and his promise to disarm the militias and other armed groups.

While he is trusted, there is little confidence in his government, which includes many ministers with close links to the militias, the death squads and other terrorist groups. Most of them were chosen because of their sectarian identity and party loyalty. We would delude ourselves if we believed that such a government could be effective in fighting terrorism and sectarian violence. Sooner rather than later Mr Al-Maliki will have to reshuffle his government by including persons known for their independence, integrity, competence and experience.

Only a competent government untainted by militia connections and enjoying the people's trust will be able to clean up the security forces and start negotiations with insurgent groups that are willing to be integrated in the political process if their concerns are addressed in a fair manner. Such a government would be in a strong position to engage Iran, Syria and other neighbours with a view to ending their interference in Iraq's affairs. It would also deal more effectively with security problems, combat corruption, end the shortages in essential services, revive the economy and take Iraq on the road to a better future.

The choice is clear: either a secular democracy or a theocratic regime that will take Iraq back to the Middle Ages.

9

Index of Speeches at the United Nations

A. Main Speeches on Palestine and the War of June 1967

1. Speeches to the Special Political Committee

11 December 1961
a) The magnitude of the Palestine tragedy
b) Historical analysis of Zionist claims
c) The true nature of Zionism
d) The Balfour Declaration – the Mandate – partition
e) The Zionist conquests of 1948
f) Responsibility for the refugee problem
g) Israel's insistence on negotiating with the Arab states and ignoring the Palestinians
h) Criticism of Dr Johnson's report on the resettlement of the refugees
i) Protection of the properties of the refugees

6 December 1962
a) Responsibility of Israel for the murder of the United Nations Mediator, Count Folke Bernadotte

11 November 1963
a) The destruction of the Arab community of Palestine has always been one of the principal aims of the Zionist movement
b) The prevention by military means of the establishment of an Arab state in Palestine

c) The building of Jewish settlements in predominantly Arab areas
d) The Zionist campaigns of 1948 to occupy as much Arab land and dislodge as many Palestinians as possible

28 October 1965
a) Attempts of Israel to restrict United Nations assistance to refugees.
b) The responsibility of Israel for the refugee problem
c) The United Nations position stated by the representatives of the Western powers and reaffirmed every year that the return of the refugees should not await the conclusion of peace and should not be contingent upon negotiations between Israel and the Arab states
d) Truce violations and conquests by Israel

4 December 1968
a) The principal issue: the refusal of the people of Palestine to surrender their ancestral homeland
b) The solution lies in enabling the Palestinians to exercise their right of self-determination
c) The Zionist myth that the Jews have a higher moral right than the Palestinians, who are therefore required to make all the necessary sacrifices
d) The necessity of extending UNRWA's mandate and the provision of adequate funds for its services
e) Priority needing be given to the problem of the recent refugees
f) The demolition of houses and the deportation of Palestinians continues

2. SPEECHES TO THE SECURITY COUNCIL

31 May 1967 – the 1345th Meeting
a) Israeli threats regarding navigation in the Gulf of Aqaba
b) Arab commitment to resolve the dispute peacefully
c) Egypt's sovereign right in its territorial waters
d) The Israeli record of persistent violations of United Nations resolutions and agreements with the Arabs and their disregard of international law and contractual obligations
e) The Arabs are ready to fight if attacked, but will not initiate offensive action

6 June 1967 – the 1348th Meeting

a) Recalling repeated Arab assurances that they will not start the war
b) Arab efforts to find a peaceful solution
c) Israel's responsibility for starting the war
d) Wrong of the Security Council to order a cessation of hostilities without first determining responsibility and calling on the aggressor to withdraw from the territories it occupied
e) US responsibility in assisting and encouraging Israeli to attack its neighbours
f) The ceasefire resolution an abject surrender to Israel

2 April 1968 – the 1411th Meeting

a) Iraq proud to help the freedom fighters of the Palestinian resistance
b) Israel has no intention of implementing Resolution 242
c) The main issue: the avowed intention of Israel to annex the occupied territories
d) Israel's disregard of the resolutions on Jerusalem and on the 1967 refugees and refusal to apply the Geneva Convention to the occupied territories
e) Israeli establishment of new Jewish settlements in the occupied territories and continued brutal harassment of the inhabitants

7 and 16 August 1968 – the 1436th and 1440th Meeting

a) Israeli attack on al-Salt and Irbid in Jordan
b) We cannot equate the legitimate activities of the Palestine resistance with the deliberate and aggressive actions of the Israeli armed forces
c) Acts of reprisal repeatedly condemned as contrary to the Charter
d) Israel's security not threatened, though that of the neighbouring Arab states is threatened
e) Israel's actions since the end of the war in June 1967 clearly showing its aggressive intention and leaving no alternative to the Palestinians but resistance
f) Israel's obstructions of all efforts to reopen the Suez Canal and its measures against the civilian population in the West Bank and Gaza

Appendix 9

3. Speeches to the General Assembly

27 June 1967 – the 1537th Meeting
a) The Israeli attack of 5 June 1967 a carefully planned and premeditated operation
b) The question whether Israel should be allowed to consolidate its aggression and permanently annex the recently occupied territories
c) Overwhelming majority of speakers call for immediate and unconditional Israeli withdrawal
d) The support Israel received from the United States
e) The US position condones Israeli occupation and its use as a means of achieving the political aims of Israel
f) Bitter Arab disillusionment with the United States
g) Israeli policy of terror in the occupied territories
h) The nature of the Arab–Israeli conflict in Palestine

3 July 1967 – the 1545th Meeting
a) The central issue: the inadmissibility of territorial acquisition by military means
b) The illegality of the annexation of Jerusalem
c) The first step towards peace the immediate and unconditional withdrawal of Israel from the occupied territories
d) The USA apparently fully committed to the perpetuation of Israeli occupation
e) Linking withdrawal to the conclusion of peace: the very long time this would take, allowing Israel to maintain its occupation and transform it gradually into permanent annexation

11 October 1967 – the 1586th Meeting
a) Israel's mistrust of the UN and its advocacy of a hands-off policy
b) Challenge to Israel's demand that the conflict be resolved through direct negotiations with the Arab states directly concerned, without UN involvement
c) Israel's responsibility for the war
d) The United Nations special responsibility, particularly with regard to the refugees
e) Israel's aim to annex the occupied territories; and seeking time to consolidate its occupation

Appendix 9

B. MAIN SPEECHES ON COLONIAL QUESTIONS

1. NON-SELF GOVERNING TERRITORIES

18 October 1955 – the 478th Meeting of the Fourth Committee
Speech delivered in the Fourth Committee

29 January 1957– the 615th Meeting of the Fourth Committee
The Portuguese colonies (this became an official document circulated to all member states of the UN and opened the debate on the subject)

1 December 1958 – the 823rd Meeting of the Fourth Committee
Speech delivered in the Fourth Committee

February 1962 – the 1112th Meeting of the Fourth Committee
Rhodesia (Zimbabwe) (this also became an official document circulated to all member states of the UN and opened the debate on the subject)

20 November 1962 – the 1170th Plenary Meeting of the General Assembly
During this speech, on a report by the Committee on Decolonization, the question of Aden was raised for the first time. I proposed a comprehensive plan for it to advance towards independence, which met with very little opposition.

22 October 1965 – the 1535th Meeting of the Fourth Committee
Aden and South Arabia

2. TRUST TERRITORIES

22 November 1955 – the 517th Meeting of the Fourth Committee
Reports of the Trusteeship Council
Togo

8 December 1955 and 10 January 1957 – the 539th and 594th Meetings of the Fourth Committee
Togo

21 November 1958, 23 February 1959, 8 October 1959 and 12 October 1959 – the 810th, 847th, 899th and 903rd Meetings of the Fourth Committee
Cameroons

Appendix 9

June 1962 – Meeting of the Fourth Committee
Ruanda-Urundi

12 December 1956, 14 October 1958 and 3 November 1965 – the 494th, 573th and 758th Meetings of the Fourth Committee
South-West Africa (Namibia)

INDEX

In alphabetizing, Al- is ignored

Abadan 76
Abduh, Mohammed 203
Abdul Hamid, Mohsen 139
Abdul Illah, Crown Price 33, 35–6
    assassination 35
Abdullah II bin Hussein, HM King of
    Jordan 123–4
Abdul Mahdi, Adel 137–9, 148
Abdul Wahhab, Ata 140
Abu Dhabi 1, 28, 106–15, 122, 126
    development of 109–12
Abu Dhabi Fund for Economic
    Development 110
Abu Dhabi Investment Authority (ADIA)
    110
Abu Dhabi National Oil Co. (ADNOC) 110
Abu Ghraib 130
Abu Musa island 107
Aden 29, 49–54, 62–4, 68–9, 74,
    77–8
Afghani, Jamaluddin 203
Afghanistan 120–1, 140, 152
Afnan, Badia 17
Aga Khan, Prince Sadruddin 17
Akimco 106
Al-Alami, Musa 22
Albania 97
Albright, Madeleine 119–20
Aleppo 12
Alexandria 5, 9–10, 13–14, 16, 24
Algeria, Algiers 19, 42, 47–8, 66–7, 108–10, 140
Allawi, Iyad 130, 141–2, 145–6, 151
Amer, Abdul Hakim 94
American University, Beirut (AUB) 14–15, 19

Amman 35
Amsterdam 11
Anbar 4
Ankara 59–60
Annan, Kofi 128, 135–7, 139–40
apartheid 27
Aqaba, Gulf of 88–9, 92, 196
Arab–Israeli War, June 1967 1–2, 67,
    84–102, 194–201
Arab League 60, 63, 79, 108–9, 121
Arab Revolt (1916–18) 8, 186
Arab–US relations 157–66, 173–4
Arabia, Southern 49, 66, 70–1. *See also*
    Aden; Yemen
Aram, Abbas 76
Aref, Gen. Abdul Rahman 61–2, 67, 75, 77
Aref, Abdul Salam 49, 58–9 61, 64
Al-Askari, Imam Hassan, shrine of 146
Al-Askari, Jafar 35
Al-Askari, Tahsin 35
Al-Asnag, Abdullah 62
Aswan High Dam 30–1, 86
Austria 13, 184, 202
Al-Ayyubi, Ali Jawdat 19, 33, 106
Al-Ayyubi, Selwa Ali Jawdat (author's wife)
    19–20, 26–7, 39–40, 106, 112–13,
    145
Aziz, Tariq 115
Azores 18–19

Ba'ath party in Iraq 128–30, 139, 169, 179
    first accession to power (1963) 49
    second accession to power (1968) 103,
    105
Ba'ath party in Syria 61

coup (1963) 49
Babylon
    Ishtar Gate in Berlin 11
Badran, Shams 94
Baghdad 3–7, 9, 15, 17, 20, 25–7, 33–7, 59, 62, 75–6, 82, 103, 105, 125, 129–30, 137, 211
    Green Zone 33
Baghdad Pact 29, 36, 74, 85
Bahrain 106–7
Baker, James 174, 207
Baker–Hamilton Study Group 207
Balfour, Arthur 185–7
Balfour Declaration 84, 185–7
Balthus 16
Bandung Conference (1955) 30
Barenboim, Daniel 16
Barzani, Massoud 127, 130
Basra
    part of Ottoman Empire 45
Bayreuth 16
Al-Bazzaz, Abdul Rahman 54, 58–9, 61, 64–5, 67–8, 75, 103
Beaumont, Sir Richard 77
Begin, Menachem 189
Beirut 5, 14–15
Belgians, Belgium 42
Belgrade 46–7
Bell, Gertrude 8
Benghazi 19
Berger, Sandy 120
Berlin 10–12
Berlin, Michael J. 103–4
Bermuda 19
Bernstein, Leonard 16–17
Beswick, Lord 51
Bevin, Ernest 22, 189
Bhutto, Zulfiqar Ali 77
Biden, Joseph 120
Blackwill, Robert 142
Blair, Tony 134
Boland, Frederick 41
Bonn 109
Bosnia 177
Braham, Noel 3
Brandt, Willy 109
Bremer, Paul 122, 127, 129–31, 134, 136–9
Brezhnev, Leonid 78
Britain, British 13–14, 18, 29–32, 34, 84, 206, 211–12
    and Aden 49–54, 74
    and Adnan Pachachi 38–9, 48–9, 60, 62–3
    and Egypt 13, 33
    Gulf policy 63, 71–2
    and Gulf war (1990–91) 168
    and Iraq 7–8, 14–15, 33–6, 74–5, 77, 206
    and Iraqi occupation (2003–) 132, 134–5
    and Iraqi oil 70–1
    and Kuwait 45
    and Palestine 161, 185–91, 193, 194
    and Suez crisis (1956) 30–2, 44, 45
Brown, George 69–72, 101, 199
Brussels 11
Bulgaria 12, 185
Bunche, Ralph 41, 88
Burns, John 144
Burundi 29
Bush, George Herbert Walker 168–70, 174
Bush, George Walker 121, 134, 136, 138, 140, 207

Caffery, Jefferson 84
Cairo 5, 18–19, 24, 47, 51, 60, 62, 64, 76, 88, 108, 123
Camp David treaty 109, 200
Campbell, A. H. 48–9
Cameroons 29, 37
Canada 21
Caradon, Lord (Hugh Foot) 51, 54–5, 62, 70–2, 101, 199
Casablanca 18–19
Castro, Fidel 41, 45
Chadirchy, Nasir 130
Chalabi, Ahmad 119, 122, 130, 134–5, 137–9, 142
Chambrun, Charles de 138
Chamoun, Camille 32, 36
Chesapeake Bay 21
Chicago 41
Childers, Erskine 185–6
China 30–1, 82, 108, 135
Chou En-Lai 30
Christians, Iraqi, 6–7, 10
Christo 110
Christopher, Warren 119
Churchill, Winston 8, 15, 187, 189
Cockburn, Patrick 128, 132
Cohen, Sir Andrew 39
Cold War 40, 46–7, 169, 176
colonialism, European 203
Concorde 26
Congo 42–4
Copenhagen 37, 108–9
Crocker, Ryan 121–2, 131, 151
Crum, Bartley 161
Cuba, Bay of Pigs 45
Cuban missile crisis 47–8
Cyprus 54, 59–60, 78
Cuellar, Perez de 118, 170, 172
Czechoslovakia 30

Dakota aircraft 19
Damascus 4, 61, 66, 68

Index

Damluji, Omar 142, 144
Daoud Pasha 4
Dawa Party 130, 148–50
De Beers–Vuitton 25
Dean, Sir Patrick 48, 50–1
Descartes, René 15
Dimichkie, Nadia 79
Dubai 106–7
Dulles, John Foster 30–2, 84–7, 157–8, 161–3

Eban, Abba 91, 99–100, 196, 198–9
Edward VII, HM King 9
Egypt 18, 30–2, 46, 49, 50, 59, 60–8, 123, 154, 193–7, 202–3
   and Britain 13
   Iraqi relations with 33–5, 60–1, 64–6, 75–8, 82, 115
   as United Arab Republic (UAR) 34, 36, 49, 62–3, 66, 67
   United Political Command (with Iraq) 75
   and US 84–95
   war with Israel (1967) 1–2, 84–102, 194–201
   war with Israel (1973) 108, 200
   and Yemen civil war 60–1
   See also United Arab Republic
Eilat 88–9, 92
Eisenhower Doctrine 32, 86
Eisenhower, Dwight 31–2, 41, 85, 87, 158
Elijah Mohammed 41
Eton 9
Euphrates 3, 74
   use of water 60–1, 74, 79–81
European Union 11–12
European values 11–12

Fallujah 141
Fanfani, Amintore 72–3, 76, 89–90
Fawzi, Gen. Mohammed 65
Federal Union of Egypt, Iraq and Syria 66
Feisal I, HM King of Iraq 3, 8
Feisal II, HM King of Iraq 33
   assassination 35, 145
Feith, Douglas 121
First World War 7
France, French 66–9, 74–5, 84, 109, 135, 137–8, 186, 193
   French Revolution 11, 13
   in N. Africa 163–5
   and Suez crisis 32–3
   in Syria and Lebanon 14–15
Franco, Gen. Francisco 12
Free Officers' coup (1958) 35–7, 68, 86
Front for the Liberation of South Yemen (FLOSY) 62–3

Gailani, Rashid Ali 14–15
Gandhi, Indira 77
Gaulle, Gen. Charles de 15, 66–8
Gaza Strip 30, 85–6, 88–9, 99, 181, 197
Geneva 10, 54, 67, 106, 115, 135
Geneva Conventions 127
Georgetown, Guyana 108
Georgetown University 24
Germany 10–15, 66, 184, 186
   Nazi 188–9
Ghazi, HM King of Iraq 8, 11, 46
Golan Heights 94, 197, 200
Goldberg, Arthur 91, 98, 100–1, 199
Greenstock, Sir Jeremy 134
Greenwood, Anthony 51
Grey, Lord (1st Viscount Grey of Fallodon) 187–8
Gromyko, Andrei 78
Gulf, Arabian 63, 71–2, 76, 79–81, 83, 115
Gulf Co-operation Council (GCC) 80, 82
Gulf War (1990–91) 17, 114–18, 137–8, 167–74

Hadhramaut 49
Al-Hadi, Imam Ali, shrine of 146
Al-Hafez, Ameen 61
Al-Hafez, Mahdi 135, 142
Haifa 92
Al-Hakim, Abdul Aziz 137, 139, 151
Al-Hakim, Ayatollah Muhammad Bakr 130
Hammarskjold, Dag 39, 42–4, 170
Handel's *Messiah* 14
Harrow 9
Harvard University 19, 34, 113
Al-Hashimi, Aqila 134
Heath, Sir Edward 17
Heidelberg 11
Henderson, Loy 18
Herzl, Theodor 183
Hindou, Paul 10–11
Hitler, Adolf 10–11, 13
Hodeida 50
Hollywood 20
Home, Earl of (Sir Alec Douglas-Home) 50
Horowitz, Vladimir 16
human rights 176–7
Hungary 78
Hurd, Douglas 39
Hussein bin Ali Al-Hashimi, Sherif of Mecca and King of the Hijaz 8, 186
Hussein bin Talal Al-Hashimi, HM King of Jordan 36

Ibn Khaldun 15
Ibrahimi, Lakhdar 140–3
Independent Iraqi Democrats party 122–3, 125, 143, 146

India 40, 77, 82, 109
Indyk, Martin 119
International Bank for Reconstruction and Development 21
International Monetary Fund (IMF) 21
Iran, Iranians 29, 54, 59–60, 62–3, 69, 73–4, 77–8, 80–2, 114–15, 119, 139, 143, 150–3, 201, 206, 208, 213
    benefits from 2003 invasion of Iraq 127
    border with Iraq 74, 76, 80–1
    and Egypt 77–8
    and Gulf 72, 74, 80–1, 107
    and Gulf islands 107–8, 111
    Shah 77–8, 107, 110
    territorial claims to Bahrain 107
    See also Iraq–Iran War
Iraq 14, 18, 20, 22, 29–30, 50, 60, 85–6, 103
    Anglo-Iraqi Treaty (1930) 14–15
    Civilian Provisional Authority (2003) 127–8, 133, 135–6, 148
    claim to Kuwait (1961) 45–6, 75, 169
    constitution (2004) 143–4
    Constituent Assembly 121, 123, 135
    early modern development 5–8
    elections 63, 68, 143–51
    at end of First World War 7–8
    a failed state 153, 205–10
    federal union with Jordan 34–6
    foreign service 18–23, 33–7
    Free Officers' coup (1958) 35–7, 68, 86
    Governing Council (2003–04) 133–41, 148
    and Gulf 63, 73
    and Gulf War (1990–91) 17, 114–18, 137–8, 167–74
    and Kuwait 45–6, 73, 75, 115–18, 167–74
    Multi-national Force (MNF), need for 206–7, 209, 211–12
    partition of 207–8
    post-conflict Iraq 179–81, 205–10
    relations with Britain 66, 69–72, 74–5
    relations with West 66, 74–5, 79, 115–16
    revolt suppressed (1991) 118
    sectarianism in 126–7, 141–7, 149–50, 153–4, 180–1, 205–13
    and Syria 60–1, 64, 68, 74
    under British mandate and rule 7–8
    under monarchy 8
    under Ottoman rule 4–5, 7–8, 45
    and United Nations 40, 43
    United Political Command (with Egypt) 61, 75
    US invasion (2003) 120–3, 125–6
    war with Britain (1941) 14–15
    weapons of mass destruction, alleged 120–1, 151, 168
Iraq–Iran war (1980–88) 46, 83, 114–15, 168–9, 201
Iraqi National Congress 119, 130
Iraqiya party 146, 151
Islam
    and modernity 202–4
    political 203, 210
Israel 1, 30, 33, 45, 64, 66, 73–6, 81–3, 103–4, 109, 115–16, 121, 123, 159, 161–3, 165, 168–9, 182–201
    and Arab–Israeli war (1967) 84–101, 194–200
    military superiority 200–1
    nuclear capability 200–1
    and war with Egypt (1973) 108, 200
    and war of 1948 191–4
    See also Zionism; United States
Istanbul 12
Al-Istrabadi, Feisal 140
Italy 12, 14, 89–90
    Iraqi relations with 72–3

Al-Jaafari, Ibrahim 130, 144, 148–9, 206
Jadid, Salah 61, 75
Jaffa 191
Japan 109
Jarring, Gunnar 99, 103, 200
Jawad, Hashim 37–8, 43
Jawdat, Ali *see* Al-Ayyubi
Al-Jazairi, Abdul Qadir 66
Jefferson, Thomas 20
Jerusalem 5, 6, 22, 96–8, 200
    as *corpus separatum* 162, 190
Jews, Iraqi 4–7, 103–4
Johnson, Lyndon B. 66, 87, 91–3, 194, 196
Joint Arab Defence Council 76–7
Jomard, Abdul Jabbar 36–7
Jordan 32, 61, 76, 87, 94, 103, 115, 123, 128, 193–4, 197, 201
    federal union with Iraq 34–6
Joseph (Polish Jewish driver) 11

Kalabdoun family 3
Kamal, Faiha 38–9
Karajan, Herbert von 16
Kashmir 77
Katanga 42–4
Kennedy, John F. 87
Keynes, John Maynard 21
Khaddam, Abdul Halim 109
Khalid, Mansoor 109

Index

Khalidi, Walid 96
Al-Khalifa, HH 'Isa bin Salman 106–7
Khalilzad, Zalmay 122, 126–7, 149
Khan, Mohammed Ayub 77
Khoi, Abdul Majeed 141
Khomeini, Ayatollah 114, 169
Kirkuk 130, 143
Kittani, Ismat 37–9
Korea 26–3
Kosygin, Alexei 78
Kruschev, Nikita 41–2, 47–8
Kurdistan, Kurds 29, 62, 67, 69, 74–5, 77–9, 81, 110, 122–3, 127, 138–9, 142–6, 151, 173, 179–81, 207
Kuwait 34, 49, 75, 96, 106, 123
    Iraqi claim to (1961) 45–6, 75, 169
    Iraqi invasion (1990–91) 17, 114–18, 137–8, 167–74

Lawrence, T. E. 8
League of Nations 8, 9, 186–90
Lebanon 5, 14–15, 23, 36, 86, 90, 111, 140
Leonardo da Vinci 10, 11
Leopoldville 42
Libya 115
Lincoln, Abraham 20
Lloyd, Selwyn 34
Locke, John 15
London 11, 20, 25–6, 28, 109
Lumumba, Patrice 42–3

MacDonald, James 161
Macmillan, Harold 41
Madagascar 50
Madrid 135
Mahdi army 141, 149–50
Maher, Ahmed 123
Makhous, Dr Ibrahim 64
Makkawi, Abdul Qawi 62
Al-Maktoum, HH Shaikh Rashid bin Said 107
Malcolm X 41
Al-Maliki, Nuri 148–51, 206, 209, 212
mandate, League of Nations 186–8, 190–1
Mehta, Zubin 16
Mello, Sergio Vieira de 128
Menuhin, Yehudi 16
Michelangelo 10
Middleton, Drew 104
Mill, John Stuart 15
Mobutu, Joseph-Desiré 42–3
Mohammera 76
Moore, A. R. 39
Morocco 26–7, 109, 159, 164–5
Moscow 37, 49, 63, 86
Mosul 3–4, 6

Mubarak, Hosni 123
Muhieddin, Zakariya 64, 93
Munich 28–9
Murville, Maurice Couve de 67
Musa Al-Khadim, Shi'a Imam 7

Al-Nahyan, HH Sheikh Zayed bin Sultan 107–11, 121, 124
    character and policies 111–12
    vision for Abu Dhabi 107, 111–12
Najaf, 141
Naples 10
Napoleon 11, 202–3
Nasser, Jamal Abdul 30–2, 41, 46, 59, 64–6, 68, 77–8
    and Arab–Israeli war (1967) 84–101, 194–7
    distrust of Ba'ath party 49, 61
National Association for the Advancement of Colored People (NAACP) 41
nationalism, Arab 15, 24, 35, 59, 65
NATO 47
Ndola 44
Nehru, Jawaharlal 41, 46
New York 17, 21, 23, 25–7, 37, 58, 68–73, 89–91, 93, 102–4, 106, 108, 137, 139–40
    World Trade Center (9/11) 120
Non-Aligned Countries, Movement of 46–7, 51, 59, 108
Nyasaland (Malawi) 29

Obama, Barack 152
oil, Iraqi 70–1, 74–5, 79–80, 82–3, 143, 148, 181
oil weapon/embargo 91, 108–9
Oran 19
Organization of Petroleum Exporting Countries (OPEC) 110
Orient Express 12
Oslo Agreement 109, 201
Ottomans 45, 184, 186, 203. *See also* Turkey
Oxford University 13–14

Al-Pachachi, Adnan Muzahim
    in Abu Dhabi (1969–93) 107–13
    becomes UAE citizen 107–8
    leads Abu Dhabi General Projects Committee 110
    member of Abu Dhabi Executive Council 110
    as UAE minister 1, 107–10
    as UAE representaive to UN 99
    antecedents 3–4
    and Arab–Israeli war (1967) 88–101

Index

and Arab nationalism 13, 15, 35, 65, 67
birth 1, 3
Britain, attitude to 13
childhood 1–8
and classical music 14, 16–17, 28–9, 44
and colonial questions 29, 37–41, 48–9
and communism 47–8
and death penalty 49
diplomatic career
   in Iraqi embassy, Washington
     (1945–49) 18–24
   as Iraqi consul, Alexandria
     (1949) 24
   in Iraqi embassy, Washington
     (1953–57) 27–32
   in Iraqi foreign ministry
     (1957–59) 33–7
   achieves ambassadorial rank 39
   as Iraqi Representative to UN
     (1959–65, 1967–69) 1, 35–57,
     98, 102–5
   heads UN Economic and Social
     Council (ECOSOC) (1965) 54–6,
     67, 69
   as Iraqi minister of state for
     foreign affairs (1965–66) 54,
     58–61
   as Iraqi Foreign Minister
     (1966–67) 62–102
   resignation from Iraqi foreign
     service (1969) 102–5
director of UN Dept, Baghdad
   25–7
draws up Iraqi Bill of Rights
   140–1, 143
early travels in Europe 10–12
education 7, 9–17
in expatriate Iraqi politics (1991–
   2003) 1, 114–25
forms Centrist Party 120
and Free Officers' coup (1958) 35–7
heads Independent Iraqi Democrats
   122–5, 144
interviews Saddam Hussein (2004)
   137–8
and Kuwait 45–6, 75
life in four phases 1–2
lobbies for Iraqi executive powers 127–
   33, 179
member and president of Iraqi
   Governing Council (2003–04) 1,
   133–41, 179
member of Iraqi Interim National
   Council (2004–05) 1,
member of Iraqi parliament (2005–10)
   1, 146–8
Nasserist leanings, alleged 35, 78
and Non-Aligned Movement 46–7
and Palestine 44–5, 54, 56–7, 84–101
and racism 21, 41
refuses interim Iraqi presidency
   (2004) 142–3
return to Iraq (2003) 1–2, 125–6, 179
and secular, Enlightenment values
   15–16
and UN ideals, attitude to 25, 40
and US, attitude to 20–1
vision for a secular, democratic Iraq
   1–2, 153–4, 179–81, 209, 212–13
Al-Pachachi, Hamdi 22
Al-Pachachi, Leila 28–9
   son Adnan 28–9
   son Faris 29
Al-Pachachi, Maysoon 19–20
Al-Pachachi, Muzahim (1890–1982) 5, 7,
   9–11, 14, 24
Al-Pachachi, Nu'man 4
Al-Pachachi, Reema 25–6
   son Said 25
   daughter Aisha 25–6
   son Kareem 26
Pakistan 29, 77, 109
Palestine, Palestinians 1, 12–14, 26–7, 40,
   44–6, 66, 68, 73, 77, 81–3, 103, 109,
   111, 160, 164, 173–4, 181–201, 203
   Arab–Israeli war (1967) 84–101, 194–
     200
   creation of Jewish state in 22–3, 160–
     3, 182–201
   PLO 61, 73, 109
   Revolt (1936–39) 12
   War of 1948 191–4
Paris 10–11, 12, 26, 59, 67–8, 140, 164
Paul VI, Pope 73
Pelletreau, Robert 119
Perle, Richard 121
Pickering, Thomas 119
Pirasteh, Mehdi 78
Podgorny, Nikolay 78
Portuguese colonies 29, 37
Powell, Colin 126, 135–6

Qadoomi, Faruq 109
Al-Qaida 120–1, 130
Qassim, Abdul Karim 43, 45–6, 65, 87
   death (1963) 49
Qatar 106–7
Quebec 21
Queen Elizabeth, RMS 26
Qur'an 203, 210

Raouf, Adnan 40
Ras al-Khaimah 107
Al-Rawi, Izzedine 38

Reagan, Ronald 174
Renaissance, European 10
Rhodesia, Northern (Zambia) 29, 44
Rhodesia, Southern (Zimbabwe) 29
Riad, Mahmoud 46, 65, 89, 109
Rice, Condoleezza 140, 149–50
Romania 78
Rome 10, 72–3
Roosevelt, Franklin D. 20, 145
Roosevelt, Kermit 84
Rostow, Eugene 91
Rostow, Walter 91
Rothschild, Lord (Walter, 2nd Baron) 185
Rubai'i, Muwaffak 137–8
Rumsfeld, Donald 120
Rusk, Dean 69, 74, 91, 193
Russia 185–6
Russian Federation 83, 135, 200. *See also* Soviet Union
Rwanda 29

Saarland 13
Al-Sabah, HH Sheikh Sabah al-Ahmad al-Jabir 106, 123
Sadat, Anwar 108–9
Saddam Hussein 17, 110, 114–16, 119–22, 128, 132, 145–6, 179–80, 208
    capture 137–8
    and Gulf War (1990–91) 167–70, 173–4
Al-Sadr, Muqtada 141, 150
Al-Said, Nuri 8, 33–6, 65
Salim, Jawad 17
Salzburg 16–17
San Francisco 19
Sana'a 50
Sanchez, Gen. Ricardo 137
Sassoon, Daoud Abdullah 4
Al-Saud, Saud Al-Faisal 123
Saudi Arabia, Saudis 3, 19, 32, 50, 59, 61, 63, 64, 67, 76, 80, 87, 108, 123, 169, 194
Sauerbruch, Ernest Ferdinand 12
Savannah, Georgia 21
Sawers, John 127
Sayn-Wittgenstein-Sayn, Marianne Fürstin zu 16–17
Schulz, George 174
Schulz-Thierbach, Peter 28
Second World War 12–14, 17, 188, 191
Seynes, Philippe de 55–6
Shakespeare 10
Shamir, Yitzhak 189
Shammar tribe 3, 142
Shari'a law 203, 210
Sharjah 107
Shatt al-'Arab 74, 76–7, 79–80
    agreement with Iran (1975) 110

Shi'a, Iraqi 80, 130–1, 136, 138–9, 141–6, 148–9, 151, 153, 181, 207–8, 210, 212
Shibib, Talib 79
Shukairi, Ahmed 61
Sinai 94, 197
Sistani, Ayatollah Ali 136
Six-Day War (June 1967) 1–2, 67, 84–102, 194–201
Skendar, Afifa 112
Sleibi, Said 59
South Africa 27
South Arabian Federation 50
South-West Africa (Namibia) 37
Soviet Union 30–2, 37, 43, 45, 49, 65, 66, 69, 74, 78–9, 82–3, 86–8, 108, 115
    and Arab–Israeli War (1967) 91, 93–8, 195–6, 198
    and Palestine 78–9, 84, 189
    See also Russia; Russian Federation
Spaak, Paul-Henri 29
Spanish Civil War 12
Staudt, Calvin K. 7
Stokowski, Leopold 16
Straw, Jack 135
Sudan 108–9
Sudetenland 13
Suez Crisis (1956–57) 30–2, 44, 86, 94, 193, 195
Suez Canal 85
Suez Canal Company 32
Sukarno, Ahmed 41, 46
Sulaiman, Ali Haidar 73
Sunnis, Iraqi 143–4, 145–6, 153, 181, 207–8, 210, 212
Al-Suwaidi, Ahmed 107
Al-Suwaidi, Tawfiq 36
Switzerland 11, 12
Sykes–Picot agreement 186
Syria 8, 12, 14–15, 32, 34, 60, 66–8, 73–7, 80–1, 86–8, 94, 108, 115, 193, 195, 197, 208, 213
    Alawites 61
    and Iraqi oil 68, 80
    union with Iraq, desirability of 82–2
    United Arab Republic (UAR, union with Egypt) 86

Tahourdin, John G. 39
Talabani, Jalal 122, 127, 130, 179
Talib, Gen. Naji 68
Taliban 120–1, 152
Tanganyika (Tanzania) 29
Tehran 77–8
Tel Aviv 162
Al-Thani, HH Sheikh Ahmed bin Ali 107
Al-Thani, HH Sheikh Khalifa bin Hamed 107

Thatcher, Margaret 16–17, 169
Tigris 3, 4, 5–6, 35, 74, 79–81
Tiran, Straits of 88–9, 92, 95, 195–6
Tito, Josip Broz 41, 46
Tocqueville, Alexis de 15
Togo 29
Toynbee, Arnold 184
Tripoli, Libya 19
Trucial States 107. *See also* United Arab Emirates
Truman, Harry 22, 161, 189
Tshombe, Moise 42, 44
Tunb islands 107
Tunis, Tunisia 19, 26–7, 108–9, 154, 164–5
Turkey, Turks 29, 54, 59–60, 74, 77, 80–1, 85–6, 186, 193, 203. *See also* Ottomans
Tyler, Patrick 128

United Arab Emirates (UAE) 1, 47, 99, 107–13, 126, 140
   formation of (1971) 107–8
United Arab Republic (UAR) 34, 36, 49, 62–3, 66, 77, 86, 88–9, 92–3. *See also* Egypt
United Political Command (Iraq and Egypt) 61, 75
United Nations 1, 13, 17, 23, 25–7, 29, 36–59, 68–9, 104, 108, 120–1, 123, 176–8, 180, 207, 209, 212
   and Arab–Israeli War (1967) 88–91, 95–102, 194–200
   and Bahrain 107
   inauguration of 19
   Decolonization Committee 41, 64
   and ECOSOC 54–6, 67, 69
   and invasion of Iraq (2003) 125–6
   and invasion of Kuwait (1990–91) 116–18, 169–72
   and Israel/Palestine 162–3, 189–90, 192–9
   and North Africa 164
   Resolution 242 98–103, 199–200
   Resolution 678, illegitimacy of 116–18
   and US occupation of Iraq 127–8, 130, 134–7, 139–41, 151
United Nations Emergency Force (UNEF) 88, 195
United Nations Food and Agriculture Organization (FAO) 21
United States 18–23, 27–32, 83, 115–16, 119, 125–6, 206–7, 211–12
   Arab–American relations 157–66, 194, 207
   and Arab–Israeli War (1967) 84–101
   CIA 43
   and communism 158–60
   and creation of Israel 161–3, 188–90, 193–4, 196–7, 199
   cultural influence in Arab world 158–60
   failures in Iraq 126–33
   and invasion of Kuwait (1990–91) 138, 168–70, 173–4
   invasion and occupation of Iraq (2003) 120–3, 125–51, 179
   pro-Israel bias 22–3, 66, 69, 73–6, 83, 109, 119–22, 169, 183
   and North Africa 164
   and racism 21, 41
   relations with Egypt 84–95
   and United Nations 40
   withdrawal from Iraq 150–1

Vichy 14
Victoria College, Alexandria 9–10, 12–13, 16
Vietnam 68–9

Al-Wali, Ibrahim 50
Warsaw Pact 47
Washington 18–24, 27–32, 85, 91–3, 119–20, 137, 139–40, 142, 149–50
Washington, George 20
weapons of mass destruction 175–8
   in Iraq 120–1, 151, 168
Weizman, Chaim 185
Welensky, Roy 44
West Bank 94, 99, 181, 197, 200
White, Harry Dexter 21
Wilkins, Roger 41
Wilson, Woodrow 186
Wolfowitz, Paul 120–1
World Bank 30

Yasseen, Fareed, 135, 140
Al-Yawar, Ghazi 142, 144
Yemen 49–50, 54, 64, 82, 95, 108, 111, 115
Yugoslavia 12, 40

Zaid bin Hussein Al-Hashimi 11
Zanzibar 29
Zionism, Zionists 22–3, 74, 95, 161, 182–94. *See also* Israel; United States